Sport in the Global So

Series Editors: J.A. Mangan and Bo

The Football Manager

NC T

Sport in the Global Society

Series Editors: J.A. Mangan and Boria Majumdar

The interest in sports studies around the world is growing and will continue to do so. This unique series combines aspects of the expanding study of *sport in the global society*, providing comprehensiveness and comparison under one editorial umbrella. It is particularly timely as studies in the multiple elements of sport proliferate in institutions of higher education.

Eric Hobsbawm once called sport one of the most significant practices of the late nineteenth century. Its significance was even more marked in the late twentieth century and will continue to grow in importance into the new millennium as the world develops into a 'global village' sharing the English language, technology and sport.

Other titles in the series:

The Football Manager

Football managers are at the centre of today's commercially driven football world, scrutinized, celebrated and under pressure as never before. This book is the first in-depth history of the role of the manager in British football, tracing a path from Victorian-era amateurism to the highly paid motivational specialists and media personalities of the twenty-first century.

Using original source materials, the book traces the changing character and function of the football manager, covering:

- the origins of football management – club secretaries and early pioneers
- the impact of post-war social change – the advent of the football business
- television and the new commercialism
- contemporary football – specialization and the influence of foreign managers and management practices
- the future of football management

The Football Manager fully explores the historical context of these changes. It examines the influence of Britain's traditionally pragmatic and hierarchical business management culture on British football, and in doing so provides a new and broader perspective on a unique management role and a unique way of life.

For those interested in the history of football and for those interested in management more generally, this book is a valuable new resource.

Neil Carter is Wellcome Trust Research Fellow at the International Centre for Sport History and Culture at De Montfort University, Leicester, UK.

For my parents

The Football Manager

A history

Neil Carter

Routledge
Taylor & Francis Group

LONDON AND NEW YORK

First published 2006 by Routledge
2 Park Square, Milton Park, Abingdon, Oxon OX14 4RN

Simultaneously published in the USA and Canada
by Routledge
170 Madison Ave, New York, NY 10016

Routledge is an imprint of the Taylor & Francis Group

© 2006 Neil Carter

Typeset in Goudy and Gill by BC Typesetting Ltd, Bristol
Printed and bound in Great Britain by
The Cromwell Press, Trowbridge, Wiltshire

British Library Cataloguing in Publication Data
A catalogue record for this book is available from the British Library

Library of Congress Cataloging in Publication Data
Carter, Neil, 1967–
The football manager: a history/Neil Carter.
p.   cm. – (Sport in the global society)
Includes bibliographical references and index.
ISBN 0–415–37538–X (hardback) – ISBN 0–415–37539–8 (pbk.) –
ISBN 0-203–09904–4 (ebook)
1. Soccer–Great Britain–Management–History.
2. Soccer managers–Great Britain–History.
3. Soccer–Great Britain–History. I. Title. II. Series.
GV944.G7C37 2006
796.334′069–dc22
2005022244

ISBN 10: 0–415–37538–X (hbk)
ISBN 10: 0–415–37539–8 (pbk)
ISBN 13: 978–0–415–37538–2 (hbk)
ISBN 13: 978–0–415–37539–9 (pbk)

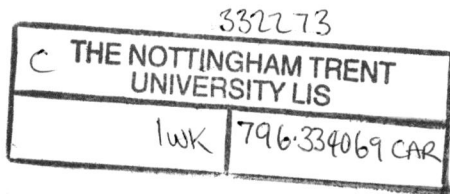

Contents

Series editors' foreword

There he is, adorning that steadfast middle class broadsheet, *The Daily Telegraph*, saturnine, solemn, supreme with his state-of-the-art Samsung 600, the hierophantic modern manager of modern association football, Jose Mourinho. The metamorphosed manager. In our media-driven celebrity culture, Mourinho, Wenger and Ferguson are the middle-aged celebrities of English soccer. They now live well but they still live dangerously. Even sporting hierophants, in all their glory, bear witness to the cold apophthegm: here today and gone tomorrow. Ferguson, for many the greatest manager of his time, had his grave, metaphorically and albeit prematurely, dug deep by the pundits during Manchester United's recent descent into a series of defeats.

It has long been thus – medal winners or mortality – as *The Football Manager: A history* makes clear, while adding to the sum of the parts of the history of association football with its comparison of the football manager with the commercial/industrial manager. Admirably, *The Football Manager* is also an exemplum of social continuity and change, revealing how football management has always been a part of wider social trends both in its subscription to a 'hands-on' work ethic (only graduates of the Muck and Brass School of Hard Knocks need apply: no graduates of the Harvard Business School, please) and its patronizing attitude to the young working class male ('Hasn't the boy done good!'). Class prejudice long permeated, indeed, saturated, association football.

A class hierarchical structure with its associated autocratic behaviour, traditional concepts of masculinity with associated anxiety over 'eviration' all once played their part in the evolution of the football manager. Within these cultural parameters, the manager 'strutted his stuff' as the 'Sergeant Major' of soccer, too often contemptuous of the cerebral and preoccupied with control, too frequently admiring brute courage and suspicious of easy elegance. Today, however, the old 'caste' certainties have all but gone. In sport, the 'Eton'-type controller has retired, slipped away or been pushed out. In soccer, the 'Sergeant Major' is almost extinct.

Today the astounding affluence of managers (and players) heralds the total takeover by a 'celebrity meritocracy' – at least at the top; survive-or-sink commercialism has demanded entrepreneurial skills, the one-eyed pursuit of profit has globalized the player pool, the media has demanded and obtained a voice in league and club decisions increasingly shaping the image of the so-called 'beautiful game'.

The manager has responded to these changes. He is no longer what he was. However, was he ever, and is he now, a significant part of the club structure? *The Football Manager* offers its answers. To provide a clue, no longer do 'manners maketh the man' but 'the media makes the man'; a telling new aphorism for our time.

The Football Manager is a welcome addition to the association football studies now available in Sport in the Global Society.

J.A. Mangan
Boria Majumdar
Series Editors
Sport in the Global Society

Acknowledgements

Many people have assisted me in the course of writing this work. I am particularly grateful to Tony Mason, who, despite his continuing anxieties over Coventry City FC, found time to offer advice and assistance. I would also like to thank Dilwyn Porter and Carolyn Steedman for reading drafts and providing useful suggestions. I am equally appreciative of the time spared by Pat Carter, and the late Jack Curnow and George Hardwick. In addition, I was aided by a number of other people who offered me advice, assistance or information: Lawrence Aspden at Special Collections, University of Sheffield, Ian Atkins, David Barber, Tony Collins, Iain Cook, Mike Cronin, Barry Curnow, Robert Day, Olaf Dixon, Eric Doig, James and Gladys Dutton, Christiane Eisenberg, Eric England, John Evans at West Bromwich Albion FC, Ken Friar, Neal Garnham, Frank Grande, Wyn Grant, Dan Hall, Graham Hughes at Wolverhampton Wanderers FC, Jeff Hill, Richard Holt, David Hunt, Martin Johnes, Pierre Lanfranchi, Andy Porter, Richard Redden, Mark Shipway at Leeds University Archive, Richard Skirrow, Terry Tasker at Middlesbrough FC, Matt Taylor, Leslie Teale, and not forgetting the staff at the various libraries and record offices around the country.

Introduction

Football managers are part of today's celebrity culture. Through the media-driven hyperbole that has engulfed the game, they have become emblematic figures: the public face of their clubs who somehow possesses mystical powers. A manager's performance, both on the touchline and in front of the media, is now analyzed as much as their team's, with their actions and words 'deconstructed' in the search for some hidden meaning. Yet the job of a football manager is a paradox. Few occupations are as volatile or as pressurized, and failure ultimately results in the sack.

How have football managers apparently become so important and do we really need them? This book will consider these questions by charting the emergence and development of the manager's role from the late nineteenth century up to the present day. It will also attempt to demonstrate how this evolution has been shaped not only by the changing nature of the football world but also by broader social changes.

With the current interest shown in them, it is perhaps surprising that football managers have been largely absent from English football's historiography. Furthermore, there have been no studies that have tried to make a link between the history of football management and other mainstream academic disciplines such as management studies, or to compare the jobs of football managers with those of managers in other industries. This work intends to bridge this gap. Social histories of football have tended to analyze the importance of the game's rising popularity and its commercial growth in a national social and economic context. In their studies, Tony Mason, Nicholas Fishwick and Dave Russell have each emphasized the development of club management but without focusing on the evolving and changing nature of the manager's role.[1]

One of the few academic studies that has dealt with the manager's developing role in some depth is *The Football World* by Stephen Wagg. As its subtitle, *A Contemporary Social History*, suggests, it is only partly a work of history as it mainly concentrates on the period after the Second World War. Wagg emphasizes the increasingly central role that the manager occupied within the game and argues that from the inter-war period 'a mystique began to be woven around the figure of the team manager'.[2]

Other academic work, such as Charles Korr's study of West Ham and Tony Arnold's business history of professional football in Bradford, has also paid some attention to the manager's role.[3] Amongst the recent economic literature on football, there has been a growing interest in the impact of the manager. Stefan Szymanski and Tim Kuypers, for example, have analyzed the sport from both an economic and a business perspective.[4]

Chris Green has written an in-depth study on contemporary football management.[5] He briefly analyzes how the job has evolved since 1945, although without placing it in its wider historical context. Green's main focus is on the lack of professional accountability as well as the absence, until recently, of any qualifications for the job, which, he argues, has resulted in a rise in managerial wastage. The importance of the manager's role has also been recognized in a number of significant biographies written in a non-hagiographical manner, unlike many books about sporting celebrities. Perhaps the best of this genre is Michael Crick's study of the life and career of Alex Ferguson.[6]

To show how football management has been part of the wider changes and continuities of British society, this work contains two main themes. The first is that football management has echoed the 'practical tradition' of British management. The second shows how the management of footballers has largely mirrored attitudes towards the handling of young, working-class men in general.

The management of football clubs had begun to take on greater significance when professionalism was legalized in 1885. However, for social as well as business historians, this begs the question, how were clubs run? Did they model themselves on any particular form of management, and what influenced the thinking and actions of committees and boards of directors? Football management has subsequently reflected the 'practical tradition' of British management, in which knowledge has been gathered and passed on through the generations by 'doing it' rather than by learning how to 'do it'. It is a tradition that has elicited much criticism concerning the quality of British management. In 1988, Charles Handy declared that,

> The conclusion that many British managers are uneducated in business and management terms is inescapable. It must also be true that management training in Britain is too little, too late, for too few. It is finally probably true that most management development is left to chance in a Darwinian belief that the fittest will survive. They probably will but it is a wasteful process.[7]

James Walvin has been similarly critical of football management. In 1986, he remarked that 'football simply reflected the experience of wide areas of British management which specifically eschewed the concept of professional managerial training and vocational education'.[8] Walvin also offered the opinion that,

Nothing illustrates more precisely the peculiar weaknesses of football than the recent history of club management. Indeed, the history of management in this one small and rather unimportant industry is a telling insight into the broader story of British attitudes towards business management in general.[9]

To a certain extent, management has both defined and mirrored developments within twentieth-century British economic and social life. A 'professionalized' meritocracy slowly emerged based on human capital where status and specialized expertise were acquired through qualifications. Management, however, unlike the law, accountancy and medicine, has not been a profession in the true sense of the word. Instead, its development, like other areas of society, has been very much subject to the vagaries of British cultural and social traditions, such as the class system, which have persisted throughout this period.

Since the nineteenth century, the history of management has been marked by a 'divorce of ownership from control', where the administration of organizations has gradually evolved from one-man businesses to companies under the control of specialist professional managers. Despite a steady decline in the number of owner-manager businesses, though, most British firms, like football clubs, have remained small in size.[10] Any developments in management, therefore, were not instantly reflected in smaller companies and the effects of any changes within the management of major companies filtered down very slowly. Because of the prevailing business culture many owners were unwilling to relinquish control of their company to professional managers. Instead, managers, with their autonomy usually restricted, worked according to the traditions of their firm rather than to the rules of any association or profession. As a consequence, the management of small firms was generally more easily influenced by the personalities and the actions of a few individuals.

Furthermore, an anti-intellectualism pervaded British management culture throughout the twentieth century. Initially, this attitude had been compounded by a 'Gentlemen' and 'Players' dichotomy. 'Gentlemen' had had a classical public school education which offered little or no preparation for management. Because of the predominance of family firms within British industry, nepotism, patronage and the old-school-tie network were important factors in the recruitment of managers. On the other hand, the 'Players' were largely uneducated, self-made owners who had gained their fortunes as practical tinkerers, and this contributed to a 'mystique of practical experience'.[11] Despite changes in the structure of industry due to the increase in professional managers, these deep-rooted attitudes towards management persisted. Most post-war managers, therefore, continued to believe that management could not be taught by formal methods. Rather,

The emphasis has always been on 'learning by doing'. . . . Great managers, in the popular view, were those who operated without reference to texts or theory. They acted spontaneously and decisively, leading by character and example, not tarrying over abstract justifications. Symptomatically, British managers have often referred to military heroes and the vocabulary of war when discussing their vocation.[12]

Until recently, many British managers lacked qualifications and instead were graduates from 'the school of hard knocks'. In comparison, whereas Britain has lagged in management education, most of its economic competitors, including France and Germany, had responded early to industrialization and catered for the demand for better-trained managers. Even by the early 1900s, differences in approach between Britain and America had also been recognized,

> Is it not again the old trouble that labour is a disgrace to a gentleman in England, whereas it is an honour in America? Or, to go further still, is there not a crying need in British construction generally for a strenuous middle man, a manager, between the architect and the labourer, to see that the one properly and promptly carries out the plans of the other?[13]

The British response, however, was limited and disjointed. A British Institute of Management was established in 1947 but it was not until 1965 that the Manchester Business School opened, with its London equivalent starting the following year. Yet the impact of this specialist preparation was mainly felt in large corporations. Many smaller and medium-sized firms still relied upon the skills of the practical man solving problems on a pragmatic, rule-of-thumb basis. There was little expertise in smaller companies.[14] The story of football management, in terms of its evolution as a profession, has been very similar.

Football management's history, though, has been as much a consequence of the game's traditions as economic traditions. From the mid-nineteenth century, cricket, horse-racing and professional athletics had become commercialized sporting spectacles, and, in one way, they provided examples of how to run a sports business.[15] Instead of commercial gain, though, early football clubs had been set up for social and sporting reasons and were part of the British liberal voluntary tradition. Furthermore, the Football Association's early administrators never considered football to be an industry, and the traditions of voluntarism, the values of amateurism, and later those of mutuality within the Football League, pervaded the management of clubs until well into the twentieth century. Once the footballing competition intensified, however, money began to play a greater part in the administration of clubs.

Elected committees ran early football clubs on a quasi-democratic basis. Later, following the conversion to limited liability, directors began to 'manage' clubs. In a sense, they made football management up as they went along. However, directors also drew upon their own work and personal experiences, which meant that they absorbed the prevailing management culture. As a consequence, it was felt that professional football managers were not necessary.

Importantly, because of their small size, many clubs were, and have continued to be, dominated by powerful directors. As the demands of running a club increased, however, the club secretary, at first, and later the manager, was given more responsibilities. Managers themselves became more powerful in the running of the club but change was generally uneven and took place in a historical context in which there was much continuity.

The book's second major idea – how a football manager's man-management methods have echoed general approaches towards the supervision of young, working-class males – highlights not only their preparation for the job but has also helped to shape the manager's make-up and image. Of course, these attitudes have mutated over time and have been dependent on the contemporary context. A managerial figure from the early twentieth century, for example, used different methods from their twenty-first-century counterpart. Regarding their management style, however, a clear hierarchical structure, autocratic tendencies, traditional notions of masculinity and the need for discipline from the players have essentially underpinned the continuum between the two eras.

The basis for this worker–management relationship within football clubs echoed the strict hierarchy of Victorian class society, where, even if they didn't like it, everyone was expected to know their place. The education system, for example, mirrored, and has continued to reinforce, crude class hierarchies where the upper classes attended public schools, grammar schools educated an expanding middle class, while the working classes went to elementary and, later, secondary modern schools. In sports other than football, social relationships have also provided the background for labour management methods. Horse-racing, for example, still exhibits strict feudal and 'squirearchical' overtones where jockeys deferentially address racecourse officials as 'sir'. Cricket's model of management has revolved around the team captain. Through the nature of their position, captains have been aloof figures, and for many decades at test level, England captains had to be amateurs, which meant appointment from the upper and middle classes. It was not until 1952 that a professional, Len Hutton, was appointed as captain of the England team.[16] Early professional football clubs were also marked by social stratification. In a class-conscious era, the directors came from the aspiring middle classes while the players represented the workers. It was the secretaries and later the managers who acted as intermediaries between the two parties. They filled a role similar to foremen and overlookers in other workplace environments. In the army it was the NCOs, especially the Regimental Sergeant-Major, who fulfilled this function.

During the second half of the nineteenth century, the thinking of some organizations concerning the handling of their workers, particularly those with uniformed workforces, was founded on a class-based authoritarianism. It also shared some characteristics with the military model of management, which in some ways was the class system writ small. Railway companies, for example, ran their uniformed labour force with discipline and through a hierarchical structure. Many of the early railway managers came from the army and were recruited for their experience in controlling large groups of men[17]. Similarly, chief constables of mid-nineteenth-century provincial police forces had had military experience. Many policemen were from the lower classes, especially farming backgrounds, and were accustomed to working in an environment which demanded obedience and a conscious identification with their masters.[18] This type of management was not restricted to men. Female nurses were also part of a system in which workers wore uniforms. On the wards, they worked under a hierarchy of sisters, matrons and doctors where the sisters and matrons enforced discipline in order to instil habits of cleanliness.[19]

Because football managers received little or no training, they adopted methods and styles of management formed from their own experiences such as personal and social relationships, military service and work – both inside and outside of football. Patriarchal figures – fathers or even grandfathers, for example – have provided important role models for generations of young men during their formative years. Fathers though, like managers, have tended to demand respect for their seniority and authority. In addition, because of the near universal experience of school, some managers may have seen their role as similar to that of the schoolmaster. A teacher–pupil relationship is still an authoritarian one but its main purpose is to impart knowledge and requires sensitivity, sympathy and understanding.

During the twentieth century many British men, including players and future managers, had a taste of life in the armed forces and experienced its tough methods of disciplining men. Moreover, these experiences had a cultural impact. Some people not only recognized that management on military principles was a way of 'doing things', they also believed in it. Many managers have consequently shared characteristics with sergeant-majors. Both tend to be charismatic, autocratic and powerful figures who like to get their own way. Both employ 'verbal authoritarianism', a mixture of violent and abusive language, direct personal castigation and scornful humour, as key disciplinary techniques in order to reinforce soldier/player subordination.[20] A 'management by fear' quickly became institutionalized throughout much of British professional football and in some ways it was admired because it appealed to some of the masculine sensibilities of working-class players and fans. As a consequence, it helped to mould the image of the football manager as an all-powerful 'Boss' figure.

One style some managers later adopted was to regard players as 'their boys', similar to sergeants in charge of platoons. It highlighted elements of both patriarchy and matriarchy as not only did managers think of themselves as father-figures but they also acted as mother-figures because, like mothers, they were always there to look after their players. Some who took on the role of the patriarch often talked about their football club as a 'family'. What they really meant, however, was that if a football club was a family, then they, as manager, were at its head. Because managers are older than the players, most feel that they are also wiser than the players, and that this merits their obedience. It has often meant that managers want to influence all aspects of players' personal conduct, preferring them to be married and settled, for example, rather than single.[21]

In line with any autocratic tendencies, managers have traditionally imposed their personalities on players. Arthur Hopcraft has actually identified the attribute of personality as the key factor in football managerial success. He has argued that,

> It is not a question of being a nice man or a nasty one, of being likeable or aloof, of being imaginative or cautious, hard or indulgent in discipline. All of these things are subordinate to the essential quality that, it seems, all the most successful have: the capacity to dominate. This is not just an over-bearing manner, a thrusting of two fists at the world: it is not just arrogance. It is a steeliness in a man's make-up, the will to make his methods tell. . . . The successful manager may have all kinds of talents, from charm to low cunning, but to stay successful he needs to be very close to indomitable.[22]

Typical of this authoritarian manner was Eddie Clamp's memory of his manager at Wolverhampton Wanderers, Stan Cullis,

> I'm sure he didn't like me – and I certainly didn't like him. I'll tell you one thing, though. I respected him. I sat scores of times in the dressing-rooms while tough, fit professional players waited nervously. And above the tramp, tramp of his steps . . . I could hear the flat Cullis voice chanting: 'I . . . will . . . not . . . have . . . a . . . coward . . . in . . . my . . . team.'[23]

The domineering nature of many managers has also been complemented and reinforced by the game's deeply rooted occupational culture. Ross McKibbin has argued that football 'lacks an organized intellectuality' due to an insufficient emphasis on education within the game.[24] Like management, football in general has been pervaded by anti-intellectualism. Instead, British football culture has generated authoritarian tendencies. As most managers were former players, they have been immersed in these habits, and as players themselves do seem to respect 'experience', they are passed on from one generation to the next.

Attitudes towards the game in Britain from schoolboy to professional level have reflected a general feeling within working-class shop-floor culture that 'practice is more important than theory'.[25] As a result, the British style of play can perhaps be best summed up in three words, 'Get Stuck In', in which a greater emphasis is placed on the physical rather than the technical side, enshrining older forms of toughness and rudeness instead of notions of fair play and sportsmanship. A football team also came to symbolize the virtues of the men who supported it, mostly from the working classes. Attributes such as hardness, stamina, courage and loyalty came to be regarded as more important than skill.[26] In comparison to European football, which has placed an emphasis

on technique, British soccer has been derided as 'kick and rush', and consequently, unable to develop enough players capable of understanding tactics,
constructive and intelligent movement and sophisticated ball control.[27] The
role of the football manager has developed within a deeply embedded culture
which is not only dominated by the qualities of hierarchy, discipline and masculinity but which also generally relies on brawn over brain.

This book, written in a largely narrative format, aims to explore how these
various themes have not only complemented changes in the manager's job but
have also been shaped in light of developments in football management. The
first chapter provides a broad overview of football management in the years up
to 1914. It analyses how clubs were then managed and who ran them, initially
when they were amateur and then after professionalism was legalized. After the
Football League was formed in 1888, the game became more competitive yet
financially more risky, and clubs formed themselves into limited companies.
However, because football clubs grew out of voluntary organizations, their management continued to be part of that more democratic tradition as opposed to
being money-making concerns.

Chapter 2 looks in more detail at early football managers, such as Tom
Watson and William Sudell, how they emerged, their social origins and why
clubs employed them. Many came from administrative backgrounds and were
employed as the club secretary – the forerunner of the manager – who was
gradually given more responsibilities for running the club on a day-to-day basis.
The relationship between manager and director, as well as that between the
manager and players, is outlined here. In addition to looking at how the job
evolved, the manager's relationship with the media and also his lifestyle will
be examined. This framework will be used throughout the other chapters.

One manager, Herbert Chapman, is the subject of Chapter 3. His career
bridged the Edwardian era and the 1930s when he helped to establish Arsenal
as the biggest and most successful club in the country. It is an attempt to empha-
size the role of the individual in this history because, it will be argued, Chapman
was the most important figure in the development of football management. He
was the first to realize that managers might 'organize victory', and marked the
starting point for football management's move towards a more professional era.

The inter-war years are dealt with more generally in the fourth chapter. Former
players, because of their practical experience, were increasingly employed as
managers during this period. However, directors continued to run clubs very
much in the mould of their Victorian predecessors. Although change was slow,
there were some, like Frank Buckley at Wolverhampton Wanderers and Jimmy
Seed at Charlton Athletic, who had similar responsibilities to Chapman. It was
during the 1930s especially, that a burgeoning sporting press established closer
links with managers.

Chapter 5 looks at the emergence of modern football management from 1945
up to 1970. It takes account of the changes within a society that was slowly
shedding its deferential attitudes; and looks at the landmark decision to abolish

football's maximum wage in 1961. During this period, managers also developed closer relations with their players, and as the game began to move closer to business, directors gradually delegated more powers to their managers. Furthermore, more people thought about the game more than ever before and new ideas on management emerged. Yet even by 1970, football management was still not a profession and a 'professional' lag emerged between British managers and their European counterparts.

The sixth chapter covers the period 1970 to 1992 when managers became part of the television age as football's relationship with the media became increasingly symbiotic. It was an era of 'big personalities' like Brian Clough, Malcolm Allison and Ron Atkinson, who enhanced their own status with frequent appearances on television either being interviewed or as 'expert' summarizers. During this period the football manager probably reached the height of his powers. Not only was he in charge of team affairs but also many managers still negotiated with players over salaries.

Chapter 7 looks at the twenty-first-century football manager and how, since 1992, football's new commercialism has radically changed the game. The formation of the Premier League and the sport's relationship with television accelerated the gap between the rich and poor, while directors now wanted to make profits from football. Directors also desired greater control over the running of the club, which caused a corresponding fall in the manager's powers. Yet, paradoxically, because of the media, the profile of the manager grew. Furthermore, with more money at stake, management became more specialized and greater resources went into preparing the players. The chapter tries to analyse how and why foreign managers managed the biggest clubs as well as the national team.

The final chapter pulls together the various themes as it examines the actual importance of managers in relation to the performance of their teams. By placing their role in its economic as well as historical context, it asks what difference does a manager actually make? Does the perception of their worth, stimulated by the media, match the reality when analysed against the complexities of football's production process? In particular, the question of whether the success or failure of management is dependent on a club's financial resources is examined.

A variety of sources have been used for this study. No manager seems to have left diaries or many letters and this has made it difficult to construct profiles of them. Furthermore, attempts to trace some of the earlier minute books of the ancestors of the League Managers' Association, the body that represents football managers, proved unsuccessful. Fortunately, I was able to consult the records – held in a variety of locations – of a number of football clubs: Arsenal, Charlton Athletic, Darlington, Ipswich Town, Middlesbrough, Walsall and Wolverhampton Wanderers. The records, mainly the minutes of directors' meetings, varied from club to club in terms of their detail. In general, the recording of these meetings became less detailed over time, yet reflected how a club's management was changing, especially with regard to the players. Arsenal also holds the cuttings and books of the journalist James Catton, which include folders of newspaper clippings, and a small amount of correspondence. In addition to its library and the minutes of various committees, the Football Association holds a range of significant materials.

Interestingly, the usefulness of the sources changed as the century progressed. Initially, at least up to 1939, contemporary national and local newspapers, like the *Athletic News* and the *Football Field*, were very informative, reflecting the close relationship between football and the press. In the nineteenth and early twentieth century, the annual general meetings of clubs were reported in great detail, and clubs often provided the main source of information for local journalists. By the 1930s, however, one can detect a change as football clubs became increasingly aware of their position and status, and information began to be more restricted. After 1945 this process increased, and was reinforced at a local level where the need for the local paper to establish a good relationship with the local club often overrode the desire to print anything controversial. Because of this, more autobiographical and some oral evidence has been used for the post-war period.

Chapter 1

The origins of football management

Between 1880 and the First World War, football underwent radical changes. From being initially a purely sporting activity, by 1914 it had begun to display the characteristics of an industry. Football, however, developed into a very peculiar business. It was still a sport but it was also partly entertainment due to the game's burgeoning mass appeal. While money was important, however, the pursuit of wealth did not characterize the game. This not only affected the game's governance but also its management. Football management, however, was a process mainly shaped by the people who ran the clubs.

Football had become a mass spectator sport by the turn of the century. The FA Cup Final had rapidly established itself as a national institution and in 1914 King George V was a spectator. It was the first time a reigning monarch had attended, giving the game the establishment's stamp of approval. The game's growing popularity had been part of the boom that took place in the service industries between 1870 and 1914.[1] In the leisure sector there was a rise in the consumption of alcohol, while music halls were increasingly placed in the hands of entrepreneurs. With the expansion of the rail network, the railway excursion became a popular day out for workers. And cheaper newspapers were published to cater for a wider market. Commercialized spectator sports themselves became one of the economic success stories of late Victorian Britain. Football began to flourish in Scotland and in the English north and Midlands. East Lancashire, in particular, the cradle of the industrial revolution, was at the forefront of the commercialization of leisure.[2]

Improvements in the nation's standard and quality of living were major factors behind these developments. Food prices in particular had begun to fall from the 1880s onwards, giving the working classes greater spending power. There were also more opportunities for leisure. From 1847, working men had increasingly gained the Saturday half-holiday at different times depending on job, employer and geographical location. Increased life expectancy further widened, and deepened, the potential market for spectator sport. By 1901, Britain's population was over 45 million, while the death rate had fallen to under 17 per 1,000. British society was also very youthful with around 30 per cent of the population under 15 years of age throughout the nineteenth century. Between

1871 and 1901, levels of urban density rose from 61.6 per cent to 77 per cent, producing further potential concentrated markets for recreational entrepreneurs. By 1915, the majority of spectators at professional football matches were from the working classes of major towns that had populations in excess of 50,000. One result of these social and economic changes was that aggregate attendances in professional football rose from approximately 602,000 during the first Football League season in 1888–9 to nearly 9 million by 1913–14.[3]

Early football clubs, however, particularly those formed during the 1870s, were not businesses but purely sporting bodies, reflecting the nineteenth-century voluntary tradition. A 'subscriber democracy' characterized these societies where the members of the club paid an annual subscription entitling them to one vote in the election of a committee and officers at the annual general meeting. By the 1870s, sports clubs were being organized on the lines of committee meetings, agendas, rules, subscriptions and members.[4]

Furthermore, the persistence of traditions like amateurism had a lasting impact on the development of football management. Amateurism itself was a Victorian invention. It meant a love of sport and was used to distinguish between those who played for pleasure and those who played for pay. Its ethos could be best summed up in two words: fair play. Amateurs, or gentlemen amateurs, were products of Britain's public schools. In the early Victorian period, those who encouraged sports in these schools wanted to create a new sporting elite and saw team games as a means to impart moral and social virtues. Games had to be played in a special way: not only had the rules to be respected but the game also had to be played in the right spirit. These were the values that the founders of the Football Association were inculcated with.[5]

Many football clubs owed their origins to various types of institutions already in existence. As a consequence, the reasons for establishing a football club ranged from the missionary, to the philanthropic, to the simple desire to spend leisure time playing football with friends. A number of clubs, like Bolton Wanderers and Everton, had connections with local churches.[6] Some came from schools. Sunderland, for example, was born at a meeting of Sunderland schoolteachers in October 1879.[7] Places of work were another point of origin. Newton Heath (later Manchester United) originated from the depot and carriage works of the Lancashire and Yorkshire Railway in 1878.[8] West Ham was first known as Thames Ironworks after London's largest surviving shipbuilding firm. The owner, Arnold F. Hills, formed a football club in 1895 as part of his strategy to develop better industrial relations with his workforce.[9] Like Aston Villa and Middlesbrough, Sheffield Wednesday had a connection with a cricket club. A football section had been established in 1866 to keep the members together during the winter months.[10] This had certain advantages for clubs trying to establish themselves. First, clubs had a pool of members who wanted to play football, and there was already a mechanism in place by which they could procure membership fees. Less visible but importantly, the name of the club as a sporting institution would have been already known and would have built up a network of contacts within the local area.

There is insufficient evidence to say whether any particular industries or occupational groups were more likely to form football clubs than others, although clerks, and their skills, were prominent in the formation of many clubs. Blackburn Rovers' membership had originally consisted of the sons of local business and professional families who had attended grammar and public schools.[11] However, the roots of local rivals, Blackburn Olympic, were more working-class. In 1883 'Olympic' became the first northern club to lift the FA Cup, defeating Old Etonians 2–1 with a group of players who were mainly skilled workers. They included three weavers, two cotton spinners, a picture framer, an iron moulder, a dentist's assistant, a master plumber and a workman.[12]

A closer look at the early history of Aston Villa, formed in c. 1874, illustrates how football clubs from this period emerged, the difficulties they encountered and who ran them.[13] Up to 1914, Villa was largely run on a collective basis, with responsibilities being shared amongst the members and later the directors. Some of the club's early committee members and players belonged to the middle classes. The club also had a strong Scottish connection and this proved important in its struggle to survive and prosper. This connection characterized the club during its early years and was represented by the choice of the Scottish lion as the club's emblem.[14] One long-serving member, Charles Johnstone, a teacher from Scotland, was later headmaster at three local schools.[15] Another prominent member was W. Margoschis, a local tobacconist who had the latest scores of away games relayed to his shop by pigeon.[16] The main influence on Villa's early development, however, was George Ramsay. He was the club secretary from 1884 to 1926 but before then he had been a player, captain, committeeman, and club chairman. Ramsay, a native of Glasgow, was a commercially trained clerk. By the early 1870s, Birmingham was rapidly developing into a major manufacturing centre and became known as the 'Workshop of the World'. Like many others, Ramsay had been lured to the Midlands in the early 1870s by the prospect of employment, taking up a position with the iron merchants, Izons.[17]

Ramsay's association with Villa began when he saw some club members playing in a public park in Aston in the mid-1870s.[18] He had previously played in Glasgow for the 'Oxford' Football Club and almost immediately he was elected Villa's captain.[19] He held this position from 1876 until 1880, during which time, on his initiative, Villa moved from playing in public parks to their first ground at Wellington Road in Perry Barr in 1876.[20] Ramsay was also keen to recruit people who could run the club, and in 1877 he persuaded William McGregor, another Scot, from Braco in Perthshire, to join. He was immediately elected vice-president.[21] McGregor was an early football entrepreneur and he later founded the Football League in 1888. He came to Birmingham in 1870 where he and his brother, Peter, opened a linen draper's shop in Summer Lane, Newtown. A teetotaller, McGregor was also a member of the local Liberal

Association during the period when Joseph Chamberlain was its President.[22] Although he occasionally played in goal during practice games, and was an umpire for the club, he had been sought for his organizational skills.[23] McGregor later exploited his involvement in football by putting his name to products such as the 'McGregor football' and the 'McGregor lace-to-toe football boot', and his shop sold football shirts and shorts. He also wrote regular columns for Birmingham newspapers like the *Sports Argus*.[24]

Another early football entrepreneur was William Sudell. In contrast to the collective efforts at Aston Villa, Sudell was the single driving force behind Preston North End's emergence as the top team in the country during the 1880s. He was the club's all-powerful chairman between 1874 and 1893, although he has also been described as 'football's first great professional manager' due to the club's success as the first winners of the 'Double' in 1888–9 (see Chapter 2).[25] Appointed the Football League's first honorary treasurer, he had already had experience of business management as the manager of a Preston cotton mill, John Goodair & Co, who employed him for over twenty-five years. After the owner's death he ran the factory himself until 1893. Born around 1850, Sudell was a freeman of the town and claimed that an ancestor had been a Guild Mayor of Preston two hundred years previously. Sudell first joined Preston North End as a member in 1867 and was elected chairman in 1874. He had been a keen sportsman in his younger days, playing cricket and rugby for the club, and on occasions he later played in goal when the team took up football.[26]

Sudell and McGregor were amongst the first people to recognize the game's commercial potential. In this sense, they demonstrated the entrepreneurial spirit that existed within Victorian service and leisure industries. In the retail sector, for example, the late nineteenth century witnessed the rise of department stores like Harrods.[27] The music hall was transformed into mass entertainment as well as big business. In 1899, for example, the Moss Empires of Edward Moss had capital of £1 million.[28] Some cricketers, like William Gunn and the Lillywhites, exploited the popularity of cricket by developing thriving businesses in the sale and manufacture of sporting goods.[29] Across the Atlantic, professional baseball had its own sports-goods entrepreneur in Albert G. Spalding.[30]

During the 1880s, a football club's administration was a relatively simple affair. Bolton Wanderers' committee, for example, consisted of the club's officers – a president and vice-presidents, captains and vice-captains, treasurer and secretaries plus eight non-playing members – all of whom were elected at the annual meeting. Their duties included the arrangement of each season's fixtures, the selection of players for all matches and the transaction of business on the club's behalf. The secretary arranged the dates for the fixtures and was responsible for collecting money owed to the club.[31] By 1882, it was stated that he had an assistant who took sole charge of collecting gate receipts. (This post may have been invented for an early professional player, as it is unlikely the work involved required two officials.)[32]

Table 1.1 Blackburn Rovers Balance Sheet, 1875–6

Receipts	£ s d	Expenditure	£ s d
T. Greenwood	0 3 0	Football	0 15 0
W. Baguley	0 3 0	Haworth Bros. for Book	0 1 0
W. Waugh	0 3 0	Cloth for Flags	0 2 0
T. Dean	0 3 0	Receipt Book	0 0 6
A. Thomas	0 3 0	Thornbers for Rules	0 8 0
J. Lewis	0 3 0	Paid Man, Allowance	0 0 6
J. Baguley	0 3 0	Goal Posts	0 8 10
H. Greenwood	0 3 0	Umpire's Expenses to Darwen	0 0 7
W. Duckworth	0 3 0	Expenses to Church	0 2 0
A. Constantine	0 3 0	Expenses to Cob Wall Post	0 1 0
H. Cottam	0 3 0	Cards and Stamps Paid for	0 5 2
Alfred Birtwistle	0 3 0	Sundry Ex.'s	0 3 5
Richard Birtwistle	0 3 0		
John Baldwin	0 3 0		
Jas. Thompson	0 3 0		
M. Brothers	0 3 0		
	2 8 0		2 8 0

Source: *Aston Villa News and Record*, Vol. IV (154), 29 January 1910, p. 380.

During these early years, a football club's finances reflected its humble origins. In 1875–6 the balance sheet of Blackburn Rovers (Table 1.1) showed that the club had an income of £2 8s 0d, entirely made up of members' subscriptions.[33] The club received no gate receipts and paid out no wages to players. In 1882, and in addition to their subscriptions, the players of Bolton Wanderers had to pay for the cost of their equipment and railway fares. The club also operated a fines system. Failure to notify the secretary of inability to play incurred a 6d penalty. In line with prevailing amateur values, anyone using bad language on the field would be fined 2d.

As the number of clubs grew, more teams travelled further away from their home towns. In East Lancashire this was easier than in most places because of the close proximity of a large number of football-playing towns. The increase in travelling, however, forced Bolton to subsidize the railway fares of their players as many were unable to afford them.[34] Because of football's growing appeal, more clubs acquired their own ground and began to charge spectators for entry. Aston Villa's landlord took note of their popularity and hiked up the rent to £8 after the first season.[35] The rise in crowds forced the club into improving and enclosing the ground. A hedge originally encircled the field but gaps in it had allowed fans a free view. In 1878 the hedge was cut down and replaced by boards, and to keep spectators back from the pitch, ropes were fastened around trees bordering it.[36]

Because of growing competition, clubs' incomes began to rise, as did their expenses. In 1879, Villa's gate receipts had amounted to £42 17s 10d. For the

1879–80 season Villa's income totalled £235 11s 9d. By 1883, gross receipts had increased to £1,720 1s 6d. From this, £443 was deducted for the away teams' share. Costs included: entertainment, £104; travelling expenses to Scotland, Wales and Lancashire, £186; and sundries such as printing and advertising amounted to £142. It was said, with probably more than a hint of irony, that 'so large are the sums of money involved . . . that the club has assumed the proportions of a large business affair'. Some clubs also found patrons from the local community. Peter Parkinson, a manager of a Bolton mill, sponsored the 'Wanderers' from 1878. During this period Villa also acquired one of its first patrons, George Kynoch, another Scot, who owned a local munitions factory – the Lion works at Witton which, at one time, employed 2,000 people. His involvement with Villa initially began when he donated some wooden railings to erect barriers at the Perry Barr ground. Kynoch was also an early visitor to Villa games where he and his wife would ride around the ground on horses while the match was in progress. Following a game against the Edinburgh team, Heart of Midlothian, he held a dinner for the club and 120 guests at his factory's dining room. Later, the 'Kynoch Wagon' was a regular fixture at Perry Barr where he entertained his guests. Kynoch was also one of the three guarantors of the ground's rent from 1880 to 1887, along with McGregor and J. Clements. He was the club President between 1886 and 1887. Kynoch, however, proved unpopular with McGregor and other committee members because of the autocratic way he wanted to run the club.[37]

At this early stage, however, perhaps the most important factor in a club's success and survival was its players: a theme that recurs throughout the history of football management. Archie Hunter was Aston Villa's most famous player during the 1880s and another example of its Scottish link. In 1887, with Hunter as captain, Villa won the FA Cup. It was claimed that he was not recruited through any monetary inducement but instead by accident. He had met the Calthorpe club when they were touring Scotland, and when he came to Birmingham in 1878 as an apprentice in the hardware trade he tried to locate them but was unable to find their ground.[38] A colleague at work who was a Villa enthusiast then suggested that he contact George Ramsay.[39]

The lifespan of many fledgling clubs, though, was short-lived. A club's survival depended on a number of factors. These included money to finance itself as well as the historical accident of location as rapid urbanization during the nineteenth century was swallowing up the potential space for clubs to play. Birmingham's first association football club, Calthorpe, had been formed in 1873 but by the late 1880s it had ceased to exist because it had been unable to secure its own ground.[40]

Although rugby was the most popular sport in the north until the 1890s, the association code was fast becoming a mania elsewhere, and by 1884 some of Villa's crowds had reached 15,000. They also took fans to away games. In 1883 Villa had played Queen's Park in Glasgow and such was the interest generated in the game that the London and North Western Railway Company ran two trains and the Midland Railway one special train from Birmingham. In addition to the struggle to keep pace with the rise in football's popularity, clubs began to compete with each other for the attentions of football enthusiasts by advertising themselves to a wider audience. At first, Aston Villa used large wall posters, but from 1886 all the club's games were advertised in the Friday edition of the *Birmingham Mail* and local sporting papers. Newspapers had actually been used early on by the club for important games. In 1881, for a game against Blackburn Rovers, an advert had been placed in the *Birmingham Mail* which announced that 'the committee of the Villa club has deemed it necessary to provide tickets for admission, in order to avoid excessive crushing at the gate'. Tickets were sold in the establishments of some club members including McGregor's drapery. Another outlet for tickets was the Crown and Cushion public house which was adjacent to the ground in Perry Barr. Ticket prices ranged from 3d for general admission to 6d for the reserved section. Admission to football games was not just restricted to standing or seats. When Villa played Aston Unity in a cup-tie at the Aston Lower Grounds in 1883, general admission was 6d and the reserved grounds or stands cost 6d extra. But if you were in possession of a two-wheel carriage, admission would cost 1s 6d, while the cost of a four-wheeler was 2s 6d – a kind of corporate hospitality of its day for the richer supporters.[41]

As crowds increased, they became more socially stratified. The majority of the spectators, who were working-class, paid the minimum admission price and stood to watch the game. Clubs, however, began to recognize that they also had to cater for wealthier patrons. In 1887, Villa built a new pavilion and new stand with a seating capacity of 700. A refreshment stand was also erected and an unreserved portion was set aside for more carriages to enter the Perry Barr ground. Similar to county cricket clubs, the club's pavilion was designated a reserved area for members. Another stand was built in 1892 which accommodated an extra 1,000 spectators. The increase in working-class spectators changed the nature of the crowd. In 1889, there had been complaints about gambling and the use of foul language at Perry Barr and the club brought in extra police to try and curb such behaviour.[42]

Accompanying the rise in the game's popularity was its increased competitiveness. Following the FA Cup in 1871–2, other local cup competitions, especially in the north, were established, and this ignited rivalries between local towns. This growth in competition and interest had caused clubs to look outside the local area for better players. Some were enticed by the promise of work and better wages in direct contravention of the FA's amateur rules. Dominated by either leisured gentlemen or professionally or commercially employed products of public and grammar schools, the FA regarded football as fun, not work, and were hostile to the idea of players being paid.[43] By the 1880s, however, the payment of players was widespread amongst northern clubs, particularly Scottish players. Scottish players attained the title of 'professors' because the game north of the border was technically more advanced than in England in the skills of dribbling and, in particular, passing.

The FA eventually legalized the payment of players in 1885, although certain rules and restrictions, similar to those in cricket, were initially imposed on the freedom of professionals. For example, they could only play for one club per season, and for cup matches they needed to have a two-year residence qualification within six miles of the club; and they could not serve on FA committees.[44] Some members of the FA never accepted professionalism and there was a long period of struggle between the amateur and professional ethos that persisted well into the twentieth century, affecting the administration of the game, and ultimately the management of clubs. In 1894, the FA Amateur Cup was established due to the dominance of professional clubs in the FA Cup. In 1907 a group of die-hard clubs, mainly from the south, broke away to form the Amateur Football Association, complaining that the FA was only interested in the business of football and that professionalism had infected the game. They returned to the fold in 1914.[45]

By contrast, William Sudell, a prime advocate of professionalism, was convinced that the public wanted to watch the best players. In 1887, he argued that,

> Professionalism has, in my opinion, benefited football. I consider football is played more scientifically now than ever it was and that is solely due to the fact that in a professional team the men are under the control of the management and are constantly playing together. Professionalism must improve football because men who devote their entire attention to the game are more likely to become good players than the amateur who is worried by business cares. No; purely amateur clubs will never be able to hold their own against a professional team.[46]

He considered that, '[football] will be played more scientifically and with less roughness and dash in the future. In short, professionalism will make such strides that football will become a science.'[47] The emphasis on science was used to show that football could be seen as a respectable activity, and not the rough and uncouth spectacle it was claimed to be in some quarters. Not only was this a comment on Sudell's entrepreneurial tendencies but it was also an indication of his attitudes to football management.

Professionalism acted as the catalyst for football's commercialization process and three years later, on the initiative of William McGregor, twelve clubs formed the Football League: six from the Midlands and six from Lancashire.[48] From 1888 onwards, the sport operated on a more organized, commercial footing. Initially, the League's objectives were limited: 'its creation was essentially a practical response to a number of difficulties in the management of clubs that had arisen following the legalisation of professionalism'. These difficulties revolved around the erratic and unreliable nature of clubs' seasonal fixture lists which mainly consisted of friendlies. Some games could be one-sided, drawing small crowds. On other occasions the opposition failed to turn up, and if a club was knocked out of the cup competitions in the early rounds it could have serious financial implications. In essence, competitive football was the aim: leagues were supposed to decrease the number of one-sided fixtures as well as providing a regular product. Thus, the Football League provided a pre-arranged and permanent schedule of games that could attract large crowds and, consequently, provide a more reliable source of income.[49] At the same time, similar to the flood of amalgamations and consolidations within industry at the time, it created 'a framework for [the] greater rationalisation and centralisation of professional football'.[50] The model of the Football League was followed by the founding of the Football Alliance in 1889 and the Southern League in 1894.[51] By 1912, the number of professional clubs had risen to 400, and there were also 7,000 professional players.[52]

Professionalism increased the rivalry between clubs from the same town or city, both on and off the pitch. With no regulation, a process of economic 'cannibalization' took place as clubs competed for the same market of fans, reflecting contemporary laissez-faire economics. As costs from paying players rose, only one or two clubs in each town or city survived and prospered. For example, Blackburn Olympic, FA Cup winners in 1883, had folded by the end of the decade, as Blackburn Rovers emerged as the town's dominant team.[53] In the 1880s, the two main rivals on Merseyside had been Everton and Bootle. Everton was one of the founding members of the Football League in 1888 but Bootle's application the following year was rejected. It was accepted in 1892 but by then Liverpool Football Club had been established. Liverpool joined the Football League the following year but at the same time Bootle resigned from the League as Merseyside could only sustain two major clubs.[54] There were similar divisions in Middlesbrough, although it was as much about amateurism as commercial factors. In 1889, Middlesbrough FC was an amateur club but some members wanted it to turn professional. The majority refused and a minority broke away to form a professional club, Middlesbrough Ironopolis. Middlesbrough responded by turning professional itself. In 1892 the two clubs agreed to amalgamate if their application to join the Football League was successful. It was rejected, however, and the amalgamation was cancelled with the two clubs again going their separate ways. Ironopolis eventually joined the League in 1893 but the following year, unable to sustain itself financially, it was voluntarily wound up. Two competing teams in the same town had not helped Middlesbrough either, and it reverted back to amateurism that same year.[55]

By 1914, the finances of English league clubs had been transformed and the professional game had developed into a not insignificant industry. In 1908 the gross income of all professional clubs in the Football League and the Southern

Table 1.2 Professional football clubs' total income, wage payments and dividends, 1908

	Gross income (£)	Payment to players (£)	Dividends and payments (£)
Division One FCs	224,906	107,107	1,551
Division Two FCs	147,602	77,511	318
Southern League FCs	98,524	64,411	
TOTAL	471,032	249,029	1,869

Source: *Sports Argus*, 16 October 1909, p. 1.

League was nearly £0.5 million, with just under £0.25 million spent by clubs on players' wages (Table 1.2). Increases in turnover grew significantly throughout the period, as illustrated by Aston Villa's finances in Table 1.3. As early as 1885, the club had generated revenues of £1,913, but by the end of the period its income was the modern-day equivalent of £1 million. Spectator sports in general were thriving and during this period Scottish football clubs and county cricket clubs generated similar amounts of revenue; yet, as in English football, some did better than others. For example, the average income of Glasgow Rangers before 1914 was £14,164 and for Hearts the figure was £7,361. St Johnstone's average income, however, was only £818. There were similar

Table 1.3 Summary of Aston Villa's balance sheets, 1879–1914

Year	Position in Football League	Revenue (£)	Wages (£)	Pre-tax profits (£)
1879		73		1
1880		235		19
1883		1,720		242
1885		1,913		11
1888		2,739	908	9
1897	1	10,935	3,999	1,299
1907	5	13,797	6,782	1,274
1908	2	11,457	5,719	443
1911	2	16,141	4,324	5,924
1912	6	12,946	5,538	1,579
1913	2	20,408	7,719	5,617
1914	2	20,167	6,726	6,777

Sources: Osbourne Newscuttings, p. 39, *Birmingham Gazette*, 22 May 1883; Osbourne Newscuttings, p. 53, *Birmingham Mail*, 4 July 1885; Osbourne Newscuttings, pp. 178, 180, *Saturday Night*; *Birmingham Gazette*, 1 June 1888, p. 3; *Aston Villa News and Record*; Szymanski and Kuypers, *Winners and Losers*, pp. 340–78; Butler, *Football League*; R. Roberts, *Schroders: Merchants and Bankers*, Macmillan, 1992, Appendix V.

Note: Aston Villa only played in Division One during this period.

differences of revenue in cricket's county championship. Between 1890 and 1914 Surrey generated an average income of over £14,000 per year whereas for Derbyshire it was £2,348.[56]

The turnover of the average Football League club in 1908 was perhaps similar to that of a small local firm.[57] By 1914, some of the leading clubs had annual turnovers of over £20,000.[58] In terms of generating income, an elite group of clubs emerged from the major urban areas, reflecting the advantages of a metropolitan location with its large pool of potential supporters and a modern transport network. It was these clubs that made up the majority of clubs in division one of the Football League, and also included London teams from the Southern League such as Tottenham Hotspur. In general, these clubs also paid the highest wages. In 1906 Villa, along with Newcastle United, had generated revenue through the gate, the equivalent of over £1 million at 2004 prices.[59]

The increase in football's competition after 1885 revolved around the players, with their wages taking up the largest portion of a club's costs, approximately 50 per cent.[60] They were a club's main assets and players quickly began to realize their market potential by selling their labour to the highest bidder. During the 1880s, a free market had existed in which some players were able to command a comparatively high weekly wage and move freely between clubs. Sunderland, for example, allegedly paid a player £5 a week in 1889.[61] By 1893, it was claimed that the average weekly wage of professional footballers was £3 during the season and £2 in the summer.[62] Wages plus transfer fees continued to rise as the footballing competition intensified. In 1898, Everton bought Johnnie Holt from Rangers for £300 and paid him wages of £6 10s per week all the year round.[63] Alf Common became the first player to be transferred for £1,000 when he moved from Sunderland to Middlesbrough in 1905.

In order to regulate football's labour market and stymie the competition for players, a retain and transfer system was introduced by the Football League in 1890, and then in 1901 the FA, who disliked the game being tainted by money, imposed a maximum wage. Both measures curtailed a footballer's freedom of movement and his earning capacity as, in theory, they prevented the poaching of players between clubs. These regulations also had a profound effect on shaping club–player relations for much of the twentieth century, and consequently how players themselves were managed. Under the transfer system, once a player registered with a Football League club he could be retained by that club for the entirety of his career unless the club decided to transfer him or terminate his contract. The length of the contract between club and player was for one year only, with the club deciding whether or not to sign him on for the following year, and if a player was offered the maximum wage he could not ask for a transfer. Accordingly, the transfer of a player from one club to another was only possible through the purchase of a player's contract. A player, or the buying club, required the permission of the player's club for an approach to be made. Furthermore, clubs could place a transfer fee on a player who had not been offered a contract for the following season as they still retained his registration.[64] The maximum wage was initially set at £4 per week. Similar to soldiers accepting the King's or Queen's Shilling when they enlisted, in order to gain their loyalty, players were also entitled to a £10 signing-on fee when they joined a new club.[65] The transfer system prevented the rich clubs from buying up the best talent because if a small club could afford to pay a player the maximum, there was little incentive for that player to move. In 1901, players were allowed benefit matches at the end of their career, or after five years' continuous service, which guaranteed them a certain sum.[66] Players later received extra benefits, together with periodic rises in the level of the maximum wage.

The imposition of a maximum wage, however, did not prevent clubs from breaching it. Between 1901 and 1911, the FA and the League investigated and punished at least seven clubs for financial irregularities. The most notorious cases were Middlesbrough and Manchester City. After an inspection of Middlesbrough's books in 1905, the FA found the club guilty of making irregular payments to players. A £250 fine was imposed and eleven of the club's twelve directors were suspended for two years.[67] Billy Meredith, Manchester City's star player, admitted that the club had paid him £6 per week from 1902, and that when City had won the FA Cup in 1904 he had received an extra £53 in bonuses. Later, in 1905, Meredith was found guilty by the footballing authorities of offering a bribe to an Aston Villa player and was suspended for one season. In May 1906, the FA launched a further investigation into the club's affairs when Meredith admitted his guilt on all charges, thus implicating the club. The FA reacted by fining seventeen past and present City players who were forbidden from playing for the club again. Two directors were also suspended and the manager, Tom Maley, was banned from football for life.[68]

The pressure to meet rising wage demands, by fair means or foul, had caused professional clubs to look for other means of raising money. One of the most popular methods was the adoption of limited liability status. During the 1890s, a rash of clubs formed themselves into limited companies. The fact that football clubs were increasingly becoming financial concerns was shown by the *Athletic News* urging all clubs with an annual turnover of over £1,000 to take advantage of the legislation. By converting themselves into limited liability companies, football clubs could sue and be sued, the individual responsibility of directors would also be limited, and a club's new status would reassure its creditors.[69] (As a members' club, the committee could have been made responsible for the club's debts.) Nearly all professional football clubs became private limited liability companies, with Small Heath being the first in 1888.[70] By 1912, the leading clubs were capitalized at over £2 million.[71]

From the 1890s onwards, football's popularity was expanding and clubs were looking to relocate to grounds with larger capacities that would then generate more income. To find a favourable location, one factor clubs had to take into consideration was the local transport network, and consequently, many grounds, like Villa Park, were situated near to a railway station and tram routes to give supporters better access. The first purpose-built football stadium was Everton's

Goodison Park, opened in August 1892 at a cost of £3,000.[72] Many clubs moved from ground to ground before finding a suitable long-term site. Sunderland moved from their ground at Newcastle Road before settling at Roker Park in 1898.[73] Before moving to Old Trafford in 1910, Manchester United played at Bank Street, Clayton. The capacity at Old Trafford was projected to be 100,000. Some grounds in Scotland also had large capacities. Hampden Park, home of Queen's Park and the venue of Scotland's home games, had a capacity of nearly 120,000 in 1909, and Third Lanark's Cathkin Park could hold over 110,000 spectators.[74]

In 1914 Aston Villa had plans to increase Villa Park's capacity to 104,000. It was hoped to more than double the club's earning capacity from £1,650 per match to £4,000. Standing spectators formed the vast majority of the crowd and paid a minimum admission fee of 6d, something that had been set by the Football League in 1890. Only 11,000 seats were to be provided, with the vast majority of spectators found on the uncovered terraces. The club had wanted to provide better covered facilities to cater for supporters who came from nearby Coventry, Worcester, Walsall, Kidderminster and different parts of the Black Country. These spectators were probably attracted by Villa's success and also by the opportunity to watch first division football. A local railway company had estimated that a Villa home game brought in approximately 1,000 spectators from Coventry alone.[75]

To what extent were football clubs like 'normal' businesses, and did they seek to capitalize on the increase in revenue? Some clubs did make profits. Everton, for example, made a profit in virtually every year between 1890 and 1915, and the club nearly always paid a dividend.[76] But others made losses. Before entering receivership in 1902, Newton Heath had been kept solvent only by loans and had never paid a dividend. A football club's commercial potential was in fact constrained by the Football Association. In order to maintain a degree of equality within the professional game between clubs, its constitution effectively restricted a club's capital base from which it could expand as a business. Rule 45 of the Football Association dealt with football club companies. Initially, all affiliated clubs' articles of association had to contain certain measures.[77] One of these, from 1896, limited the payment of dividends to shareholders to 5 per cent, rising to 7.5 per cent after 1918. Furthermore, and importantly, directors could not be paid. In effect, directors were still, and continued to be up until the 1980s, part of football management's voluntary tradition. The main aim of clubs, however, was to win football matches. As a consequence, many clubs did not obey strict economic rules. Instead, they can be classified as 'utility-maximizers' as opposed to 'profit-maximizers', and were willing to sacrifice profits for the sake of winning games and championships.[78] Losses, at least before the introduction of the maximum wage in 1901, were probably the result of bad management as clubs paid more than they could afford. Profits, on the other hand, were mostly ploughed back into the club for buying new players or investing in the ground.

To what extent then were commercial considerations a motive for share-holders and directors to get involved in football? Shareholders in English foot-ball clubs before 1914 were predominantly drawn from the local population, the majority being middle-class, although the largest occupational group that held a stake in their clubs was skilled labour, consisting of 28.6 per cent.[79] Of Everton's 453 shareholders in 1892, however, 56 per cent were from skilled manual or skilled non-manual occupations.[80] Most working-class shareholders held only one or two shares, and their reason for purchasing them can be attri-buted to identification with their team.[81] In this respect, football was one of the few industries that had working-class shareholders.[82]

Football club directorates, however, largely mirrored shareholdings, that is those who held the greatest number of shares, rather than the make-up of a club's shareholders. The next highest group of shareholders, in socio-occupational terms, were proprietors and employers with 26 per cent, including 6.9 per cent associated with the drinks trade, but in terms of shareholdings they accounted for 46 per cent compared to 13.7 per cent for skilled labour. Before 1915, approximately 50 per cent of football club directors belonged to the pro-prietor and employer category, and the proportion of professionals and managers on club boards considerably exceeded that of skilled workers.[83] The make-up of Middlesbrough's directorate changed between 1892 and 1914 from being pre-dominant working-class to being dominated by industrialists and proprietors from the alcohol and tobacco trades.[84]

The drinks trade actually used football to market its product, and was an important stage in the commercialization of sport. Players, both past and present, were given public houses to increase custom, products were advertised at grounds and financial support was given to teams to boost awareness and sales of beer.[85] Manchester City, for example, was known as a brewer's club during the Edwardian period. Its chairman, John Chapman, owned half a dozen public houses, and the club secretary, Joshua Parlby, was a publican. The club's chief benefactor was Stephen Chester Thompson who was the managing director of Chester's Brewery. It was one of Manchester's biggest brewers and controlled many pubs in the Ardwick and Gorton areas of the city. Furthermore, the club's headquarters was the Hyde Road Hotel in Ardwick.[86]

With an increasing proportion of businessmen and professional people becoming directors, it can be assumed their motives were different from those of working-class shareholders; but what were they? A brief survey of the litera-ture on the subject reveals a great variety. Robert Lewis, in his study of the early development of football in Lancashire, has argued that 'football as a leisure industry although organized as a business to cater for a mass audience, seldom created any profits and can hardly be viewed as a normal commercial enterprise'.[87] On the other hand, Tischler proffers the view that 'directorial par-ticipation in football was in most cases characterized by the implementation of many of the same income-producing methods outside of sports'. However, he is unable to substantiate his claim that, despite the limit of a 5 per cent dividend, directors were able to get round this and conceal extra income due to their familiarity with business techniques.[88]

The formation of a small number of clubs, like Sheffield United in 1889, did owe something to financial opportunism and showed that money could be made out of football. One notable opportunist was John Houlding. As president of Everton, he was also landlord of their Anfield ground. In 1891, he increased the rent and, following a complex dispute, the club's members were outraged enough to leave Anfield and make a new home for the club at Goodison Park in 1892. With a stadium and no team, Houlding decided instead to form his own football club, Liverpool. The outcome was that Houlding's Sandon Hotel next to Anfield was still frequented by football spectators for every home game, and being chairman of the football club complemented Houlding's position as a leading local Conservative.[89]

Another example is that of Chelsea, formed in 1905. In 1896 Henry Mears became owner of Stamford Bridge, the home of the London Athletic Club. Mears, a large contractor from south-west London, redeveloped it as a football ground using his own company. He also owned the catering company that supplied the large crowds at Stamford Bridge between 1905 and 1915. Mears was also the landlord and charged the football club an annual rental of £2,000.[90]

In 1903, Bradford City was formed after originally being a rugby club, Manningham. The club's committee had decided that the association code was more profitable after the club's failings on the rugby field. Manningham had joined the second division of the Northern Union League in 1902 but the club failed to obtain promotion despite spending heavily on players' wages, and, as a result, went bankrupt. Some club members, in conjunction with the Football League, the Bradford FA and local schools, then started a campaign to establish a first-class team in the local area, culminating in Bradford City's formation. By 1906 the gate receipts of the new club were five times higher than in the last three seasons of rugby combined.[91]

Some directors, therefore, did benefit from the game financially, from secondary profits and modest share dividends. Others used their position on the board to award themselves and their companies contracts to undertake the club's catering and to build new stands. Many directors also acted as guarantors. In 1900, Middlesbrough's directors had to place a personal security of £40 with the bank if the club was to receive an overdraft.[92] The chairman of Manchester United, the brewer John H. Davies, spent £20,000 on financing the club without receiving any reward.[93] In general, the reasons for becoming a football club director were multifarious but generally not of a profit-orientated nature. Russell has argued that serving on a club board was akin to a civic duty and he has argued that, 'profit-maximisation . . . was not a major consideration for the football club directors of Victorian and Edwardian England'.[94] Mason has suggested that a professional football club can be looked upon as 'a family firm with both shares and directorships passed down [the] generations', rather than a profit-making concern.[95]

Although football clubs were peculiar types of businesses, they did share many characteristics with other small firms. Football club directors, many of whom were small businessmen, based their ideas of managing football clubs on their own social and business experiences. They largely eschewed the hiring of pro-fessional management, and although directors delegated some of their authority to others, there was still a close relationship between the control of a firm and its ownership.[96] As a result, clubs were mainly run by directors who wanted to enjoy the privileges of ownership, and regarded selecting the team as a perk of the job. Yet, they also spent much of their time working on behalf of the club, travelling many miles up and down the country. Furthermore, directors were unwilling to hand over more responsibilities to salaried officials whom they regarded as socially inferior and tainted by earning a wage from football.

There were notable differences, however, between clubs and local firms that stemmed from the markets that they operated in. For their income, football clubs relied on supporters for whom 'the supreme appeal of football lay almost certainly in its expression of a sense of civic pride and identity', and this was very unlikely to change.[97] Clubs also represented an institution within a local community, whereas the people who owned family firms were ultimately respon-sible only to themselves. In his study of West Ham United, Charles Korr states that the directors' prima facie freedom was an illusion, 'the club had become almost a captive of the community in which it existed and which the directors purported to serve'.[98] As a consequence, the job of a football club director was not dissimilar to a public service. Moreover, football clubs were also part of the Victorian philanthropic tradition, and this continued into the twentieth century as Football League clubs made donations to a number of national causes, like the Titanic Fund and the Ibrox Disaster in 1902, as well as local ones, which cemented their standing in the local community.[99]

Despite converting to limited liability status, the management of many clubs continued to be rooted in the voluntary tradition. Many football club directors were former members of clubs and their main interest was in the welfare of that club. Initially, just one general committee had run Aston Villa. In 1887 this numbered nine plus the officers of the club, the president, vice-presidents, treasurer and the secretary.[100] When Villa became a company in 1896, it was run by a board of five directors. Despite the adoption of limited liability status, most clubs continued to be run by committees. As the business of football increased, however, so did the work of committees. For the 1892–3 season, Wolverhampton Wanderers' board of directors numbered twelve, with a players' and a finance committee. Before embarking on their first season in the Football League, Middlesbrough had three committees: finance and emergency, players' and ground. The players' committee had five elected members, the other two committees had three, while the chairman and the vice-chairman were appointed to all three as ex-officio members. For the following season the players' committee was reduced to three.[101] The workload and enthusiasm of the directors were reflected in their attendance at directors' meetings. In 1906–7, for example, Aston Villa's directors held forty-one meetings.[102] When Middlesbrough decided to turn professional and join the Football League in 1899, the increase in financial responsibilities brought with it an escalation in management duties. The workload of the club's directors increased dramatically, and during the summer before the new professional season began, meetings were held two or three times a week.[103]

Management, however, differed from club to club. At Preston North End there was a reverse in style when William Sudell, once the dominant figure in the club, lost overall control when it became a limited liability company in 1893. A general committee had initially run North End but in 1886 the number of committee members was reduced from twelve to four with Sudell as chairman.[104] Sudell had probably wanted the executive to be streamlined so that he could run the club the way he managed his cotton mill. And because of the success of the team, his style did not elicit any criticism from the members.[105] It is not inconceivable, however, that vanity began to cloud his judgement, because after the 1889 annual general meeting (AGM) there was not to be another one for four years. As the 1880s came to a close, the club was experiencing greater financial pressures, and suffered a steady decline in the 1890s. Between 1889 and 1893 it ran up a deficit of £752, precipitating Sudell's request at the 1893 AGM that the club become a limited liability company.[106]

Individuals, however, still heavily influenced the direction of clubs. Football clubs, like other firms, are 'organic institutions' in the way that they evolve. Moreover, they were, and continue to be, relatively small firms where the potential for an individual to influence direction is much greater than in larger companies. Fred Rinder, for example, was the dominant personality on Aston Villa's board for over thirty years. He was known for his austere manner and had a reputation for being brusque with people. Yet, he probably found being a football club director more interesting than his other line of work (see below). Football also represented a chance to climb and mix in higher social circles. It perhaps had a touch of glamour as well as improving the perception of a director's own status. Together with his work for Villa, Rinder held senior positions on FA committees such as the International Selection Committee and he was also on the Football League Management Committee. Only a few months before he died he had travelled 1,000 miles in a week on football matters.[107] Like other football administrators such as Arthur Oakley at Wolverhampton Wanderers, Charles Sutcliffe from Burnley and John Bentley, but, admittedly, unlike most other directors, football became a way of life for Rinder, 'almost a surrogate profession in itself'.[108]

It was noted earlier that some directors had had a long connection with their club from a time when members paid subscriptions. Rinder, for example, was elected a member of Aston Villa in 1881. He became a member of its committee in 1893 and eventually chairman of the board in 1899. Rinder, who succeeded another long-serving member, J.E. Margoschis, was a surveyor with Birmingham corporation. Coming from a non-conformist background, it was ironic that, as a teetotaller, he was a technical adviser to the Licensing Justices and, in 1912, he was appointed surveyor of licensed premises.[109] Rinder gave the club free advice on the building of the grandstand at Perry Barr in 1887, and laid out the designs for Villa Park when the club moved there.[110] Unusually, Villa had two former players, John Devey and Howard Spencer, on the board. Both had required special dispensation from the FA to become directors, as professional players had previously been barred from serving on club executives. After finishing his playing career, Devey entered the cinematography industry with another former Villa player, Harry Hampton, forming the Winson Green Picture House Company.[111] Spencer entered the coal trade and was managing director of a Birmingham coal and coke company.[112]

The make-up of many club boards reflected a unitary civic culture. William Sudell represented the traditions of both civic duty and pride within Preston which were well established within the town during the Victorian and Edwardian periods. In Lancashire, the scope of local government grew during the nineteenth century and councils became increasingly dominated by new industrial elites that replaced the landed gentry. Moreover, 'many among the industrial bourgeoisie were to hold firmly to a vision of themselves as the custodians of a unique industrial civilisation'.[113] Lancashire towns also became pioneers of a kind of municipal socialism that involved local government controlling local gas and water supplies. In the late nineteenth century, Preston was characterized by the active presence of a central urban elite. Whereas a suburban elite would have had no interest in the town, residents of Preston still relied on the town itself as a place of recreation and of day-to-day living. This meant that powerful families showed an active concern for their neighbourhood.[114] By contrast, those in the urban middle ranks involved themselves at less prestigious levels of local government, for example, as members of health boards and Poor Law administrators.[115] In a sense, Sudell's role with Preston North End reflected this trend as the football club grew in importance as a local social institution. As football's popularity increased, however, so did his popularity, elevating Sudell to the status of local celebrity.

Sudell had also joined his local Volunteer Force in 1874, rising to the rank of major by 1895.[116] The Volunteers had a reputation for primarily being an excuse for its members to enjoy social and recreational activities, and some regiments, most famously the Third Lanark Rifle Volunteers, had established football clubs. One of Liverpool's original directors, John McKenna, also joined the Volunteers and became a sergeant-major in the South Lancashire Artillery Volunteers. In 1883, a rugby club, connected to the battery, was formed and McKenna acted as its chairman.[117] Frank Watt, later secretary at Newcastle United, had helped form a football club with the 3rd Edinburgh Rifle Volunteers in 1874.[118] In addition to his connection with the football club, Sudell also held positions with other sporting institutions, including vice-president of the Preston Bicycle Club and the Preston Swimming Club, plus an array of cricket and football clubs.[119]

Many directors were also involved in local public life as town councillors or magistrates. For example, two prominent Villa directors, James Lees and Jack Jones, were members of local councils. Lees, a Conservative, was a member of Aston Urban District Council for three years.[120] Some football club directors also tried to exploit their connections to gain election to public office. At Manchester City, John Chapman and John Allison attempted to become Conservative councillors by using the alleged support of the club's players. Another Manchester City director, Chester Thompson, was a local politician. He was also agent for A.J. Balfour, the MP for Manchester East until 1905 and Conservative Prime Minister between 1902 and 1905, whom Thompson persuaded to become patron of the club.[121] The most notorious connection between football and politics occurred in 1910 and concerned the Middlesbrough chairman, Lieutenant-Colonel T. Gibson Poole. He was found guilty of offering a bribe to Sunderland before a game because he felt that Middlesbrough winning that particular game would be crucial to his chances of becoming the Conservative and Unionist MP for the town. Middlesbrough won the game but the Liberals won the election. Poole was later banned from football for life.[122]

The period up to 1914 laid the foundations for football management for the rest of the twentieth century. Developments that took place after the First World War were subject to the traditions and attitudes established in this period. Although there was some money to be made from football, most directors were not dissimilar to unpaid volunteers running a local social institution, and regarded their position as one of the perks of civic life. The management of a club was moulded by the professional, commercial and social experience of its directors and combined with the peculiarities of the football business. In general, directors preferred to manage the club themselves rather than to delegate, and this had a profound impact on its management culture.

Chapter 2

The pioneers, 1880–1914

Fledgling football clubs, although not businesses in the true sense of the word, needed managing when players began to be paid. The management of clubs was at an embryonic stage and, initially, it was the club directors who ran the clubs from top to bottom. However, as clubs struggled to come to terms with football's growing popularity and commercial demands, early managerial figures did emerge although their roles differed markedly from club to club.

Football itself was not isolated from the outside world, and in late Victorian England, changes in workplace relations had been set against a background of growing class conflict as both football and British industry struggled to control its 'human element'. The Employers and Workmen Act of 1875 had begun the slow process of changing the law of master and servants to that of 'employers' and 'workers'. Change, however, was complex and uneven as the language and notion of master and servant pervaded workplace culture well into the twentieth century. Middle-class football club directors regarded professional, working-class players as their social inferiors, and became increasingly reluctant to deal directly with them on a day-to-day basis. Instead, it became preferable for an intermediary to be used in this capacity and this role was usually split between the trainer and the club secretary. The gradual emergence of football club intermediaries mirrored the increasing role of foremen in industries like shipbuilding and construction, and overlookers in the textile industry. In addition to intermediaries, some managers assumed a more prominent role in their industry. There had been a rapid growth in the railways in the 1840s, for example, which created Britain's first wave of professional managers.

Because there was no management model for football to follow, defining what or who constituted a football manager before 1914 is complex. Instead of trying to identify distinct managerial figures similar to their modern counterparts, football management during this period needs to be seen in its contemporary context. Although the professional game was developing rapidly, any managerial responses to a club's changing circumstances were based on the motivations of its committee members or board of directors. Early managerial figures did emerge but their evolution was a slow process. The club secretary was the forerunner of the football manager. He initially ran the club on a day-to-day basis while a trainer looked after the players. Secretaries were decidedly deferential and subservient to their directors, and their role was limited and only developed gradually and in an uneven manner.

Early references to football management were usually in the context of a club's financial affairs, and managers were regarded as committee members or directors. Football League President John Bentley commented that, 'In the early eighties . . . club managers realised the fact that it was necessary to have a "star".'[1] Football managers were still associated with a club's finances later in this period. In 1906 Aston Villa's programme reported that, 'Football managers have found it exceedingly difficult to persuade any player of average merit that he is not worth the maximum of £4 per week . . .'.[2] Players also needed supervising, and on away trips, Bentley remarked that, 'The manager takes full charge of him from leaving home until he returns. . . . That is part of the business of football.'[3] At most clubs, however, it was initially the directors who carried out this task.

Although most of football's early paid officials carried the title of secretary, it can perhaps be claimed that Aston Villa's George Ramsay was the sport's first paid manager. In 1886, the club placed an advertisement in the *Birmingham Daily Gazette*, which stated,

WANTED, MANAGER FOR ASTON VILLA FOOTBALL CLUB who will be required to devote his whole time under direction of Committee. Salary £100 per annum. Applications with reference must be made not later than June 23 to Chairman of Committee, Aston Villa Club House, 6 Witton Road, Aston.[4]

Ramsay got the job yet throughout his career he was known as Villa's secretary. This may have been because the job title of 'secretary' was regarded as more prestigious than 'manager'. Whereas managers dealt with the workers, the secretary was running a company in alliance with its middle-class directors. There was similar confusion over the career of Tom Watson of Sunderland and Liverpool. On his will he was given the title of secretary but one of his obituaries remarked that, 'Tom Watson had been given many titles and in his football wares was the title of secretary. This was not strictly correct. Tom was a manager pure and simple.'[5]

Notwithstanding the claims of George Ramsay, Watson was perhaps football's first prototype of the modern manager. He had probably been an iron moulder by trade like his father but he may have also had clerical and retailing experience.[6] Watson's football career spanned both the amateur and professional eras. Before having a successful professional career with Sunderland and Liverpool, he was a prominent figure in the rapid growth of football in the Newcastle area during the 1880s. In 1881, Watson had founded Rosehill Football Club in the mid-Tyne district and by 1885, he was representing the club on the Northumberland FA Challenge Cup committee.[7] The following year

he was Newcastle West End's representative after being elected honorary secretary at its 1886 AGM.[8] During his time at 'West End' he had helped to secure
the lease of a ground that was to become St James's Park.[9] In December 1887,
however, he resigned his position. This seems to have followed an FA Cup tie
between the Newcastle team, Shankhouse, who had been loaned St James's
Park, and Aston Villa, where a crush occurred. The arrangements for the
admission of the public were presumably Watson's responsibility and these
had received some criticism.[10] By the start of the 1888–9 season, Watson was
honorary secretary at Newcastle East End. His time at West End and East End
coincided with an infusion of money into both clubs. As a result, Watson
recruited several Scottish professionals for the clubs, inducing them with a £5
signing-on fee plus the promise of a factory job on Tyneside.[11]

Because professional football was a new industry, clubs were initially looking
for someone who had experience of being involved in the game, and, as a result,
early managerial figures came from diverse backgrounds. A small survey of
secretaries of north-east clubs during the 1880s, shown in Table 2.1, reveals a
relatively even mix of occupational categories. Unsurprisingly perhaps, clerks,
with their organizational and administrative skills, formed the largest group,
with skilled workers next. Men with clerical and administrative experience
were also prominent at other clubs. John Nicholson, for example, Sheffield
United's secretary-manager from 1899 to 1932, originally worked as a clerk in
the local deputy coroner's office, while Sam Allen, who held a similar position
with Swindon Town between 1902 and 1933, had been a clerical worker at the
local Great Western Railway works. Another pre-1914 managerial figure, Sam

Table 2.1 Sample of occupations of north-east football club
secretaries, 1885–6

Occupational category	No.
Higher professions	3
Lower professions	2
Employers and proprietors	2
Administrators and managers	3
Clerical workers	9
Foremen, supervisors, inspectors	0
Skilled manual workers	7
Semi-skilled manual workers	3
Unskilled manual workers	4

Sources: *Newcastle Daily Journal*, 22 August 1885, p. 4, 23 September
1886, p. 3; *Ward's Directory of Newcastle* (1883–8); Bulmer, *History and
Directory of Newcastle-upon-Tyne* (1887); Censuses 1881 and 1891.

Notes: Based on occupational categories in G. Routh, *Occupation and Pay
in Great Britain 1906–60*, 1965, pp. 155–7.
The sample was taken from two years: 1885 in which there were forty-
three clubs, and 1886 in which there were fifty.

Hollis, had worked in a probate office and also the Post Office. A number of managers and secretaries were qualified as accountants, one of the few professions that offered some management training. Derby's secretary-manager from 1900 to 1906, Harry Newbould, was actually a qualified accountant, as was Arthur Turner, Spurs' secretary from 1906 to his death in 1949.[12] Celtic's long-serving manager, Willie Maley, had trained to be a chartered accountant while still a player with Celtic but he later abandoned accountancy to work full-time at the club.[13] Some managers had also been teachers. Both Wolverhampton Wanderers' secretary-manager, Jack Addenbroke, and Frank Brettell, secretary of Bolton Wanderers and later manager of Portsmouth, Plymouth and Tottenham Hotspur, relinquished positions as schoolmasters before entering football management.[14] Will Settle, on the other hand, belonged to the merchant class, selling coal. He had first been a director of Bolton Wanderers but became manager in 1910 for five years.[15]

It was mainly after the first generation of footballers had retired, usually post-1918, that a recognized path into management emerged. One exception was John McCartney. He had played for, amongst others, Rangers, Luton and Barnsley where he became secretary-manager in 1901. In addition, he had also worked for the Caledonian Railway Company as a clerk.[16] Another Scot, John Cameron, was one of the first, perhaps the first, professional player to combine playing with the duties of club management when he became the player-secretary-manager of Tottenham Hotspur in 1899. An international, Cameron had originally joined just as a player in 1898. Initially an amateur with Queen's Park and then Everton, whom he joined in 1895, he also worked for the shipping firm Cunard and was an early secretary of the Players' Union. It was said that his amateur status caused friction amongst Everton's professionals. They thought that being an amateur gave him some social advantage over them and his team mates refused to pass to him. This, apparently, forced him to turn professional.[17]

In addition to their organizational abilities, education was another important sought-after quality among these pioneers. Nothing, however, highlighted the stratification of Victorian class society more sharply than the education system. Whereas the upper classes went to public schools and middle-class children to grammar schools, the bulk of the population attended elementary schools, compounding their rank, sex role and lowly social position.[18] It was only in 1880 that attendance at elementary school was made compulsory for all children over 5 years old. Few members of the working classes received a secondary education let alone went to university. It is likely, therefore, that early managerial figures enjoyed a better schooling than future managers because directors later deemed a manager's practical experience gained as a player more important than educational qualifications. It is reasonable to assume that, even up to 1939, the general educational levels of football managers were relatively poor, reflecting the experience of the majority of working-class men.

Some prominent early managers did receive a better education than their contemporaries and this was perhaps reflected in the stature of the clubs they managed. William Sudell, for instance, received a private education at a Cheshire boarding school where he was likely to have had a classical liberal education in the public school tradition.[19] Ernest Mangnall, who became secretary-manager of Manchester United in 1903, and later managed Manchester City, was a pupil at Bolton Grammar School.[20] On his appointment at Tottenham, it was noted that John Cameron 'has splendid business experience and his educational credentials are far in advance of most of the other candidates'.[21] Tom Watson attended a local school and also one in York. It is likely that his father, a skilled worker, was part of the independent educational tradition that sent its children to church, chapel or voluntary schools. Within respectable working-class households, learning was sought as a means of advancement and the schooling of children was seen as normal before it became compulsory.

The role of these nascent football managers was largely determined by their relationship with the club's directors. Before 1914, football management was not impervious to changes within the game or society but any change was slow and subject to each club's management culture. Directors ran the clubs and this control was highlighted by the regular number of committee or board meetings they held in order to conduct business. However, as the game's popularity and competitiveness increased, so did their workload. More time needed to be devoted to the administration of business on a day-to-day basis and, as directors either had jobs or their own businesses to run, this was increasingly left in the hands of secretaries, and later secretary-managers. This process was evident by the 1890s as clubs began to outgrow their amateur roots. Following their conversion to professionalism in 1899, Middlesbrough's directors found that they could not handle the increased workload. For the next season they decided to upgrade John Robson from his honorary position to secretary-manager.[22] In 1888, Sunderland's members felt that they needed to appoint someone who could devote all his time to the club as, it was calculated, 'the work of a football club secretary absorbed 16 to 17 hours of his time weekly' and, 'There was no reason why such work should be done voluntarily.' At the 1889 AGM, one member claimed that 'the [secretarial] duties had so greatly increased that a match secretary was imperatively required'.[23] As one of the few people with experience in a fledgling industry, Tom Watson was an ideal candidate and Sunderland appointed him shortly after.[24]

Growing commercial and competitive pressures were not insignificant influences on club management. It was perhaps no coincidence that Watson's appointments at Sunderland and then Liverpool, in 1896, were at times when both clubs were facing competition within their own areas. On his arrival on Wearside the club was engaged in a spiteful battle with Sunderland Albion for local supremacy. On two occasions, for example, the two clubs had been drawn together in cup competitions with 'Albion' having home advantage.

Sunderland, though, withdrew from both, preferring to 'scratch' rather than ensure large gate receipts for 'Albion'. Furthermore, to obtain a more lucrative fixture list than Albion, Sunderland increased the expenses paid to opposing teams. Sunderland even withheld the publication of the following season's fixture list so as not to give any advantage to their rivals.

Moreover, despite the lack of emphasis on making money, the financial risks in football were increasing. Some clubs began to realize that a talented managerial figure could make a difference. Tom Watson, for example, was hired by Liverpool because of the successful job he had done at Sunderland. At first, John McKenna had acted as honorary secretary and seems to have run the club along with John Houlding's son, William, who was the club's chairman, with his father as President. But McKenna was also a director and the board realized that they required someone else with more experience in the football industry. It was William and McKenna who 'head hunted' Watson. He continued his success at Liverpool, winning the Football League on two further occasions, 1900–1 and 1905–6. This made him the first manager to win the championship with two different clubs.

Tottenham Hotspur had turned professional in 1895, and in 1898, under the direction of Charles D. Roberts, it converted from a members' club to limited liability status. In 1899, Roberts became chairman and moved the club to a new ground, White Hart Lane.[25] To gain a return on their investment the directors felt that, to improve the team, they needed a football specialist, and appointed John Cameron player-secretary-manager that same year. As we have seen, most other secretaries had a background in administration, and Cameron, having worked for Cunard, also had this experience. In addition, though, he had played football at the highest level. However, Cameron's relationship with the Spurs directors was still based on deference. He claimed that, 'The manager is not the sole governing authority. As regards his status, he is indubitably the servant of the club directors.'[26] Cameron also recognized the voluntary work undertaken by directors on the club's behalf. By 1906, the Spurs directors, because of the growing demands of the job, felt that Cameron should concentrate more on the team and appointed him team manager while they made Arthur Turner secretary.[27] The following year Cameron resigned citing various differences with the board.[28]

Commercial pressures, however, only had a limited impact on the management of clubs. Before professionalism, committees had carried out team selection, and this tradition continued when clubs became companies. Directors regarded picking the team as their prerogative and were unwilling to relinquish what they deemed as their duty. Secretaries may have offered their opinions on this matter, some of which may have been informed, but at this stage autonomy over team selection was not thought of as part of the secretary's job. In 1903, for example, following a series of poor results, Newcastle United's chairman, James Telford, even asked the club captain, Colin Veitch, and two other players, Andy Aitken and Jack Carr, to pick the team, thus overlooking the club's secretary, Frank Watt.[29] In the same year the newly formed Bradford City's board of directors consisted entirely of former members of Manningham rugby club. They realized they lacked any substantial knowledge of soccer, and allowed the players to elect their own captain.[30] Interestingly, on taking up his new position at Anfield, it was suggested by a local paper that Tom Watson should be given greater autonomy: 'The new secretary ought to be allowed as free a hand as possible and not be hampered in his work so long as he goes all right. It should be remembered that too many cooks spoil the broth.'[31] Although his role at Liverpool seems to have become more influential as time went on, it is unlikely that it extended to autonomy over team selection as a committee of directors and the manager was picking the club's first eleven into the 1950s.[32] John McCartney was actually given control over team matters at Barnsley and two Scottish clubs he managed, St Mirren and Hearts. Yet McCartney was an exception to the general rule, and he later resigned his post at Tynecastle in 1919, claiming that the directors were interfering with his team selections.[33]

Despite some responsibilities for the team, the job of these early managerial figures was largely administrative. They dealt with the ticketing and fixture arrangements, and the club correspondence, and took the minutes of meetings. As one of his tasks, George Ramsay informed Villa's players by telegram whether they were playing or not and about the forthcoming travel arrangements for an away game.[34] At Sunderland, Tom Watson was responsible for organizing the club's sports days, something which he had had experience of at Newcastle. Before one game at Bolton he had also arranged an excursion party, although this was dependent on getting a guarantee of 200 people. In 1895 Watson tried to arrange a tour to America. Despite corresponding with various clubs, the tour seems to have fallen through, probably because financial terms could not be agreed.[35] At Liverpool, Watson's main task was to ensure the smooth running of the club on a financial level, and between 1900 and 1915 Liverpool made a profit every year.[36] Much of Watson's time was taken up travelling by train, which indicates that the committee members either did not have the time or were unwilling to devote their time to the club's business any more. In contrast, Middlesbrough's directors supervised the players on trips to away games.[37] At Aston Villa James Lees undertook this task for a number of years, and during the 1904–5 season he travelled approximately 3,000 miles with the team.[38] Watson, between September 1891 and May 1892, covered over 14,000 miles, both travelling with the team and also to Football League and FA meetings in his capacity as the club's representative.[39]

One of football management's main functions, probably its most important, has been to build a winning team. During the 1880s, clubs explored various avenues in order to recruit players. One method was to place advertisements in newspapers. In 1880, William Giffen and John Devlin went to Bolton Wanderers after responding to advertisements in the Glasgow press. One had been promised work as a bookkeeper in a spinning mill, the other as an engineer.[40] Another means was for club committeemen to be informed of promising players through a network of personal contacts, and then approach the player themselves. Some early managers, referred to as 'postcard writers', signed players they had not seen on the recommendation of a friend or contact. Clubs also used agents. Middlesbrough employed a Mr Ferguson who was paid a £5 commission for every player he recommended who then went on to play for the club.[41] The judgement of agents, though, could be fallible. In 1893, an agent's recruitment of some sub-standard players for Aston Villa, who had not been seen by its committee members, caused much controversy and led to the committee resigning. The new committee, including Fred Rinder, later took on more responsibilities in signing players.[42] Directors in general played a significant role regarding the recruitment of players. They travelled to games to watch and report on prospective players, a practice that they continued well into the twentieth century. When Liverpool was first established, a sub-committee had signed the players.[43] However, some secretaries and managers were gradually given more of these responsibilities. John McCartney, for example, gained a reputation as a team builder. At Barnsley, in a bid to sign new players, he took it upon himself to sell season tickets door-to-door. He raised £10 and went to the north-east and bought fourteen players, and in the following season Barnsley won the Midland League.[44]

Before the First World War, Scotland was the major source of footballers. In the early 1880s Scottish 'professors' had become renowned for their combination play and their ability to keep possession of the ball by passing it amongst themselves. Up until then the game in England was dominated by an emphasis on individual players dribbling the ball, resulting in possession being frequently lost. Scotland dominated the annual fixture with England during the 1870s and 1880s through superior teamwork and passing. In October 1882, the FA's assistant secretary, N.L. Jackson, responded by forming the Corinthians club. Made up of players who had attended public school and university, it later provided the bulk of the England team. Jackson believed that its formation would give them more opportunities to practise together and thus regularly beat the Scots. Despite the club's amateur ethos it could not hide the competitive sentiment behind its creation.

When, in 1999, Chelsea first fielded an all-foreign team, it was accompanied by some xenophobic undertones in the media. However, this 'foreign invasion' was nothing new. During the 1880s, Preston North End, known as the 'Invincibles', was largely made up of Scots, while 'Team of the Macs' was the sobriquet given to Liverpool's original side. Football's increased competitiveness quickly dissolved the idea that teams should be comprised entirely of local players. Tottenham's team of 1900–1, for example, did not include one player from London.[45] From the summer of 1883, Preston's policy of recruiting Scottish players centred on Edinburgh, with other Lancashire clubs focusing on Glasgow. Sudell had acted on the advice of Tom McNeill, a native of Edinburgh, who was a foreman in the *Preston Herald*'s composing room.[46] By 1884, there were fifty-eight

Scottish players in England and, of these, eleven represented Preston North End.[47] Players, however, had to be induced to come over the border, and at 'North End' they were found jobs by club members. Its most famous player, Nick Ross, joined the club from Heart of Midlothian in July 1883, and took up a position as a slater in Preston with a Mr Bradshaw.[48] To avoid being caught paying players, their wages were refunded to their employers by the club treasurer and deducted from the gates receipts before they were entered in the club's books.[49]

Shortly after taking up his position as secretary at Sunderland in May 1889, Tom Watson, together with its treasurer, and one of the club's benefactors, Samuel Tyzack, went to Scotland to recruit players. The result was the 'Team of all the Talents'.[50] In addition to wages, Sunderland also gave the players jobs at the J.L. Thompson shipyard. Watson claimed that the players were paid on average 30s per week, plus a £10 retainer fee.[51] However, the case of John R. Auld, a Scottish international, suggests that the Sunderland players received more than this. On signing for the club in 1889, he claims he received a cheque for £300, which was his wages paid two years in advance, and then a further £170 as a signing-on fee. Auld then requested, and received, a place of business. This turned out to be a boot and shoe shop in Sunderland for which the club paid the first year's rental of £50 and it also put in the fixtures. After his second year with the club he received a £200 loyalty bonus. In addition to this, he also received playing bonuses of 10s for an away win, 7s 6d for a home win, and 5s for a draw.[52]

When clubs began to pay players, it brought with it unique labour management problems. Footballers were young men, many of whom liked a drink, and, from the club's perspective, needed discipline. Yet, this was complicated by the fact that the players were the club's main assets. Thus, in terms of managerial strategy, directors and managers needed to use the carrot as well as the stick. Management–worker relations within football clubs were cemented by the prevailing class system. Virtually all professional footballers were from the working classes while the majority of directors had middle-class backgrounds. On one occasion, the Aston Villa club programme, reporting on a banquet, commented on how well one of the players, Joseph Bache, spoke for a 'footballer'.[53] In 1909, the players threatened to strike over the maximum wage and the retain and transfer system. In response, one member of the Football League Management Committee, Charles Sutcliffe, wrote an article titled, 'Who Shall Be the Masters – Players or Clubs?' By implication players were still regarded as servants to their clubs despite the fact that they had signed a contract with their employers. The restrictions imposed by the transfer system also added to the players' sense of frustration. Furthermore, footballers were declared workmen under the Workmen's Compensation Act of 1906. As a result, players were now entitled to compensation if they sustained any injuries 'while following their employment'.[54] A certain tension existed between the two parties, and directors were to increasingly use their secretaries in dealings between the club and its players.

The most obvious way to discipline players was through their pockets. As early as 1885, Villa's committee had wanted to reward or punish players through their wage packets. The club's poor performance was being blamed on the poor physical condition of their players. The committee was forced to resign and it was proposed that players should be fined for not attending practice. A graduated scale of pay was suggested where professionals received a match fee, a bonus for a win and bonuses for every goal scored. It was also proposed, however, that any player who played while out of condition should not be paid at all.[55] The proposals were not carried.

On a day-to-day basis, the club trainer was in charge of the players. Some early trainers had a background in coaching athletes and, therefore, had a sound knowledge of training methods. However, their experience was usually in dealing with individual athletes and was inadequate for dealing with a group of young men. Other trainers had been in the army. A typical example was Hubert Dillon, whom Birmingham appointed in 1910. He had served in the army and had previously worked as a chief physical instructor in an education college where he had taught Swedish Drill.[56] Trainers were quasi-NCO figures and, in addition to maintaining the players' fitness, their main function was to keep an eye on them and make sure they kept out of mischief. The Middlesbrough trainer regularly reported to the board and was questioned on the condition of the players.[57]

A trainer's authority was limited, however, and clubs used other methods to monitor and control the players. Aston Villa resorted to spying on their players and occasionally they were spotted in pubs when they should have been training.[58] Rules with reference to training and playing were also introduced. Any player of Wolverhampton Wanderers, for example, who did not undertake his weekly training would forfeit a day's wages, his daily meals and he would be liable to suspension.[59] Clubs also insisted that any players who claimed that they were too ill to play or train had to provide a doctor's certificate.[60] Middlesbrough also made players sign their names in a book on training nights.

Some rules reflected temperance and non-conformist attitudes of a club's management. In 1899, for example, Middlesbrough adopted the rules of Aston Villa, and supplemented these with a ban on players betting on matches.[61] William McGregor had wanted Aston Villa to make a rule banning professional players from 'serving in public houses'.[62] At the same time the welfare of the club's players occasionally conflicted with the interests of those directors that worked in the drinks trade. It is reasonable to assume that, in keeping with his working-class background, frequenting pubs was one of a footballer's main leisure activities during this period. All too often for a club's liking this interfered with football, and in conjunction with any prevailing non-conformist attitudes inside the club, management aimed to stamp down on the players.

In 1893, during a poor season for Villa, Fred Rinder claimed that, 'Drink was the curse of the team', and that players had been drunk when training. He also complained that some members of the committee used 'filthy, obscene and profane' language to the players, and that some of them had been seen drinking with the players.[63] By looking through the minutes of Middlesbrough it is clear that drink was a major problem for them and no doubt other clubs.[64] Following the imposition of the maximum wage in 1901, many players had had their wages reduced. Some, like Derby County's famous inside-forward, Steve Bloomer, resorted to turning up drunk at training on a number of occasions as a submerged form of protest. Bloomer sometimes prepared for important matches with a few pints of beer at a local hostelry.[65]

A number of clubs adopted paternalistic methods as an attempt to gain both control and the loyalty of the players. By providing leisure facilities and other benefits for workers, many nineteenth-century employers sought to keep their workforce happy and loyal. During the 1892–3 season, Villa built a club-house at their Perry Barr ground that provided amenities such as a billiards table, and card and writing rooms, plus non-alcoholic refreshments. Its main purpose, however, was to keep an eye on the players. In welcoming the initiative, the *Birmingham Mail* commented that the sooner it was open the better, 'for several of the team require to be under pretty constant supervision'.[66] When the club moved to Villa Park more recreational facilities were also provided. A large room under the grandstand was fitted up as a gymnasium and the players' recreation room was connected to another room that was to be utilized as a reading room and library.[67] When Fred Rinder proposed the redevelopment of Villa Park in 1914, he announced that the players' dressing rooms were to be moved to the other side of the ground and situated in the corner of the new stand nearest to the offices, gymnasium and recreation rooms. Training was to take place on a piece of land on the other side of the offices, and as a result all the players' facilities were to be situated in one corner of the ground. Rinder then added, 'The training quarters and recreation rooms would then be under the easy control and supervision of the trainer without him having to walk to the opposite side of the ground to see how things are going on.'[68]

In 1892, Sunderland shipbuilders opened a Workmen's Rest Home that provided a reading room, a library and games facilities.[69] In the same year Sunderland Football Club purchased a house adjoining the club that was then fitted up as a billiard room. The club aimed to give the players somewhere to spend their leisure time in the (probably optimistic) hope that it would keep them out of trouble.[70] Tottenham Hotspur also opened a social club for the players in 1899. The club provided billiard tables and card tables plus facilities for reading and writing. There the players were under the control of a club steward, Troop-Sergeant-Major Sinton, who had served twenty-one years in the 1st Royal Dragoons and who in his own person embodied the notion of the military model of management.[71]

Other forms of paternalism included financial compensation. Preston North End's first Scottish import, J. Belger, broke his leg in November 1884 and was forced to retire from football. At its 1886 AGM, the club voted to pay him a final settlement of £50: previous to that he had been receiving £2 per week from the club since his injury.[72] Belger had already received a cheque for £200 on leaving hospital in January 1885 which had been donated by the club's followers.[73] Compensation was probably common among football clubs as Aston Villa had dispensed gratuities to injured players as far back as 1879–80. Professional clubs also appointed medical officers (i.e. the club doctor), albeit in an honorary capacity, a number of whom sat on the club's board. Any serious injuries, such as cartilage operations, were his concern, and he would refer players to specialists for surgery.

Throughout this period, however, football's industrial relations were moving away from a paternalistic model to one drawn on capital and labour lines that reflected the unrest throughout industry as a whole. In March 1902, for example, Stockport County's players bypassed the club's committee and picked the team themselves, after their wages had not been paid for over a week.[74] In 1896, by contrast, Manchester City prohibited its players from working at any other job other than football, in order to increase their fitness levels. Players also became more militant regarding their working conditions. An early players' union, the Association Footballers' Union, had been established in 1897 with John Cameron as secretary. It enjoyed the support of the *Athletic News* but was wound up in 1901.[75] The union was revived in 1907–8, though, and after the players threatened to go on strike in 1909, clubs reluctantly recognized that more time needed to be devoted to dealing with the players. In addition, directors were increasingly unwilling to haggle directly with working-class professionals over something as unseemly as money.[76] It demanded, therefore, a different approach to management and an increasing number of clubs used their secretaries or employed secretary-managers to handle the players.

What also stimulated management pressures was the game's growing competitiveness and the desire of clubs to improve the team's performance. At this stage, however, preparation of the players had little to do with the secretary-manager. Instead, the club trainer fulfilled this role. The recognition of the importance of preparation and training of sportsmen was not new. In the late eighteenth century, for example, the pugilist, Tom Cribb, used the champion pedestrian, 'Captain' Barclay, as his trainer for some fights. Aston Villa had recruited Joe Grierson as their trainer in 1893 when he was lured from Middlesbrough Ironopolis. Grierson was noted for specialist goalkeeping and weight-training routines. During the 1880s, Preston North End hired Jack Concannon, a well-known distance runner from Widnes. He put the players through a physical preparation similar to that of professional boxers, runners and oarsmen.[77] Preston also employed a shoemaker who once travelled with the team to Scotland for a game against Renton to adapt the players' boots according to the state of the pitch.[78] Tottenham's trainer under John Cameron was Sam Mountford who had also been a professional athlete, winning Sheffield sprint handicaps. The training that the Tottenham players underwent, however, was fairly representative of the period. During the season it was thought that walking and some 'practice at kicking' with the occasional sprint was enough to maintain a player's fitness.[79] For important games, teams retreated to hotels for a week to prepare themselves, where they were under the supervision of the trainer and secretary. The first team to do this was possibly Blackburn Olympic in 1883, which organized a pre-match preparation before their victory in the cup final.

When Preston won the cup in 1889, their preparation and training included ball practice, combined with some walking and running exercises, although it ceased on the Thursday before the game. In an attempt to engender team spirit the players drove twelve miles in an open wagonette to Lytham on the Friday before the semi-final where they had tea at 'The Ship'. Travelling to other games, however, was usually a rushed affair with teams getting to the ground just before kick-off and then leaving soon after the game finished in order to catch the last train. In the saloon before Preston's final league game in 1888–9 at Aston Villa, the players had chatted and smoked around a card table, but after the train passed Wolverhampton they changed into their kit. Following a four-hour journey, they were then driven in an open conveyance to the ground, arriving just in time for the 3.15 p.m. start. The following week the train journey began at 8 a.m. for Grimsby. To make sure the players got to the station on time cabs were sent round to their homes. They reached Grimsby at 2 p.m., leaving enough time to have a bowl of soup and to change. After the game there was only thirty minutes to catch the 5.30 p.m. train home.[80]

Around the turn of the century, books on the training and conditioning of footballers began to be published that reflected a growing awareness of the need for a more scientific approach to the training and coaching of sportsmen (and women) in general. In 1901, for example, *The Training of the Body*, written by F.A. Schmidt and Eustace H. Miles, attempted to analyze the mechanical movements in humans in activities as diverse as bowling and climbing. Another pioneer in this field was Sam Mussabini, one of the first British athletics coaches. He also coached cyclists and, in 1913, his first book on athletics, *The Complete Trainer*, was published. Later, Mussabini used cinematography to study the techniques of runners.[81] An early lecturer on football had been Robert Campbell, Tom Watson's successor at Sunderland. Campbell made many speeches in support of the game and also wrote a short series of pamphlets on various aspects of football, such as *Football: Physical, Social and Moral Aspects*, published in 1897.

One consequence of these new ideas was that more consideration was given to the player's physical well-being. Billy Meredith actually took this upon himself. He followed a strict match-day diet of a glass of port before and a boiled chicken after the game and this helped to prolong a career that lasted over thirty years. Meredith also took advantage of the revolutionary heat treatment of sporting injuries offered at the Matlock House Hydro near the Manchester City ground in Hyde.[82] A book written by John Cameron put forward theories about the training and preparation of players and it also indicated how clubs had become concerned with the effect of vices on the well-being of their players, although, in the twenty-first century, not all the advice given would meet with approval. Robert Campbell advocated that players should be tee-totallers, while Cameron advised players not to consume excessive quantities of alcohol, probably with little effect. Smoking was 'a matter which is left to the men's common sense'.[83] Cameron also regarded diet as important. He recommended that 'a substantial meal should be taken at least two hours before a match'. This was to include a well-cooked beef steak, stale bread and vegetables with no potatoes. It was argued that this would enable the players to 'play right through the game without . . . feeling fatigued'. Players also had to be kept together, have regular hours for meals and go to bed early.[84] Managers would subsequently become more responsible for this area of management and these ideas pointed towards the direction this would eventually take.

Some early coaching of footballers had been undertaken by team captains like Archie Hunter at Aston Villa and Jimmy Ross at Liverpool.[85] The main role of the captain, however, was that of leadership and to make tactical changes on the pitch. At Everton, Nick Ross was in disagreement with the committee over his role as captain. He felt that as captain and a professional he should pick the team and decide their positions on the field, but instead the Everton committee undertook these tasks.[86] Despite the emergence of new ideas on the coaching of players, any improvements generally took place on an *ad hoc* basis. In 1908, one newspaper columnist bemoaned the repetition of players' mistakes, and was convinced that 'the first club who can secure the right man to give the team lectures with a blackboard on points of play and then take them on to the field to practise one point after another, will speedily rise to the top of the tree'.[87] Preston North End, however, had already done this. Nick Ross, along with Sudell, has been credited with introducing the blackboard into the dressing room, and with being a clever tactician.[88] Furthermore, Sudell used chessmen set out on a billiard table to illustrate tactical plans.[89] On another occasion, Sudell hired a bus and four horses and, along with other members of the committee, drove the team to Blackburn to watch them play Everton so that the players could 'spy' on both teams.[90]

During its early years, football was still a very vigorous game. It lacked the finesse and skill of the modern game and was generally marked by rushes and an emphasis on physical contact. Heavy shoulder charges were very much part of the play and goalkeepers, unlike today, received no protection. Games could sometimes be rough affairs. On one occasion when Preston played Everton, the 'Toffeemen' were accused of inaugurating 'a series of malpractices from the start of the game'. This met with retaliation from the Preston players, bringing the socially driven comment that 'such disgraceful exhibitions . . . tends to lower the respectability of the game and disgust the better class of onlookers'.[91]

However, Preston were also noted for their distinctive style of play, underlining Sudell's promotion of a more cultured and scientific form of football. Essentially, the team cultivated a short passing game partly as a consequence of having Scottish players. Early pioneers of the passing game, or combination play as it was known, were the Royal Engineers, and in particular, Queen's Park of Glasgow during the 1870s. Their formation had consisted of two backs, two half-backs and six forwards, although by 1884 English teams had learnt to counter it. Preston were the first team to consistently play with three half-backs and only five forwards; the extra half-back had previously been a centre-forward. It became known as the attacking centre-half formation and endured until 1925 when the offside law was changed. Importantly, through its passing, this formation brought a greater cohesion and emphasis on teamwork.[92]

Preston's style contrasted with that of the majority of their opponents. In a game against Bolton in 1885, it was reported that North End was 'machine like . . . in working the ball along the ground', whereas their opponents did 'their work in rushes'.[93] Before their 1888 cup tie, Aston Villa were advised to harry and bustle North End to prevent them dominating the game through their measured passing. It did not work as Preston won 3–1.[94] The 1889 FA Cup final brought a comparison between the two sets of forwards: 'While the Wolverhampton men went in for hard – very hard – and determined play, North End plodded away with a distinct system.'[95] A system was only as good as its players and in centre-forward John Goodall they possessed one of the pioneers of this more scientific approach. Players at other clubs were also formulating their own tactical plans. At the turn of the century, full-backs began to play an 'offside game', probably invented by Morley and Montgomery of Notts. County, and later perfected by Newcastle United's Billy McCracken.[96]

Football's popularity coincided with, and was reinforced by, the expansion of the newspaper industry during the late nineteenth century, and this had major implications for the game as well as for managers. Tony Mason has stated that, 'there is an important symbiotic relationship between the expansion of the game, both amateur and professional, and both the growth of a specialized press and the spread of football coverage in the general newspapers'.[97] The press became part of the sporting sub-culture and through reporting on matches it gave football a cultural legitimacy. Following the success of the Bolton-based *Football Field*, football specials became common in towns with a professional football club after 1884. First published in 1875, the *Athletic News* was a strong supporter of professional football. Its headquarters were in Manchester and between 1893 and 1900 John Bentley, the President of the Football League from 1894 to 1910, was its editor.[98] It was known as *The Times* of football and many of its writers were influential FA or League officials. Sports coverage as a whole became more widespread in the national and, especially, the Sunday papers during the 1890s. It was during this decade that the Northcliffe Revolution took place and by the turn of the century no paper aiming for a popular audience could neglect sport.

It was the club secretary, then later the manager, who became the link between the press and the football club, and consequently, a fount for stories. Bentley's successor, James Catton, for example, regularly corresponded with Tom Watson and other managers in his quest for articles.[99] John McCartney's dealings with the press bordered on the modern. He had a regular column with the *Evening News* in Scotland and was also known for his colourful literary quotes – something, as a former journalist, he knew the press would appreciate.[100] Yet it was a two-way process as information was sometimes passed on to promote the club. It was also important that the club kept its local audience informed of any ongoing news, such as the transfer of players or ticket arrangements for important games. The publicity generated by keeping the club's name in the headlines was another important factor.

Tom Watson had recognized the value of publicity from early on, and that the best way to convey it was through the press. When he was involved with Rosehill it was announced in 1885 that, as a publicity stunt, the club intended to engage a Highlander in costume to play the team on to the ground.[101] Sometimes at night, and because the club did not have enough money to pay a printer's bill, Watson advertized forthcoming games by painting their details on walls.[102] At the 1887 AGM of Newcastle West End, one member took exception to reporters being present and moved that they should leave. Watson strongly objected. He insisted that the club was a public body and that, instead, the press should be allowed to freely publish and criticize the club's proceedings.[103] Watson enjoyed a long and fruitful relationship with reporters and, like modern managers, he used it to cultivate his own reputation. Jimmy Catton, the editor of the *Athletic News*, remarked that,

> No secretary contrived to be mentioned in print so often as Tom Watson of Liverpool. He loved to see his name in good type. It was a little weakness of his – and quite pardonable, for most people have their spice of vanity, although they take pains to conceal it.[104]

In 1891 it was reported that a prominent FA Councillor, J.C. Clegg, had asked Watson who he was. The reporter, slightly ironically, commented, 'Fancy the great Tom Watson of Sunderland not being known.'[105] When he left Sunderland the local reporters presented him with an inscribed, gold carbuncled pin and a silver matchbox as a mark of their appreciation and their relationship.[106]

At this early stage, football clubs were usually reported in terms of their directors. Newspapers would announce, for example, that the directors had selected the team for Saturday, thus indicating who ran the club. Yet a few managers were already associated with their team. When Preston North End won the FA Cup in 1889, it was reported as Sudell's 'great victory'.[107] Sudell was also recognized as the club's dominant figure, and before the following season, the

Athletic News predicted that 'Mr Sudell will keep the team up to its present high standards'.[108] Liverpool were also referred to as 'Tom Watson's men', thus giving at least a perception of an association between a manager and his players. When the club won the League in 1901 the rejoicing crowds at Lime Street station in Liverpool attempted to shoulder him.[109] Furthermore, Watson was immortalized in a painting by Thomas Hemy, in a scene of a match between Sunderland and Aston Villa in January 1895.

Even if directors and committees ran clubs, it was still believed by some that a manager could make a difference to the team. When Aston Villa had problems with its committee in 1893 it was argued that the club lacked someone like Major Sudell or Mr Tom Watson who could improve its fortunes.[110] At Burnley's AGM in 1894 it was remarked that some of the players were guilty of disobedience and misconduct and that it required a manager to look after the team. It was then claimed that,

> Mr Sudell . . . was in the main responsible for the decision of the meeting. The argument was that while Mr Sudell was the manager, the North End were the champions. Therefore, if Burnley have a manager, Burnley will become the champions.[111]

In the majority of clubs, though, directors and committees were unwilling to loosen the reins of power. However, the game's increasing competitiveness and the growth in newspaper readership also correlated with a rise in scapegoating, as fans wanted someone to blame when their team was not doing so well. Club directors began to look for another figure to represent the public face of the club so that they instead became the focus of the fans' ire.[112] Aided by his increasing profile in the press, this helped to project a public perception of the manager as an important figure within the club despite the fact that the main source of power was still located in the boardroom.

With its growing profile and the game's peculiar business that demanded weekly results, football management developed pressures all of its own. And these manifested themselves in various ways almost from the start. For William Sudell, it ended with him being sent to prison for three years in April 1895. He had been found guilty of embezzling money from his mill and falsifying the accounts over a four-year period from 1889 to 1893. Both the prosecution and the defence agreed that Sudell did not gain personally from his felony. Instead, he had diverted the money into the coffers of the club and used it for entertaining football officials and visiting teams.[113] Because of football's increasing competition, the management of Preston had started to overwhelm him.

The nature of the business could also fray the nerves. During the 1889 FA Cup semi-final against West Bromwich Albion, it was reported that Sudell and the club trainer, Tom Livesey, 'kicked about like a pair of restive ponies' due to pressure from Albion.[114] On another occasion Preston were losing 2–0 to Notts. County and Sudell encouraged or perhaps berated the players from the touchline.[115] Similarly, Tom Watson was also nervous about the result of a match, and 'for a long period could not bear to look at a game in which his team was engaged until assured that a good lead had been obtained'.[116] He was highly strung and it was common for him to leave the ground or walk around the grandstand because he could not stand the strain.[117] This stress, combined with a weight that was between 18 and 20 stones, may have resulted in the pleurisy that caused his death.[118] By contrast, John Cameron took a more relaxed attitude, and was still imbued with the amateur spirit. Before the 1901 Cup final, he was the last of the Spurs team on to the field, casually walking with his hands in his pockets and with an air of indifference about him to the biggest game of the year.[119]

Although early football managers did not enjoy the profile of their modern counterparts, by 1914 they had begun to form a distinct group and had their own aspirations. In 1907, for example, a secretaries' and managers' association was established, although it was more characteristic of a friendly society than a professional body and it did not last long. This fledgling identity was also evident in a rise in their salaries, improved lifestyles and their social mobility. It was probably a more exciting way to earn a living compared to their previous jobs and, like club directors, gave them the opportunity to travel and mix in different social circles. Before 1914, there had been a lack of mobility from the working classes to the middle classes, and it was unusual for someone from a working-class home to become a member of the middle class. However, it seems that, in terms of income, many football managers became part of the lower middle classes, earning similar salaries to teachers, for example. Tom Watson had originally earned 35s a week (£89 per year) at Sunderland, later rising to £150.[120] He also took over a tobacconist's shop in the town and it was in this shop's office that football business was conducted.[121] On moving to Liverpool, his annual salary was £300, which at the time was considered the most anyone in football had ever earned, and this figure had probably increased by the time he died in 1915.[122] By comparison, business managers and foremen earned about £200 per year by 1914.[123] During the Victorian and Edwardian periods, the status of public figures was greater than today and this was mirrored in their salaries. In 1913, for example, the Chancellor of the Exchequer's salary was £5,000.[124] John J. Bentley, when he became secretary of Manchester United in 1912, earned £300 per annum.[125] George Ramsay was also earning £300 by 1900 but by 1914 this had probably increased to around £500 while his assistant may have earned about £150 per annum.[126] These were managers of the bigger and more successful clubs, however, illustrating a nascent meritocracy within football management. Lower down the scale, John Robson of Middlesbrough earned a salary of £156 that was more in keeping with the status of a clerk.[127] In 1895 Frank Watt was offered the position of secretary at Newcastle United with an annual salary of £140 plus a house owned by the club chairman, James Telford, that was rented to the club. Watson had earlier turned the position down because he earned more at Sunderland.[128] Until the imposition of the maximum wage, the wages of the top players were higher than those of secretaries or secretary-managers, indicating the officials' lack of importance.

The idea of class, however, is not merely defined by economic indicators such as income, occupation or education. Instead, as E.P. Thompson has argued, class needs to be seen as a social and cultural formation that men and women define as they live their own history.[129] Foremen, for example, identified more with the lower middle class than with artisans or workers, and they were often owners of small properties and frugal savers. Some also became freemasons.[130] Football managers probably held similar aspirations. It was claimed, with more than a hint of irony, that, 'Some secretaries sport big watch-chains, glittering rings and cigars the size of a policeman's truncheon.'[131]

Managers' aspirations were also reflected in the local societies and institutions that they joined. Freemasonry, for example, was an important part of civic culture. A number of football directors, like Fred Rinder, had joined the fraternity, and it is likely that with their assistance a number of managers were invited to join.[132] Tom Watson, for example, was a freemason and shared the same lodge, 'Sincerity', as Liverpool director John McKenna, who probably invited him.[133] McKenna, himself, was probably invited to join by John Houlding, another freemason.[134] The founder of Sunderland, James Allen, had also been an active freemason.[135] Watson also attended church regularly and was a keen bowler.[136] He had been chairman of the Liverpool Parks and Garden League, and a former President of Liverpool and District Bowling Association.[137] For his long service as a manager Watson was awarded the Football League's Long Service Medal in 1910 for twenty-one years in football management.[138] Ernest Mangnall was also awarded the medal in 1921.[139] Furthermore, Watson's funeral was an occasion not just for the local community but for football as well. As a managerial figure, Watson had become part of the football establishment. The Football League, local FAs and the major clubs were represented, as were members of the press. The number of wreaths numbered over one hundred (this at a time of war). Seven former Liverpool players, including Alex Raisbeck, Ted Doig, and the club trainer William Connell, acted as pall bearers.

By 1914, the role of a football manager, in line with similar developments throughout industry as a whole, had gradually gained more importance. The business of football clubs had increased, and directors, with their own firms to run, were unable to meet the rising demands of managing a club on a day-to-day basis. Secretary-managers consequently took on more duties and responsibilities. Any development, however, was on an *ad hoc* basis, and differed from club to club. Directors were still in control, and generally made all the important decisions, including team selection. Football's managerial figures learned their job 'on the job' as it did not require any formal training or qualifications, or even much in the way of basic education. Managers, however, through the expanding press coverage of football, had begun to forge a professional and, as a result, a middle-class identity.

Chapter 3

'Organizing victory'

Herbert Chapman and football management modernity

Herbert Chapman's career was a watershed in the development of the football manager and marked the beginning of the game's gradual divorce from its amateur past and a more professional approach. In terms of the history of football management, Chapman provides an example of the impact that human agency can have on the process of social change. Although his career was not a linear progression and needs to be seen in light of its contemporary setting, more than anyone else, Chapman shaped the image and role of the modern manager.

His career spanned the years 1907 until his sudden death at 55 in 1934, during which he had been the first to 'organize victory'.[1] Chapman's achievements are still unique, being the only manager to win both the Football League championship and FA Cup with two different clubs, Huddersfield Town and Arsenal.[2] His overall impact has been acknowledged across the generations. When he was manager of the club, George Graham impressed on his younger players the image of Arsenal that Chapman had shaped.[3] In comparing him with others, Manchester United's Matt Busby described him as a 'man of stature . . . who in transforming Arsenal transformed the game of football'.[4] Bernard Joy, a former Arsenal player, recognized his wider contribution,

> Herbert Chapman not only put Arsenal on top of the soccer world. He did more for professional football than any man since William McGregor, the founder of the Football League. The C.B. Cochran of football, he swept it from the committee and roped-off enclosure stage to be a leading entertainment industry and he showed that teams run by amateur directors could not match those run by expert managers. He looked beyond the cloth-capped supporters and made big soccer games as fashionable as Wimbledon or a Test Match.[5]

In addition to his achievements on the field, Chapman therefore grasped the idea that football should, and could, be modernized into something more akin to the entertainment business, and he tried to attract and then cater for a wider audience that was less stratified and more heterogeneous. He claimed that,

> The old idea that a club may sit back and wait for the crowds to come should have died long ago. In these days you have to fetch them by making an irresistible appeal and in this respect, at least, we do not differ greatly from other entertainment promoters.[6]

In other service industries, entrepreneurs had also placed an increasing importance on the dramatic in order to attract customers. One of the most famous entertainment promoters of Chapman's day had been the theatre impresario C.B. (Charles Blake) Cochran who had made his name promoting Harry Houdini. Cochran was not a businessman but his visual sense and good ear for music provided the basis for his success as an entertainer. An early pioneer in the field of retail had been the American, Gordon H. Selfridge. He was a showman who loved display and opened Selfridge's department store on Oxford Street in 1909, which became an example of American marketing techniques.[7] Moreover, in the field of management, the emergence of men like Josiah Stamp of the London, Midland and Scottish Railway and Harry McGowan who, in 1926, along with Alfred Mond, formed Imperial Chemicals Industries Ltd, put the idea of the dynamic business manager to the fore of the popular consciousness after the First World War. Despite the fact that football clubs were tiny organizations by comparison, Chapman's emergence and reputation partly echoed this trend.

Herbert Chapman's background was not untypical of contemporary football managers. Born in 1878, he was the product of a Methodist, working-class upbringing in Kiveton Park near Sheffield, where his father was a miner. Herbert had one sister and four brothers, one of whom, Harry, played for Sheffield Wednesday, winning Football League honours in 1903 and 1904, and an FA Cup winner's medal in 1907. He was also manager of Hull City between 1913 and 1914.[8] Herbert enjoyed a more moderate playing career, frequently moving between clubs.[9] However, he did show an early knack for the spectacular by playing in light yellow boots.[10] Chapman had little other preparation for management. Initially, he had attended the local colliery school before working at the colliery itself. To supplement his football wages he took other jobs such as a solicitor's clerk. He later embarked on a mining engineer's course at University College, Sheffield. Chapman did not complete the course due to his playing career but it indicated a certain level of intelligence and aptitude at a time when working-class boys did not automatically receive a secondary education.[11]

His experience in industry, which he squeezed in during his football career, also marked Chapman out from his contemporaries. During the First World War, he took a position at the Barnbow munitions factory, the Number One National Shell Filling Factory, just outside Leeds. In wartime, the Ministry of

Munitions sought people with managerial experience, and Chapman was chief storekeeper, in effect a sub-manager, with responsibility for the stores, the box factory plus the farm.[12] At Barnbow, Chapman would have taken note of a more progressive form of industrial management that emphasized the importance of workers' welfare and health.[13] This new attitude towards the workforce had been initiated by Seebohm Rowntree, the head of the Ministry's Industrial Welfare Department, and was similar to that at his York Cocoa Works. Directly after the war, Chapman's football management career went into abeyance. He resigned from Leeds City in December 1918 and began work as superintendent of labour at Europe's largest seed crushing mills, the Olympia Oil and Cake Works in Selby, owned by Joseph Watson, his managing director at Barnbow.[14] In 1920, however, the oil mills were sold. Chapman found himself out of a job and went back to football.[15]

Although Chapman built his reputation at Arsenal, it was at his first three clubs – Northampton Town, Leeds City and Huddersfield Town – that he laid the foundations for his later success. At each of these clubs there are a number of common factors that give insights not only into how Chapman's career evolved but also how modern football management developed.

First, Chapman's appointment at all three had been preceded by financial as well as football problems. Despite this he was successful at each, and the difference that Chapman made was almost immediate. In 1909, two seasons after his appointment, Northampton Town won the Southern League and finished in the top four in each of the next three seasons.[16] Yet, when he joined the club, Northampton had just finished bottom of the first division and only maintained its status through the re-election process.[17] Similarly, in 1912, following Chapman's lobbying, Leeds survived a vote of re-election after finishing bottom of the Football League.[18] In the next two seasons Leeds finished sixth and fourth in the second division.[19] In 1921, he joined Huddersfield Town, a team struggling in the first division, but by the following year, it had won the FA Cup and then it won the Football League in 1924 and 1925, bringing Chapman national attention.

Moreover, Chapman's management alleviated these clubs' off-the-field situation. In the season prior to his arrival, Northampton Town's income, for example, was £1,855. In his final season it had increased to £5,309.[20] Following an EGM in August 1912, shortly after Chapman was appointed, Leeds went into voluntary liquidation. The club's total losses since 1905 amounted to £11,320. A new company was formed with Norris Hepworth, eldest son of Joseph, the tailor, as its benefactor. Norris cleared the club's debts and injected some new capital. By the end of his first season, Chapman had persuaded the financially prudent Leeds directors to part with £3,000 for transfers. This was to pay a dividend, literally, as the club finished sixth and attendances increased to the extent that there was a profit of £400. Unlike the other two, Huddersfield Town was a first division club. By 1919, however, crowds averaged only 4,000 and the club had spent over £21,000 on ground improvements resulting in total accumulated losses of £6,650.[21] Even after winning the FA Cup in 1922, it still made a loss on the season of £1,707.[22] Nevertheless, and despite a rise in unemployment due to the economic depression that had hit the town's textile industry, there was a profit of £1,814 the following year.[23]

Furthermore, Chapman's first three clubs had been in competition with the local and more well-established rugby clubs who on his arrival enjoyed greater popularity than their association counterparts.[24] One visible consequence of this had been that the local press gave preference to the rugby club in its coverage. By 1921, however, gates at Huddersfield Town were outstripping those of the rugby club, and by 1923, as at Northampton Town, it was the football club that enjoyed preferential press treatment.

How was Chapman able to make this difference? Clubs like Aston Villa, West Bromwich Albion and Everton epitomized football's management culture. They had a tradition of directors dealing with team affairs, with the secretary handling day-to-day matters. Nicholas Fishwick has argued that only those clubs that lacked a strong tradition of director involvement or in which a crisis occurred, would experiment with new ideas.[25] In contrast to Aston Villa *et al.*, Chapman's clubs were formed later, and were perhaps more inclined to try out new methods, such as employing a manager. At Northampton Town, a joint board of guarantors and members of the old committee had been appointed to manage the club in 1906. Northampton was then the only club in the Southern League that relied on gate receipts and patrons for its income: others relied on shareholders and directors. The guarantors included the officers of the club who controlled the club's financial affairs while the overall responsibility for the team fell to a selection committee. But due to its continuing problems, by the following year the guarantors, in return for further funds, made it 'a condition that a Playing-Manager should be secured' who had experience of professional football. It was reported that 'it was the intention of the guarantors to give him a free hand' in terms of his management of the team, replacing the amateur-dominated selection committee.[26]

Chapman later claimed that he had the responsibility of choosing the team at all the clubs he had managed.[27] However, this is unlikely, and may have been an example of someone embellishing his reputation. At Northampton, for example, he was new to the job and a perception that he was immediately all-powerful needs to be balanced against football's prevailing attitudes towards management in which directors or committee members were unwilling to completely abdicate duties which they felt were a reward for their efforts. Northampton Town itself was dominated by its chairman, A.J. ('Pat') Darnell, the local coroner, and a charismatic figure who had influence in all of the town's sporting clubs. At board meetings, Chapman would have revealed his team selection but it is likely, as at other clubs, that his selection would have been questioned. Furthermore, Chapman still operated within a social framework in which managers were not only subordinate but also socially inferior to their directors. Early football managers in general aspired to the bourgeois status of their directors. To improve his social and professional standing, for example, Chapman became a member of a local freemasons' lodge.[28] Nevertheless, Chapman held a relatively strong position at Northampton and his other clubs. This was due in no small part to his strong personality. He was articulate and had great powers of persuasion and, because they were small organizations, it illustrated how forceful individuals could catalyze changes within football clubs.

Initially, his position at Huddersfield Town had been relatively marginal. The directors took an active part in the club's management with team building and team selection being reported in the press through their actions. However, the directors were sufficiently impressed by Chapman's management skills to later give him the responsibility of selecting the team.[29] The football competition was also intensifying, and as the directors had their own jobs and businesses to run, the demands on their time increased. They may have reasoned that the situation demanded someone with specialist football knowledge to take a bigger role in running the club. The directors were also not above criticism, and this was circulated through readers' letters in local newspapers. Furthermore, the Huddersfield players had shown signs of militancy. In 1922, the Football League Management Committee had decided to reduce the maximum wage from £10 to £8. There was little sign of a national strike but at Huddersfield Town the players had discussed the possibility of taking some form of industrial action.[30] This perhaps indicated to the directors that they needed to improve their relationship with the players, and that by giving the manager more responsibility he could foster better relations. Or it may have simply been that as middle-class professionals they did not want the stress of dealing with proletarian footballers face-to-face.

In dealing with professional footballers, Chapman, unlike other early managers, believed that it was necessary for a manager to establish a close relationship with his players in order to gain their confidence. At Leeds he inaugurated the team talk, believing that players should give as much thought to football as they did to playing billiards and gambling at cards. Before every home game the Leeds players would assemble on a Saturday morning at a city centre hotel to talk amongst themselves. Chapman presided but he encouraged every player to express his views on the previous week's game. At the same time, he recognized that the majority of northern and Scottish working-class players were shy and reticent about speaking in group situations, and that private interviews were another way of gaining their confidence. At Leeds he also had a diagram of the field painted on a table in his office where he would discuss the game with individual players.[31] Chapman also has some claim to being the first 'tracksuit' manager as 'in his more active days he dressed for the part and went out to practise with a player whose deficiencies he wanted to remedy'.[32] One of these players was Northampton's Fred ('Fanny') Walden, later of Spurs and England, who Chapman helped to improve his crossing of the ball.[33]

Despite these efforts to form closer relations with players, Chapman was also a disciplinarian. He wanted his players to behave themselves both on and off the pitch. He warned them away from women and told them to quit smoking, although he did allow the players a glass of sherry the night before a game. It is unlikely, however, that the players – young working-class men – totally adhered to this relatively spartan regime. Before a game, Chapman sometimes gave the players a glycerine tablet, perhaps more for the placebo effect than any chemical assistance it might induce.[34] With control over the team's selection, Chapman employed psychological methods together with some gentle persuasion in an attempt to improve performance. If a player had had a good game, for example, Chapman would later ask him if he was not feeling well, and tell him that he had better have a rest. Conversely, after a poor game, he would praise a player for his efforts.[35]

However, it was Chapman's influence as a manager in developing a tactical plan 'to organise victory' that was one of the most notable landmarks in the history of football management.[36] As a player, he could only remember an occasional chat between two men playing on the wing about tactics, but Chapman was to make match preparation the sole responsibility of the manager. He later extended this by developing more long-term tactical ideas, and his tactical acumen gave something extra to all the clubs he managed.[37] In contrast, English football during this period was characterized by an emphasis on individual play, i.e. dribbling, and any tactics were usually devised by the captain on an *ad hoc* basis. At Northampton Town, he sowed the seeds of his future strategies by developing a more team-oriented style of play. But just as important as his plan was Chapman's ability to get it across to the players so that they understood it and believed in it. He achieved this through an ability to convey his arguments in an articulate manner, but one in which the soft tones of his Yorkshire accent betrayed a certain steeliness.[38]

At Huddersfield Town the signing of Clem Stephenson in 1921 turned out to be crucial to their success. Stephenson became the first in a line of purchases who Chapman essentially built the team and its system around. Stephenson, at inside-forward, was given a roving role, and at Arsenal Alex James was similarly important. The impact of both Chapman's and Stephenson's arrival at Huddersfield was immediate as the team finished the season strongly.[39]

Perhaps the best gauge of Chapman's impact is the reaction when he left for other clubs. One Northampton newspaper, for example, recorded on his departure that his management skills had 'lifted Northampton out of the furrow of failures and placed them among the strongest sides in the south'.[40] Another remarked that it would 'conclude a period marked by sound ability, tactful management and financial acumen'.[41] After he decided to join Arsenal, a letter to a Huddersfield newspaper noted the manager's contribution: 'Everyone must admit that, with all due respect to our players, if any man has played an individual part in bringing Huddersfield Town to its present heights that man is Herbert Chapman.'[42]

If Chapman achieved national recognition at Huddersfield Town then Arsenal was his *tour de force*. In eight years he turned a mid-table team into the greatest footballing power in the land, and the most famous club in the world. Overall, this transformation had important consequences for football as the game became more business-like and moved further away from its amateur roots. However, Chapman's management skills were not the only ingredient in this process. Arsenal's success was dependent upon other factors. Supported by an extensive transport network, for example, London offered access to a large supporter base. Moreover, during the inter-war period, the capital did not suffer from the depression like some areas in the north and Wales, and its level of employment actually increased.[43]

Even before Chapman's arrival, Arsenal had been keen to exploit this potential and break the north's footballing monopoly. Arsenal's chairman in 1925 was Sir Henry Norris. Although a solicitor by profession, he was a rich property developer, and between 1918 and 1922 Norris was MP for Fulham East.[44] He became chairman in 1910 and in 1913 moved Arsenal from south London to Highbury, pouring £125,000 into the club by 1915.[45] Norris was also a very forceful personality. Chapman's predecessor, Leslie Knighton, left the club complaining that Norris had persistently bullied and interfered with his management of the club, telling him which players he could or could not buy.[46] Moreover, before Chapman's appointment, the advertisement for the job in the *Athletic News* specified that 'Gentlemen whose sole ability to build up a good side depends on the heavy and exhorbitant [sic] transfer fees need not apply.'[47] Soon after taking the job, however, Arsenal signed Charlie Buchan from Sunderland for £3,900 even though he was aged 34.[48] It was perhaps because, unlike Knighton, Chapman had a record of achievement, and this forced Norris to accept the limits of his own authority, and enabled Chapman to persuade the chairman to break his embargo. Knighton himself claimed that Chapman was 'exceptionally clever with finances and could . . . charm off a donkey's hind leg'.[49]

By 1927, however, Norris's association with Arsenal was at an end as he and fellow director William Hall were suspended *sine die* by the FA for paying their chauffeurs' wages from club funds.[50] As a result, directorial interference in the club's management was further diminished. In 1928, for instance, Chapman and the new chairman, Sir Samuel Hill-Wood, were delegated full powers by the board concerning the transfer of players, although the acquisition of new players was later left entirely to Chapman.[51] Despite his recommendations being subject to directors' approval, there is no suggestion that any of Chapman's recommendations were ever rejected.[52] Moreover, he picked the team without any interference from directors, even barring them from the players' dressing room on match days.[53] In terms of the club's management, there was now a clear separation of its functions. Chapman had sole responsibility for the players and provided the link between them and the directors.

Tensions, though, still existed within the club. Chapman's relationship with one director, George Allison, for example, seems to have been relatively cool. In 1930, Chapman had been late in putting forward Allison's nomination for the FA Council and was later sternly instructed to get the 'matter going in time for the following year'.[54] It is also interesting that in his autobiography Allison rarely mentions Chapman and certainly not in the glowing terms that others have used.[55] Allison liked to style himself as a 'gent', and the other directors who succeeded Norris also could be described as gentlemen. They included Lord Lonsdale, Colonel Sir John Norton-Griffiths and Colonel Sir Matthew Wilson.[56] Given their social background, they were probably happy to allow Chapman to run the club with minimal interference, and not have any involvement with working-class footballers. Instead, they seemed to be more concerned with trivial matters like whether or not to allow their chauffeurs into the boardroom after a game for tea.[57] Another director, John Edwards, was more proactive and had some responsibility for the redevelopment of the ground. Of course, the Arsenal directors still held ultimate responsibility for the club and also acted as financial guarantors. A hierarchy did exist and, as at his other clubs, the directors could dismiss Chapman because he was a salaried official. During the season, the directors held fortnightly board meetings where Chapman would give a manager's report, and the language used during these meetings – such as 'the manager was empowered' and 'the manager was instructed to' – still suggests that Chapman was a subordinate.

Nevertheless, allied to his sole responsibility for team selection, the directors backed Chapman's judgement of players by providing the funds for him to spend. In 1929, he bought David Jack from Bolton Wanderers for a record £10,650, and a few months earlier Alex James came from Preston North End for £8,750. These two transfers generated a more competitive era within football as other clubs tried to emulate Arsenal's success. In 1930, for example, Chelsea paid Newcastle United £10,000 for Hughie Gallacher. During Chapman's eight years at Arsenal, he spent £101,400 on transfers, although £40,000 was reclaimed. It was a policy of speculating to accumulate, and under Chapman it was successful. Not only did Arsenal win two League Championships and an FA Cup, but between 1925 and 1934 it made an average yearly profit of £10,000.[58]

Successful football managers have needed to be good judges of a player, and despite the heavy outlay on James and Jack, Chapman did not just buy established stars for large fees. He also had the ability to identify players who played for lowly clubs but would fit into his overall scheme. Herbie Roberts, for example, was bought in December 1926 from non-league Oswestry Town for £200.[59] Full-back Eddie Hapgood cost Arsenal £250 from Kettering, while Cliff Bastin, aged 17, was a left-winger, who came from Exeter City for a fee of £2,000. In 1930, centre-forward Jack Lambert completed the forward line. His eventual selection for that position had been more problematic for Chapman, and perhaps owed something to luck. He was originally bought as an inside-forward from Doncaster for £2,000 but, at first, he spent most of his time in the reserves. Chapman did not think Lambert was the ideal centre-forward and spent £20,000 on three other players. None proved as effective as Lambert, however, who, although not as skilful, complemented the team's overall pattern with his robust style. Chapman was convinced that a footballer's all-round intelligence was just as important as his playing ability.[60] He also wanted his players to reflect his own sober lifestyle and would lose interest if the answers to pointed questions were not satisfactory. On first meeting Eddie Hapgood, a future Arsenal and England captain, Chapman asked, 'Well, young man, do you smoke or drink?'[61]

In recent years, critics and fans alike have regarded a manager's tactical acumen as a litmus test of his ability. As we have already seen, Chapman was in the forefront of this development by making himself, as the manager, responsible for his side's tactics. At Arsenal, it has been argued that his tactical ability in exploiting the new offside rule from 1925 was a major reason for the Gunners' success.[62] In 1924–5 they had finished twentieth in the League, the following season they were second. The change in the offside law had produced a sudden increase in goals being scored.[63] Acting on a suggestion by Charlie Buchan, Chapman countered the goal frenzy by turning the centre-half, Jack Butler, from a midfielder player into a purely defensive one, renamed a 'stopper' or a 'policeman'. This changed the team's whole system, producing the so-called W/M formation. The 'W' represented the five forwards, with the 'M' as the defensive system with the wing-halves marking the opposing inside-forwards, and the full-backs, the wingers. The centre-half would occupy a central defensive role as Chapman believed that it was in this area that 90 per cent of goals were scored.[64] In the 1930s, Herbie Roberts replaced Butler, who Chapman had converted from wing-half; Roberts was more of a defensive player than Butler. Another suggestion by Buchan led to the introduction of a linkman, a roving inside-forward between defence and attack. Alex James was later purchased to fulfil this role. Chapman believed that this position was the vital ingredient to his tactical plan, and in James he found the ideal player.

Chapman also believed that teams could attack for too long. The essence of his plan was to create space behind the opposition's defence that could be exploited by swift counter-attacks built on accurate long passes and the element of surprise.[65] This style was more direct and Arsenal eschewed the short-passing game that had previously been the fashion. Wingers were also encouraged to cut inside and shoot for goal rather than cross from the by-line.[66] Arsenal's style not only had its imitators but it ushered in a new era as football became faster and more physical.[67] Chapman did not confine his tactical input to team discussions. During a cup-tie against Aston Villa in 1931 played in foggy conditions, the two captains had agreed with the referee to forgo half-time and turn straight round. With Villa leading 2–0, though, Chapman rushed to the touchline and ordered his players to the dressing room for a tactical reappraisal. Arsenal went on to draw the game and eventually won the replay.[68]

Because of the size of their investment it was important that Arsenal got the best from the players who were their main assets. Chapman's response was to develop a closer relationship with them. On signing Charlie Buchan, for example, Chapman was keen to hear his opinions on the Arsenal team. The skills of Chapman's predecessor, Leslie Knighton, had lain more on the administrative side.[69] Commenting on the different temperaments of players, Knighton once described football stars with a temperament as 'just hell'.[70] As a sign of the warmth former players held for him, Eddie Hapgood refers to Chapman as the 'Old Boss' throughout his autobiography.

In 1929, Arsenal had been invited to tour Argentina, and it is interesting that Chapman actually consulted the players to ascertain their feelings on the matter before reporting back to the board. The question of the tour was left with Chapman and the invitation was eventually declined.[71] On a personal level, Chapman's approach was different according to who he was dealing with. George Male had been a wing-half who he converted to right-back, and who later played for England. In getting Male to overcome his doubts about the switch, Chapman called him to his office. Male later confessed, 'By the time I came out of that room, I was not only convinced I was a full blown right-back, I knew, without doubt, that I was the best right-back in the country.'[72] On Chapman's style, Male said, 'he was the boss, and you knew it, even though his voice was so quiet. When he talked to you there was no bullying. He could persuade you in the quiet way he'd talk to you.'[73] On another occasion, however, Chapman took Male aside before a train journey and told him to 'pull his socks up' because he was 'playing for his place'.[74]

Chapman was still essentially an authoritarian figure, using his personality to demand discipline. However, not every player conformed to his ways. He found Alex James particularly troublesome. In 1931, for example, he had refused to re-sign unless Arsenal offered him more money.[75] James continually challenged Chapman's authority and made their disagreements public through the newspapers, something that infuriated Chapman. James, however, was a special player and because football was a peculiar business it was highly unlikely that Chapman would transfer him. He was less forgiving of those who were expendable. For instance, his first trainer at Arsenal, George Hardy, shouted out a tactical instruction to the players during a game in February 1927. On the Monday Chapman sacked him as he did not want to give the impression of his authority being undermined.[76]

Nevertheless, in order to secure a player's loyalty the club also invoked a more paternalistic approach. Arsenal operated a house purchase scheme whereby Chapman bought houses on the club's behalf that he thought suitable for players. This was perhaps another example of how he wanted to mould the players in his own image. Many properties were located in the newly developed suburban areas of north London like Hendon, where Chapman himself lived.[77] Chapman also launched a savings scheme where £1 of the players' weekly wage was deposited with the club at an interest rate of 6 per cent.[78] A similar scheme had earlier been instituted by Lord Hawke at Yorkshire County Cricket Club, and reflected the prevailing notion that employers knew what was best for their workers. Chapman also realized that, as the club's main assets, the players' physical welfare was paramount. Dressing room and training facilities were improved and the club later installed modern medical electrical apparatus such as sun-ray equipment.[79] Tom Whittaker, the club's trainer, had studied anatomy and massage. He became an expert in his field and later became England's regular trainer.

Chapman's role did not just embrace football matters. He held the title of secretary-manager and ran the club on a day-to-day basis. In this sense he was also all-powerful. Following Chapman, managers demanded this complete control of running the club without any interference. Chapman's control over his administrative staff, which admittedly probably only numbered a handful, was as firm as that over the players. No member of staff was permitted to leave until they had telephoned his office at six o'clock and asked for permission to go.[80] He held wide responsibilities that entailed a variety of bureaucratic tasks. Some of this was very trivial work, ranging from sorting out the arrangements for the opening of the new tearoom to dealing with pirate chocolate sellers.[81] Chapman was the public face of the club and on one occasion visited a local resident after his fence had been damaged following a game, to 'point out in a friendly manner we [Arsenal] can not be held responsible for damage at such a distance from the ground'.[82]

The legacy of Herbert Chapman, however, was not just restricted to the management of his teams. He embraced football modernity and was full of ideas about the future development of the football business. He saw the press as an extension of advertising and in 1929 Arsenal hired a publicity agent, F.J. Coles, for £100, who also doubled as the club's programme editor. Coles was expected to attend the majority of home matches and ensure that a report of the game was published in London's morning and evening papers. He had to telephone Chapman every day for any information on the club that could be published in order to keep Arsenal's name in the news.[83] Chapman also acted as the club's public relations officer and would ring up newspapers to query some of their stories regarding Arsenal.[84]

The growth of the BBC in the 1920s provided a medium for Chapman to publicize his views on football and its future. In 1926 he gave a talk on the BBC about some of his ideas. Peter Batten also interviewed him on 'My Greatest Hour'.[85] Arsenal's home game against Sheffield United in 1927 was the first to be broadcast on radio by the BBC. The BBC applied directly to clubs for broadcasting rights and Arsenal willingly granted permission for certain games.[86] The club had a strong interest in broadcasting. While Chapman was a personal friend of the BBC's Outside Broadcasts Director (OBD), Gerald Cock, George Allison, an Arsenal director, was an early football commentator.[87] Unsurprisingly, the tension between Chapman and Allison seems to have spilled over regarding the BBC. In 1932, Allison had been invited by Cock's successor as

BBC OBD, S.J. de Lotbiniere, to arrange football talks for the radio for the programmes on football management but Allison never recommended Chapman.[88] Furthermore, on one occasion de Lotbiniere had inadvertently phoned Chapman when wanting to speak to Tom Whittaker concerning a football talk. De Lotbiniere told Allison that Chapman was 'obviously anxious to have a finger in the pie but I think all will go well'.[89]

Despite his disagreements with the BBC, Chapman sought other ways to make football and Arsenal more popular. Perhaps his shrewdest move was to persuade the London Electric Railway to change the name of their Piccadilly Line station adjacent to the Arsenal ground from 'Gillespie Road' to 'Arsenal' in 1932, giving the club instant, metropolis-wide publicity.[90] He also had a regular column in the *Sunday Express* to vent his ideas, something that helped to cultivate his own reputation and progressive image. For example, he advocated the use of a white ball that would be easier for the crowd to see at the end of dark winter afternoons, and that the players' shirts should be numbered.[91] In 1933, on the suggestion of the *Daily Mail's* cartoonist, Tom Webster, Chapman changed Arsenal's shirts from all red to red with white sleeves to make them more distinctive and modern.[92] Floodlights were installed at Highbury after he saw them used on the continent in 1930, and realized how they could benefit the English game.[93] For those chilly nights he even proposed that the stands should be heated. It would be over twenty years before most of these measures were adopted in England.

Given his modern ideas, he also believed in the value of coaching and had been impressed with an FA scheme staged at Highbury in 1930. Initially for public school boys, Chapman wanted it to be extended to elementary schools and for the FA to distribute a film on coaching.[94] Chapman was aware of the progress of football on the continent and envisioned a West European Cup. He himself has a claim to have been England's first manager, if only on an unofficial basis. In 1933, England visited Italy and it is claimed that the FA member in charge of the England team, Arthur Kingscott, invited Chapman to Turin to act as team manager, although without the FA's blessing.[95] It was Chapman who gave the players a team talk before the game, and also at half-time.[96] During the game Chapman stood on a chair to shout and urge the players on, indicating how the stress and pressure of games affected him not only in this international but probably also in domestic fixtures.[97]

What can we say about Chapman's lifestyle while Arsenal manager? In appearance he sometimes resembled a country gent with his plus fours complementing a portly figure and round face. His aspirations were partly reflected by an increase in salary. His initial wage at Arsenal was £83 per month, the equivalent of an annual salary of approximately £1,000.[98] In 1933, he was awarded a new salary of £2,000 per year, then the highest in football, and about £90,000 at today's prices. (At the same time, the maximum wage for players was £8.) This was the salary of a high-flying business executive, and a reflection of Chapman's importance to the club. In addition, there was a possible £500 bonus if Arsenal won the Cup and £250 for the League.[99] Chapman also had aspirations for his family. He had two daughters and two sons who both played rugby union, indicating that they attended grammar or private schools. The eldest, Ken, born in 1908, played for the East Midlands and later became President of the Rugby Football Union. Bruce meanwhile represented Middlesex. Herbert regarded Bruce's qualification as a solicitor as his proudest moment.[100] He can have had little time for a family life, however, as he was a workaholic. It was perhaps this commitment that led to his early death when he contracted pneumonia and died suddenly on 6 January 1934, aged 55.

What was the legacy of Herbert Chapman? In the short term, despite his death, Arsenal built on his foundations and continued to prosper during the 1930s. They won the League on three other occasions and the FA Cup again in 1936. No other club had been as dominant before. Inevitably, perhaps, it created envy, particularly amongst football supporters in northern areas suffering from the Depression and for whom Arsenal represented the apparently well-heeled south. This image was not totally inaccurate as in the six years leading up to the war Arsenal made an annual average profit of £22,000, enabling the club to open a new stand in 1936 at a cost of £120,000.[101] Not only was it fitted with all modern facilities but it was also designed in an art deco style that represented the aesthetic side of modernity.

In one sense, Chapman's success with Arsenal was an historical accident, a product of circumstances. Some managers, like John McCartney, may have been bestowed with similar powers, but Chapman's impact, and therefore legacy, was determined by his success, which others could not match. Things just fell into place for him, which was not the case for managers at other clubs. Arsenal was a unique club. It was prepared to spend a lot of money in procuring success and was aided by its London location. Once Henry Norris had left, Chapman enjoyed unprecedented powers and influence. Yet he also had to prove he could manage, and in this respect he was uniquely successful, not only at Arsenal but also at his other clubs, especially Huddersfield Town. Chapman himself was unlike most other football managers. In addition to his experience as a player, he was better educated, more articulate and had had a broader experience of life than most, including working for five years in industrial middle-management. Arsenal may have had more resources than other clubs, but this in itself was not a guarantee of success. It was Chapman's management that was the key ingredient in Arsenal's rise to the top.

It was how he defined the role of the manager, however, that was perhaps Chapman's most important legacy. This was not felt immediately, however. In general, directors of other clubs resisted any 'Chapmanization' process. Even Arsenal reverted back to the old model following Chapman's death by appointing a director, George Allison, as his successor, and left Tom Whittaker, the trainer, to deal with the players. Nevertheless, Chapman provided the template for future generations. His hands-on style and increased powers ensured that the manager became a football club's central figure. It also became a job for obsessives and carried great pressures that left little time for self or family. In terms of how a club was run, managers would want to be in charge of every-thing, from the tea-lady to the first team. Players would come to rely on 'the Boss' and, like the press and the fans, they would identify the manager as the most important person in the club. Largely because of Chapman's success, directors would come to regard a manager as someone who could change the fortunes of the team. Paradoxically, it would mean that a manager's job would become less secure as directors would search ever more frantically for the 'right man'.

Chapter 4

The emergence of the football manager, 1918–39

During the inter-war period the idea of the football manager became more popular and the number of managers increased significantly following the First World War, corresponding with a rise in demand for consumer goods like football. Between 1921 and 1940 nearly 200 men managed at least one Football League club at one time or another, and after 1930, they increasingly represented the first generation of professional footballers.[1] However, there was little 'Chapmanization' as most directors preferred to retain the privileges of ownership and run clubs as they saw fit. A small number of Chapman 'disciples' did emerge but any change was generally slow and specific to individual clubs.

In management generally, the economic vicissitudes that characterized Britain during these years had a modernizing impact on industry. In an attempt to increase efficiency there was a phase of 'rationalization' plus a wave of mergers. In 1923, for example, the 120 railway companies merged into just four gigantic enterprises.[2] It signalled the start of a 'professionalization of management' as the day-to-day running of companies was gradually transferred from the owners to career managers in bureaucratic hierarchies.[3] Between 1921 and 1951, the number of managers and administrators nearly doubled from 704,000 to 1.25 million. During the 1930s a managerial middle class emerged.[4] But instead of technical expertise, the most sought-after qualities in managers, especially in small firms, were social confidence and the ability to lead men. These were attributes formed on the rugby pitches of grammar and minor public schools, and this ensured that the belief in the 'cult of the amateur' survived well into the twentieth century.[5]

The inter-war years as a whole were marked by severe regional fluctuations in the economy. A short boom after the First World War was followed by a collapse. Subsequently, from 1921 until 1938, unemployment remained above one million, reaching a peak of 2.8 million in 1932. During the 1920s, there had been a shift away from northern staple industries reliant on exports, towards high productivity industries mainly situated in the south and the Midlands, such as manufacture of motor vehicles and consumer durables that depended on the home market.[6] Despite the worst years of the Depression between 1929 and 1932, the 1930s was a decade of continual growth with the real incomes of consumers rising. Demand for leisure commodities during these years was buoyant and there was a 15 per cent increase in consumer spending on the theatre, cinemas and sporting events. Football attendances also increased considerably, closely mirroring the fortunes of the national economy. In 1927, 23.4 million people watched Football League games; for the 1937–8 season, it was 31.4 million. The level of a worker's disposable income was the main determinant of consumer demand, and as a football club's main source of income was gate receipts, its support was partially dependent on local economic circumstances such as levels of trade, employment and wages.[7]

Nevertheless, there were only modest changes in the overall geographical balance of footballing power during this period. The rise of southern football, for example, can be largely attributed to the success of Arsenal. Despite this, a club's fortunes partly reflected the state of the local economy. Tottenham Hotspur's revenue, for example, increased from £37,087 in 1927 to £52,144 by 1934, during which time Spurs were mainly in the second division. Middlesbrough, however, was deeply affected by the Depression, and between 1927–8 and 1932–3, when unemployment in the town was 46 per cent, the football club's attendances fell by 44 per cent. Revenue also dropped from £36,792 in 1930 to £24,611 in 1934. Yet throughout the 1930s, Middlesbrough, along with other teams from the depressed north-east, Sunderland and Newcastle, maintained their first division status.[8]

The main reason for football's relative resilience was the protection offered to clubs by the Football League in its role as a cartel and its equalization policies. As well as maintaining a competitive edge, promotion and relegation provided clubs with opportunities to increase their income by playing at a higher level. Moreover, not only did the retain-and-transfer system and the maximum wage regulate football's labour market, but it also limited, to a certain extent, the concentration of football talent in the richer clubs. During the First World War, the principle of pooled resources had been established, and in 1924 this was extended. League President, John McKenna, devised a scheme whereby 20 per cent of the home club's net gate was to be paid to the visitors. In addition, the gate receipts for FA Cup games were shared. Within this framework, however, football clubs were still 'dynamic business enterprises', with the management of resources and the team as more significant factors in achieving success than the prevailing socio-economic forces.

As the demand for football managers increased, 'northernness' was a recurring characteristic, reflecting the sport's early development as their geographical diffusion closely mirrored the spatial origins of professional footballers. However, this geographical distribution of players and managers also reflected the shifting economic performance of the north and the south.[9] With managers coming from an increasing number of different locations, like London and South Wales, there was a definite, if slow, 'nationalization' process.

In their quest for a manager, one simple equation directors worked on was that the better the player, the better qualified he was for the job. For example, a number of players from the famous Newcastle team of the Edwardian period had become managers by the 1920s. Of the players who became managers, a relatively high percentage was made up of former internationals. Interestingly, it seems that no particular type, defender, midfielder or forward, was favoured.[10] The exception to this was goalkeepers who perhaps suffered from the prejudice that they were not 'real' footballers.

Through their knowledge of the professional game, directors believed that players would 'know the ropes' and understand all about players from the 'practical side', such as detecting 'malingerers'.[11] Other attributes, though, were also sought, including experience, leadership qualities and evidence of a better education. However, as most players came from working-class backgrounds, it meant that few potential managers had had a secondary education, the great majority having left school at 13 or 14. A few, like Colin Veitch and Andy Ducat, did have a secondary education behind them, and the proportion of managers with a secondary education was probably higher than that of footballers generally. A superior education and a successful playing career, however, were no guarantees for success and Veitch left after eighteen unsuccessful months at his only club as manager, Bradford City.[12]

It was not compulsory for managers to have been players, and many came from a variety of other backgrounds. Bill Beer, for example, spent ten years as a sheep farmer in Australia before managing Birmingham City. Others were hired for their knowledge of local football or were promoted after having previously served the club in some other capacity, as player, trainer or secretary. Charles Foweraker, for example, was appointed Bolton's secretary-manager in 1919. He had originally been a gateman for the club and later became assistant secretary. In 1930, Bristol Rovers appointed Captain Albert Prince-Cox as their manager. In addition to having been in the Royal Flying Corps, he had been a referee and, therefore, had some understanding of handling men. Prince-Cox also held a professional qualification as a meteorologist.[13] Fred Everiss had not been a player either, and had left school at 13 in 1895 after passing the Labour Examination. He first worked as a decorator and then as a printer's errand boy before joining West Bromwich Albion as an office boy at 4s per week in 1896, and was only 20 when he became the club secretary. Like Herbert Chapman, Everiss worked in a local munitions factory – John Spencer's in Wednesbury – during the First World War, where he was placed in charge of the production of shells.[14]

For former players, their experience in football provided the main form of preparation for football management. It also conditioned some of their attitudes to the job and tended to perpetuate as well as consolidate contemporary attitudes on how players should be managed. In addition, following the First World War, many footballers had served in the army and it is likely that some managers with military experience used this in their handling of footballers. Frank Buckley, for example, was awarded a commission in the 17th Footballers' Battalion and was later promoted to major and acted as second-in-command.[15]

On his first managerial appointment at Norwich City, Buckley actually advertised for players from the Footballers' Battalions.[16] Previous to that, he had served as a sergeant-instructor in the 2nd Kings Liverpool Regiment during the Boer War. In addition to his army background, Buckley owned a farm in partnership with his brother Chris. He also dressed like a farmer, wearing a tweed suit with plus fours. He was always addressed as 'the Major' throughout his career, even by his wife. Three other members of the Footballers' Battalion also became managers: Jack Tresarden, Angus Seed and Charlie Bell, who, like Buckley, was given a commission.[17] Seed's brother, Jimmy, also joined the Cyclists' Corps at Sunderland during the war.[18]

Demand for managers was not confined to England. In 1920, Glasgow Rangers appointed Bill Struth, a stonemason by trade and the club's trainer, as their manager. He retired in 1954, and under him Rangers surpassed the success Celtic had enjoyed under Willie Maley.[19] Moreover, it was not just in Britain that the number of football managers was increasing. Through its trading links as well as the military, the British exported football to all corners of the globe. Interest and competition in the game grew in these new footballing countries and so did the need for expertise to aid their development. In contrast to British football's amateur and practical traditions, European football was a 'manifestation of technical progress'. Engineers established many clubs, and from early on this established a technocratic mentality towards management and coaching.[20] In addition, the game in Europe was a 'white collar' game whereas in Britain it had strong working-class roots. Nevertheless, because they were the pioneers of football, British coaches were at the forefront of turning football into the world game.[21] One of the early pioneers was William Garbutt. He had been a player with Woolwich Arsenal and Blackburn Rovers in the early 1900s before moving to Italy to coach Genoa between 1910 and 1915. He later managed Naples from 1929 and 1935 having helped to prepare the Italian team for the 1924 Olympics.[22] Fred Pentland became famous as manager of the Spanish Basque team, Athletic Bilbao, winning two titles in 1930 and 1931. In 1920 he had coached the French Olympic team before managing Racing Santander. Pentland has been credited with introducing the short-passing game to Spanish football.[23]

Jimmy Hogan was probably the most famous of the British coaches who worked abroad. He began in 1910 coaching a club in Holland before taking charge of the Dutch national team. He moved to Austria in 1912 where he began a long association with Hugo Meisl who has been described as the Herbert Chapman of European football. Hogan was peripatetic and also coached in Germany, Switzerland and Hungary. In 1936, he coached the Austrian side that reached the 1936 Olympics final.[24] European managers also began to emerge between the wars. Hugo Meisl had been a pioneer in Austria and his brother, Willy, later assisted him. Vittorio Pozzo was the leading coach in Italy. As a young man he had worked in Bradford but preferred to watch

Manchester United, especially Charlie Roberts. Back in Italy he first worked at Torino before managing the national team that won the World Cup in 1934 and 1938 and also at the Olympics in 1936.[25]

Both European and South American countries concentrated more on the training and preparation of players than the British. Furthermore, greater emphasis was placed on the national team rather than the club game. In Italy, admittedly assisted by a Fascist regime that used football for political purposes, the national team under Pozzo assembled three weeks before a game for practice and tactical preparations.[26] In Holland all potential internationals were card indexed and then underwent a thorough preparation consisting of blackboard demonstrations and ball practice.[27] English coaches returning from the continent to management positions, like Tom Bromilow at Burnley, faced cultural resistance from players to the methods they had used in Europe.[28] Similarly, Jimmy Hogan had returned to England in 1934 to manage Fulham but was dismissed after only one season. The players did not respond to his methods and the directors agreed with them that experienced players did not need coaching.

English football generally was at a more mature stage of development than in Europe. Its management culture was more deeply embedded and despite the increase in the number of managers, it would be wrong to assume that a change in their relationship with club directors was inevitable. During the inter-war period, the amateur, voluntary tradition of English football management persisted, with directors unwilling to concede the perks of their position. On his appointment as Aston Villa manager in 1936, Jimmy Hogan had wanted to revert from a defensive back to an attacking centre-half but the club chairman would not allow it.[29] At West Brom, the directors continued to select the team albeit with an input from the secretary-manager, Fred Everiss.[30] In one sense, this is not surprising. Many directors were professionally qualified or successful businessmen who had a lot of self-esteem and thought they knew a lot about football, and some did, having played it at a reasonable level. Harold Hardman, for example, a director of Manchester United, had been an England amateur international. In comparison to footballers, directors were also better educated and more experienced in life generally. Any claims of interference in the manager's job by directors is perhaps a case of 'history with hindsight' because directors had always taken responsibility for running the club and expected to continue to do so. Some directors, like James Taylor at Preston North End, dominated their clubs during this period. At nearby Blackburn Rovers, former England captain, Bob Crompton, was honorary manager between 1926 and 1931 as well as being a director of the club at the same time.[31] Newcastle United's tradition of directors being in charge of the team was continued by former player, Stan Seymour.[32] George Allison of course had been a director before relinquishing this position to become Arsenal's full-time manager. At Rangers, however, Bill Struth held the largest individual shareholding and in 1947 he was able to oust the club chairman, James Bowie.[33]

Management changes were unique to each football club, however. In 1938, for example, the Barnsley directors gave Angus Seed sole power over team selection for a certain period. They had decided to experiment because of poor results, and after performances improved they continued to allow Seed to pick the team.[34] Frank Buckley initially had to defer to the directors of Wolverhampton Wanderers when he became manager in 1927. It was not until 1933–4 when the team was having a poor run of results, together with changes in the boardroom, that he was accorded full powers to select the team.[35] Peter McWilliam also became Middlesbrough's manager in 1927. It was claimed that he was to be given total control of team selection without any interference from the board, and it was actually stipulated in his contract that he was to have full powers to select both the first and second teams. The reality, however, was rather different. When Herbert Bamlett, his predecessor, had been manager, the directors had selected the team, and when they disagreed on this, or on the recruitment of players, they took a vote. McWilliam was also faced with the problem of directors questioning his selection and having to change the team at their behest.[36] Similarly, on taking up the post of secretary-manager at Sheffield Wednesday in 1933, Billy Walker felt that his position was one of full power and full responsibility. When the club was later relegated to the second division in 1937, however, the directors began to interfere with Walker's handling of the team.[37]

In contrast, Jimmy Seed, who was appointed manager of Charlton Athletic in May 1933, virtually ran the club, in a fashion not dissimilar to Chapman at Arsenal. This can be concluded from the actual number of directors' meetings Charlton held between 1935 and 1939: only one every two months. Middlesbrough's directors, on the other hand, met once a week during the playing season, making interference more likely. In 1932, Charlton had been taken over by two brothers, Albert and Stanley Gliksten, who were millionaire timber merchants from London's East End. They were probably too busy running their business to manage the football club and so left it in the hands of Seed.[38] In 1932, Charlie Paynter had been appointed West Ham's team manager. He continued, though, with his duties as club trainer while the recruitment of players became the responsibility of two directors, Messrs Liddell and Leafe. This division of labour represented a dilution of the responsibilities of the previous secretary-manager, Syd King.[39]

The manager's role was partly shaped by the game's increasing bureaucratization. Between 1900 and 1939, for example, the Football League evolved into a central regulatory body, gaining formal control over player conditions relating to employment, pay, discipline, movement and welfare.[40] With football's increasingly bureaucratic labour market and the growth in its transfer market, the main job of the football manager was not unlike that of a personnel manager. It also underlined the need for an expert, to buy the right player.

Managers were often compared to 'horse traders', someone who bought and sold players. Who they bought or sold, however, was usually dependent on the directors. When the post of manager of Wolverhampton Wanderers was advertised in the *Athletic News* in 1927, it was unequivocally stated in capital letters, that 'A SPENDTHRIFT IS NOT NEEDED'.[41] And during Frank Buckley's tenure this set the tone for the club's long-term policy. When he took office the club owed the bank £14,000, and had made a loss for the 1926–7 season of £1,500 with first team receipts totalling £15,000. By 1935–6, the club had made a profit of £17,000, were in credit with the bank to £4,000 and gate receipts had increased to £32,000.[42] Buckley had built himself a reputation for 'wheeling and dealing' in players, and, importantly, finding talent. Between 1935 and 1938 the club's income from transferred players was £110,658, an overall profit of £68,000.[43] At the centre of this turnaround was the Wolves scouting system and Buckley's ability to sell on players for large profits. In 1938, for example, Wolves sold Bryn Jones to Arsenal for a record £14,000. On his appointment as Charlton manager, Jimmy Seed was told by the Glikstens of their ambitious plans to make Charlton's ground, the Valley, the best in the country, but their motivations later changed. When they first assumed control at Charlton they had taken an active role in all the club's affairs, and later, in the form of two debentures, the Glikstens invested £105,000 in Charlton.[44] However, instead of making further investments they aimed to reclaim the loan. Seed claimed that, as a result, the club had 'a policy against big spending'.[45] In his twenty-three years as manager of Charlton, Seed spent £55,000 on players but sold others worth £170,000.[46]

Football clubs also adopted a more systematic approach to the recruitment of players. For example, many began to develop scouting networks that extended across the British Isles, and the richer the club the more sophisticated the network.[47] Jimmy Seed arranged for scouts to cover most of Britain on behalf of Charlton. He was particularly keen to cultivate the north-east, generally regarded as a breeding ground for professional footballers. Seed appointed his brother, Anthony, as the chief to the other five scouts there.[48] Sam Bartram, for example, Charlton's longest-serving player, was recommended to Seed while playing for Boldon Villa in county Durham. Professional clubs also began to develop links with local junior clubs and adopted them as nursery clubs which cultivated the talent of young professionals. Charlton's nursery club was Bexleyheath and Welling, while Middlesbrough had first refusal on Scarborough's players.[49]

In addition to scouting reports, Jimmy Seed kept a record of every Charlton first team game, in which he gave brief comments on each player from both sides. Seed signed Don Welsh from Torquay United in February 1935 for £3,250, and earlier that season, when Charlton met Torquay, Seed remarked that Welsh was the best player on the pitch, a 'brilliant player in defence and attack'. Other opponents were judged more harshly. In October 1936, the performance of Manchester City and England goalkeeper, Frank Swift, 'did not inspire confidence' apparently.[50] At Middlesbrough, the directors as well as the manager and his scouts took an active role in reporting on potential players.

Their comments placed great emphasis on a player's social and physical characteristics as well as his technical ability. In 1927, for example, Peter McWilliam reported that the Wolves full-back, Shaw, had two good feet 'but is very weak at close quarters'. On reporting on Boyd of Newcastle United, one director, a Mr Rand, observed that 'the player struck him as lacking in pluck, otherwise a good player'. McWilliam made his own enquiries and came to the conclusion that 'he was a very good footballer but a bit timid'. Armstrong of Jarrow was reported as having satisfactory ability but a poor physique as he was only 5 feet 6 inches tall and weighed 9 stones and 10 pounds. A report by a Middlesbrough scout on Ballantine of Partick Thistle detailed some of his personal habits. He was a married man who was strictly temperate and a non-smoker but was inclined to be moody. Follow-up reports confirmed his footballing ability but also a hasty temper that led him to commit too many petty fouls.[51] Age was another significant factor when Middlesbrough decided to sign a player. It was common for players to mislead clubs regarding their actual age for fear that they might not be taken on. Jack Curnow was 25 when he joined Wolves in 1935 but he had told the club's scout that he was 23. The scout then said that this would be too old, and told Curnow to tell Frank Buckley that he was in fact 21. Buckley believed him.[52] In 1930, the Middlesbrough chairman, Phil Bach, wanted to see the birth certificate of any player that they were interested in who was around 30 years old. In 1933, the club cancelled the contract of E.P. Taylor on the grounds that he had wilfully misled the club over his age. In the following year, Middlesbrough finally decided to obtain all the players' birth certificates.[53]

A football club's labour relations also partly reflected industry's gradual shift during the inter-war years from old-style paternalism towards a more rational system of welfarism. Although in football as elsewhere,

> the extension of welfare schemes [between 1900 and 1939] to cover accidents, pensions, sickness or death was not the work of idealistic paternalists but of hard-headed employers intent on maximising the efficiency and ensuring the dependence of their workforces at the lowest possible cost.[54]

Other employers, particularly the railways, took greater steps to monitor and control their workers by imposing fines, placing workers under surveillance and subjecting them to medical tests and examinations of competence. Regarding the attitudes of clubs to players' welfare, some were more progressive than others. In 1936, for example, Charlton was one of only two London clubs that took advantage of the FA's arrangement with the Board of Education and London County Council to provide educational classes for London's professional footballers.[55] Other clubs, though, continued to play a traditional paternal role. Wolves' players were encouraged by Buckley to save their wages and also to send some money to their parents.[56]

However, football's labour management methods were still fairly rudimentary. In terms of man-management techniques, a football manager's personality was still his most important tool, something he shared with foremen in industry, amongst other characteristics. In a paper given to the psychology section of the British Association in 1923, Alice Ikin listed thirty-two qualities that were felt to be desirable in a foreman. These included an ability to swear, to teach, organize and inspire confidence, as well as qualities such as character, personality and self-control.[57] At Rangers, it was claimed that Bill Struth was a charismatic personality who would accept neither criticism nor advice. He also ruled the team through a hierarchy of older players who were given petty privileges.[58] Frank Buckley was perhaps the prime exponent of the military method, unsurprising given his army background. The word 'martinet' was never far away when describing his managerial style. Following a defeat by Mansfield in the Cup, Buckley once humiliated the players by forcing them to walk through Wolverhampton town centre in their kit.[59] Don Bilton, who joined Wolves just before the outbreak of the Second World War, said that Buckley ruled by fear and that 'if you had a rotten game you'd hardly dare go in at half-time, you were going to get the biggest bawling at . . . [he] cursed and swore at you. So from that point of view he was a terrible chap.' Jackie Sewell described Buckley as 'a very frightening man', when he was his manager at Notts. County, who could 'make grown men have tears in their eyes'.[60] Conversely, Bilton also recognized acts of kindness, when Buckley, on occasions, supplied young players from poor backgrounds with new clothes. When he was at Blackpool, the supporters' club had complained about Buckley's style of management. They suggested that the players had lost their enjoyment of the game and that this was the reason for the team's lack of success.[61] Other managers, however, were more sympathetic. Matt Busby, for example, was greatly influenced by George Kay, his manager at Liverpool during the 1930s, who displayed much loyalty towards his players and treated them with consideration. Kay's approach contrasted sharply with the malicious atmosphere Busby had experienced at Manchester City.[62]

Most football managers had little daily contact with the players and were regarded as 'ivory tower' figures who remained in their offices while trainers continued to supervise the players on a day-to-day basis. Tommy Lawton recounted how as a young player he had tried to put in a transfer request at Everton. First, he had to make an appointment just to see the manager, Theo Kelly, who was actually more of a secretary. At the meeting, Lawton was belittled by Kelly who insisted that he go out and knock before entering his office. He then told Lawton he had been trying to give him away for four months, and not to waste his time again.[63]

Football clubs also wanted to control the players' lifestyles outside the club and continued to issue them with bigger and bigger rule-books. At Hull City, for example, players were not allowed to enter public houses after Monday or attend dances after Tuesday.[64] For Wolves players, dancing after Wednesday night was 'strictly forbidden'.[65] In addition, Buckley had a network of spies throughout Wolverhampton's pubs and clubs to observe whether the players were behaving themselves and not breaking any curfews. It was further claimed that Buckley wanted to know when and who a player was going to marry. Interestingly, at one point, in 1937, Wolves did not have one married man amongst the forty players on their books.[66] Buckley was almost obsessed by having control and his office was situated in the foyer of the main stand so everyone had to go past it. In 1938 he created a hostel for the club's young players complete with recreational facilities, in order to keep them under the one roof and make supervision easier.[67]

Buckley was the sole authority at Wolves when it came to player supervision. The club trainers were directly under his command and they feared him as much as the players did. The role of the trainer, however, as seen at Arsenal with Tom Whittaker, generally took on an increasing importance. Jimmy Seed delegated many supervisory duties to his trainer, Jimmy Trotter, and on a day-to-day basis it was Trotter who was in charge of the players. Many trainers were former players, although some came from the army, bringing with them experience of handling men. A trainer's overall authority, though, was limited, and at some clubs senior players would take advantage of this fact. Charlie Cole was Middlesbrough's trainer throughout the inter-war years. George Hardwick said later that, 'He had little or no authority. The players ruled him rather than him ruling the players. Poor Charlie, he had a hell of a time because everyone was taking the piss out of him.'[68]

As many managers were still administrative figures, the players usually devised the tactics, as was the case at West Bromwich Albion.[69] In this area, the captain played an important role, often acting as an intermediary between the manager and players. Jimmy Guthrie claimed that he, as captain, and the trainer, Jimmy Stewart, looked after team affairs at Portsmouth. The manager, Jack Tinn, knew very little about tactics and was more of an administrator.[70] Similarly, when Jimmy Seed was captain of Sheffield Wednesday between 1927 and 1931, he admitted to having been given 'unlimited licence' to introduce his own methods and ideas. The manager at the time, Bob Brown, was mainly employed for his secretarial skills, and he never interfered with any of Seed's decisions. Once a week they would have a chat and Seed would then convey Brown's views to the players. As a manager, Seed tried to bridge this gap, and, like Chapman at Arsenal, introduced tactical discussions. However, Seed also believed that a captain should be a manager on the pitch who decided the tactics.[71] Similarly, Bill Struth left tactics to the Rangers players on the pitch.[72] Stan Cullis was made Wolves captain at the age of 19 by Buckley who told him that he was to be the 'boss' on the field, and to make any necessary tactical changes. As an example of the ongoing tensions within the club's management, Cullis once overturned a director's tactical decision at a reserve game but later received Buckley's backing for his action.[73]

Football's industrial relations were characterized by a lack of player militancy during this period. Union membership was generally low and there were also fluctuations between clubs. Some, such as Manchester United and Manchester City, were almost always unionized, whereas the opposite was the case at Everton and Liverpool. It has been suggested, although there is little evidence, that powerful individuals had an influence over the extent of a club's union membership. Will Cuff, for example, ran Everton. A prominent member of the Football League Management Committee, he was a very forceful personality. Similarly, the lack of union activity at Wolves may have been due to Buckley's influence. Arsenal players were also inactive but, instead of Chapman's influence, the more obvious reason may have been that Arsenal were successful and that the players were doing all right. If there was a lack of militancy amongst players, it did not stop their disgruntlement over the transfer system and the maximum wage. In 1938, for example, Tranmere Rovers won the third division north but on the eve of the new season the players went on strike until they received an extra £2 per week.[74]

One problem that managers had not previously encountered was taking into account the wishes of players' wives. As a result of their political emancipation in 1918, and then having their franchise extended in 1928, women were becoming more assertive generally. Football clubs also recognized that a player's family life might influence his performance on the pitch. Tom Bromilow had agreed with two players to their transfer to Burnley but in both cases they had just been fixed up with new houses and their wives were not willing to move, having just got settled in. In what he described as 'quite a ticklish little job', Bromilow had to persuade the women that the transfer was to everyone's advantage.[75] Billy Walker also had problems with getting players' wives to settle in a new town. On one occasion, a wife had complained because there was no electric fire in the house.[76]

The actual training of players at most English clubs was still relatively basic. It mainly consisted of lapping, i.e. running around the ground, and was notable for the absence of any work with a football. This was partly due to the widely held belief that by not seeing a ball during the week players would be hungry for it on a Saturday, and also because very few trainers actually had any qualifications themselves. Even in the 1950s, Nat Lofthouse, the former Bolton centre-forward, remarked that when Saturday arrived they did not know what to do with the ball.[77] Occasionally, some players would indulge in a game of head tennis. The debate over the merits of coaching had been in progress for a number of years, yet it met considerable resistance throughout the professional game from both management and players. Nevertheless, on the initiative of its secretary, Stanley Rous, the Football Association began coaching courses in schools in 1934–5.

Frank Buckley, like Herbert Chapman, was one of the few managers who had recognized the benefits of coaching much earlier. He gained a reputation as a pioneer of modern training methods and had an obsession with physical and mental fitness. Soon after his appointment at Blackpool in 1923, it was reported that a 'pleasing feature of the training . . . is that the manager dons the jersey and joins the boys giving them advice and practical demonstration of what to do and how to do it'. Buckley also held practice games on Friday afternoons aimed at developing a better understanding between the players.[78] Later, at Wolves, he introduced mechanical innovations to supplement training sessions; a rowing machine was an early example. Buckley also had a machine purpose-built that fired out footballs at different angles for players to control. A room under a stand was fitted with rubber walls at which players kicked a ball that would then return at unpredictable angles, again with the aim of improving their ball control. One of Buckley's most peculiar practices was to encourage players to go ballroom dancing. This, he believed, would improve their balance and movement. On occasions, he would insist on players dancing with each other in training. Buckley was very keen that all players, including goalkeepers, should be able to kick proficiently with both feet. In practice matches, for example, right-wingers would play on the left wing for this purpose. He wanted his players to be versatile and would play them in a number of different positions.[79]

Buckley's most infamous innovation, or, some may argue, stunt, was to inject his players with monkey gland extracts. It was later sensationalized in the popular press.[80] Buckley began using the treatment on Wolves players in 1935. He refuted accusations of using chemical assistance to improve the team's performance and claimed its purpose was to increase a player's resistance to colds and other minor illnesses.[81] Buckley's wife claimed that he had the injections himself and that they worked wonders for him.[82] The use of medicinal substances was not uncommon in football, although there is no evidence that they helped to improve performance. At Blackpool, Buckley had handed out pep pills to players before a cup-tie in the mid-1920s.[83] Leslie Knighton also gave pep pills to Arsenal players before a cup-tie with West Ham in 1925.[84]

Other aspects of pre-match preparation that gained more importance included the treatment of injuries, highlighting the growing attention that was given to health and medicine in general during this period. Jimmy Trotter at Charlton followed Tom Whittaker's lead, and also qualified as a masseur and physiotherapist. In 1922, West Bromwich Albion appointed Bill Gopsill as trainer. In the war he had been a sergeant in the Royal Army Medical Corps, indicating that his experience of treating injuries was an important factor behind his recruitment.[85] Albion players who required cartilage operations were sent to Mr Stewart, a knee specialist from Newcastle who also treated players from other clubs.[86] Most trainers, though, had been former players and were sympathetic appointments, hired for their past services to the club, and they had little if any knowledge of physiology or anatomy.

Some clubs experimented with psychology in the 1930s. It is likely that this was a passing fad and that the expertise hired and the benefits it brought were dubious. Some clubs, including Arsenal, Brentford and Sheffield Wednesday, used the Reverend M. Caldwell, a chaplain to two large London mental hospitals who was described as an expert in practical psychology and gave lectures on what he termed 'psychotactics'.[87] At one time, Wolves players also attended regular sessions at a local psychologist in an attempt to build up their confidence.[88]

Following Herbert Chapman's innovations, tactics was another area where managers began to take more responsibility. Other managers tried to copy Chapman's methods but with varying degrees of success. Many other clubs, however, still developed tactics on a match-to-match basis without any long-term plan. After the change in the offside law in 1925, a greater emphasis was placed on speed and athleticism, and not conceding goals. The need for tactics, therefore, became greater. As a result, the immediate goal explosion that accompanied the law change subsided, and by 1937–8 the number of goals scored per game fell back to less than three for the first time since 1924–5.[89] After 1925, many teams attempted to use Chapman's W/M formation. They tended to place the emphasis on its defensive aspects as opposed to its attacking potential, mainly because other clubs did not have Arsenal's quality of players. Under Jimmy Seed, Charlton were criticized for playing negative football. When he was captain of Sheffield Wednesday, Seed had developed a tactical plan that was to be used at Charlton in which an inside-forward would drop back into defence. Its chief aim was getting men behind the ball when the other side had it.[90] Seed, like Chapman, regarded the centre-half as an essentially defensive player.[91] Others, like Brentford's Harry Curtis, still saw the centre-half as the team's pivot, at the heart of the team's defence and attack.[92] During the inter-war years, however, this was a fading belief, as centre-halves increasingly came to be seen as a third back or stopper with the job of close-marking the opposing centre-forward and preventing goals.

Frank Buckley's tactics reflected his personality – direct with little close inter-passing as the accent was on attacking, high-speed football.[93] Others termed it 'long ball' or 'kick and rush'. Attacks were launched by the full-backs while the centre-half, Stan Cullis, would support the forwards. Like Arsenal, Wolves' wingers would also cut in from the wing and make for goal diagonally.[94] Because of Buckley's training methods, his teams were also renowned for their high levels of fitness. To take advantage of their stamina, Buckley regularly flooded the pitch before every home game. He claimed later that a softer pitch would lead to fewer injuries.[95] Another major characteristic of the Wolves style under Buckley was its emphasis on the physical. Football during the inter-war years could be violent and certain players, like Frank Barson, gained reputations as 'killers'. The football authorities, however, wanted to stamp out these tendencies, partly in an attempt to widen football's appeal. This conflicted with an acceptance by many players of the legitimacy of football's physical approach: they still saw it as a 'man's game'.[96] Wolves came under particular scrutiny. In 1936–7 their players had seventeen cautions, more than any other club. As a penalty, the FA vetoed the club's proposed continental tour.[97]

If during the years before 1918 the seeds of the relationship between the manager and the press had been planted, then by 1939 they had established firm roots. It was one of the most significant developments in the manager's role during this period as not only did dealing with the press become an important part of the job but also for future generations of fans this relationship helped to shape the perception of the football manager.

Developments in the media had aided the game's increasing commercialization during the inter-war years and the media became an agent in football's nationalization process. In addition to the press, the broadcasting of games on radio widened football's potential audience.[98] Partly aided by a circulation war, this period was marked by a continuation of the expansion in newspaper readership that had begun before 1914. Football was particularly important to Sunday papers such as the News of the World and the People as they carried the results and reports of Saturday's games that fed the fans' appetites. There was also an increase in gossip and hyperbole. Before 1914 the front page of the Athletic News had also been dominated by tittle-tattle. Any criticism it offered, however, was relatively benign. The language now used in the reports became more aggressive and sharper. Through the American influence of 'Sportuguese', reports were jargon-ridden and replete with violent words.[99]

Moreover, there was a further proliferation of specialist local sports papers such as Saturday evening 'Greens' and 'Pinks'. These were also vehicles for fans to offer their opinions on the team's situation, and thus provided a framework for discussion. Many supporters' clubs had also sprung up in the 1920s and 1930s, although these were non-threatening organizations. When the National Federation of Football Supporters' Clubs was formed in 1926, it adopted the motto, 'To Help and Not to Hinder'.[100] Football clubs, however, were (and still are) very sensitive to criticism, and on occasions this affected their relations with the local press. In 1930, the Middlesbrough board received a letter from a player, R. Bruce, who asked for a transfer due to the continual barracking from the crowd and criticisms in the local Evening Gazette. The directors decided to forward a copy of Bruce's letter to the paper's local competitor, the Northern Echo.[101]

Nevertheless, the game's image was changing and public relations became an increasingly important aspect of a manager's job as he gradually became a club's public face as well as the first point of contact with the press. In addition to the increase in football coverage, reporters needed a regular source for their stories and the manager was the obvious choice. With directors withdrawing from the spotlight, the FA also cracked down on players making any public comments during this period.[102] The press, therefore, had an interest in managers having sole charge of the team, as the more autonomy managers enjoyed the more inside stories reporters were likely to get. By the 1930s, the football manager, through the press, was becoming more closely associated with the team's performance, and manager–reporter relations gradually became institutionalized.[103] The press began to report on a club's activities in terms of its 'managerial activity'.

However, it is important to remember that the press constructed reality, as well as reflecting it, and that the powers that managers actually held did not always reflect the media's perception of these powers.[104]

The impact of the BBC on football was not as great as that of the press but its influence grew steadily throughout the period. In 1924 licences were held by 10 per cent of British households but by 1939 this had increased to 71 per cent. Under John Reith, the BBC was driven by a strong sense of moral purpose that included the raising of cultural and educational standards. Broadcasting was also intended to bring different classes together, promote social unity and enhance a sense of national identity through the coverage of major national events such as the FA Cup final, first broadcast in 1927.[105] The radio provided managers with limited opportunities of exposure to a national audience. In 1932, as part of a series on football, Leicester City manager, Peter Hodges, gave a talk on 'Team Building and General Managerial Worries or Practices'. (De Lotbiniere had actually preferred Fred Everiss.)[106] In 1944, Frank Buckley was interviewed by Dennis Moore on the radio programme, 'Strike a Home Note', and talked about the idea of a British League. He also predicted that there would be a European tournament with clubs travelling by aeroplane.[107] In 1946 a banquet was held to celebrate Fred Everiss's fifty years' association with West Bromwich Albion, and this was featured on a local radio programme, 'Midland Region'.[108]

With this burgeoning profile, how did the lifestyle and status of the football manager change? During this period, there was an increasing gap in salary between managers of top clubs and those in the lower divisions. This reflected not only a club's size, status and economic fortunes but also a manager's importance to the club. On succeeding Herbert Chapman at Arsenal in 1934, George Allison was awarded a five-year contract worth £3,000 per annum, reputedly the highest in the game.[109] By contrast, a player's maximum basic weekly wage was £8 during the 1930s. On accepting the position of secretary-manager at Bolton Wanderers, Charles Foweraker's salary was £400 in 1919 which was comparable with the salaries of those players on the maximum. Yet, unlike the players, his contract was for five years and he later received annual increases of £25.[110] Managers with lower division clubs, however, were not paid much more than the players they managed. In 1934 Walsall's new manager-coach, Andy Wilson, was paid £5 per week whereas a year later the club's star player, Gilbert Alsop, was offered £6 per week.[111] Darlington's manager, George Collins, was paid £4 per week in the playing season and only £2 10s in the summer of 1936. In contrast, one player, R. Strang, was getting wages of £5 per week between September and May.[112]

Some clubs from the third division, however, were ambitious and able to offer bigger salaries. Ipswich Town, backed by the brewers, Cobbolds, entered the Football League in 1938. The year before they had offered the position of manager to Frank Buckley. He eventually refused and the club then turned its attention to the Manchester United manager, Scott Duncan. He was given a seven-year contract at £1,500 per annum plus a 5 per cent commission on the sale of all players, together with bonuses if Ipswich gained entry to the Football League and any subsequent promotions.[113] Success also brought greater rewards. In 1936 Jimmy Seed's annual salary was increased to £1,040 following Charlton's successive promotions to division one.[114] Frank Buckley was re-engaged by Wolverhampton Wanderers in 1933 for five years on an annual salary of £800 plus £200 expenses.[115] In 1938 he stated that he would be happy to stay at Wolves for the entirety of his career but he left in 1944 for Notts. County who offered him an annual salary of £4,500, then the highest salary paid to a football manager.[116] This compared well to the Chancellor of the Exchequer who during the inter-war period (as in 1913) had a salary of £5,000.

During the inter-war years these figures compared quite favourably with the salaries of the majority of conventional managers. The average salary of a manager in 1922–3 was £534 and the median salary was £483. By 1938–9 these figures had declined to £490 and £444 respectively, perhaps indicating a rise in the number of managers overall. At the top end of the scale, however, it was calculated that 4,240 managers received an average salary of £8,290 and some top company executives earned substantially more.[117] In 1926 Josiah Stamp, for example, was offered a salary of £17,500 on taking up the position of President of the executive of the LMS Railway. At ICI, Harry McGowan's annual salary as chairman and managing director averaged £57,000 between 1931 and 1937, and in 1937 he received £64,410.[118]

In terms of income criteria, most football managers now belonged to the middle classes, as it was (crudely) calculated that the middle class began and the working class ended at £250 per year. What constituted 'middle-classness', however, was complex and social indicators such as education (especially in a grammar school), fertility, lifestyle, manners and social aspirations were considered just as important to people who did not fit the financial indicator. For example, what mattered to clerks about being middle-class was the status of their occupation, social aspirations and manners and, importantly, a very strong sense of not being working-class.[119]

To what extent Jimmy Seed, someone with a strong working-class background, considered himself middle-class after becoming a football manager is difficult to gauge. Yet his lifestyle does indicate a certain level of social mobility. For example, he sent his daughter, Gladys, to Brooklands Preparatory School and from there to Bromley County School for Girls. Seed and his family also lived in a detached house on an estate opposite a golf course in Bromley, Kent, and their neighbours included an anaesthetist and a doctor. His house was fitted with consumer durables such as a washing machine and telephone, and they later owned a television. Seed had also owned a car since the 1920s when he was a player. Private car ownership stood at 100,000 in 1919 and had reached 2 million by 1939, although the majority of working-class families were unable to afford one.[120] Unsurprisingly, Seed's home life took a back seat to his job and its demands. Even during the summer he was away from home on club tours to Sweden and the USA. Gladys and her mother usually stayed with relatives in the north-east. On other occasions the family went to Jersey and once on a cruise. Christmas was also a difficult period for family gatherings as matches were played on both Christmas Day and Boxing Day. Furthermore, Seed hardly ever sat down with his family for meals or helped his wife with the housework. He never discussed football at home although Gladys did attend Charlton home games. Seed's interests outside of football seem to have included golf, gardening, bridge and sketching and he could also play the piano.[121]

Another aspect of middle-class life during the inter-war period was a propensity for joining clubs. Membership became synonymous with friendship, and in middle-class communities membership of these mainly masculine associations was almost regarded as obligatory.[122] After the failure of the previous organization, football managers and secretaries re-formed the Football League Secretaries' and Managers' Association (FLSMA) in 1919. Membership required five years' service in club management and, perhaps surprisingly, in 1935 this comprised 90 per cent of all secretaries and managers in the League. It lacked any pretensions to further its members' professional credentials, however. In essence, the FLSMA was a friendly society. Fred Everiss was elected chairman in 1935. He declared that, 'It is not a trade union. We have nothing to do with agreements, salaries or quarrels with employers which we consider a domestic matter.'[123] Its own members, therefore, did not regard football management as a profession.

Despite the increase in their material well-being, managers were ultimately judged by results. Notwithstanding the limit of their powers, the intensification of competition brought with it a steady increase in managerial insecurity.[124] There was a decline, for example, in the number of men who gave a lifetime of service to one club.[125] The stability of some clubs contrasted with others who employed several managers over the period. For instance, Walsall hired nine managers between 1921 and 1937 and during the 1930s Manchester United had four.[126] The pressures of the job could also take their toll on a manager's health. Matt Busby recollected George Kay at Liverpool sitting on the trainer's bench 'shouting, beseeching, wringing his hands, holding his head in apparent anguish, and making an excellent attempt to head and kick every ball in the match'.[127] Kay himself was forced to retire in 1951 on medical advice. The case of Syd King at West Ham, however, was extreme. King, secretary-manager since 1901, was suddenly sacked in November 1932 following a board meeting. He had arrived drunk and insulted the directors. King, a regular at many local pubs, took the news badly, and less than a month after his dismissal he committed suicide. An inquest was held and he was found to be of 'unsound mind' and to have been suffering from persecution delusions that had begun in the previous season when West Ham had been relegated.[128]

By 1939 most football clubs employed a manager who was increasingly subject to similar stresses as the sport became more competitive and commercialized. Five years earlier the growing importance of managers had been recognized when Dick Ray, then manager of Leeds United, was chosen to manage the Football League team against the Scottish League.[129] More importantly, and on a larger, national scale, managers were leading out their teams in the FA Cup final by 1939. It had become more widely recognized that there needed to be some buffer between directors and players. Clubs began to look to former professionals to provide this cushion, and, through the media, the manager's role became more visible. But because directors were generally resistant to change, few clubs followed Arsenal's lead and allowed managers the range of powers accorded to Herbert Chapman.

Chapter 5

The modernization of football management, 1945–70

Following the Second World War, Britain was marked by fundamental economic and social changes. After war and peacetime austerity, the 1950s saw the beginning of a more consumer-based and affluent society in which living standards doubled between 1946 and 1973.[1] Greater prosperity amongst the working classes brought a decline in deference and a growing confidence, epitomized by the film, *Room at the Top*. The creation of the welfare state with its cradle-to-the-grave provisions spawned a more egalitarian ethos that permeated the public consciousness. Not only was cricket's anachronistic Gentlemen versus Players game abolished in 1962 but by 1968 a comprehensive education system had been partly established. Libertarian measures, such as wider access to contraception, and a burgeoning youth culture added to a growing permissiveness within a country in which, according to Philip Larkin, 'sex was invented' in 1963. Overall, people did what they wanted more often than ever before.

When the Football League restarted after the war, football management had changed little since 1939. The directors were in charge and to a large extent managers were employed on a 'front man and office boy' basis.[2] By 1970, however, there had been a change in the public's perception of football managers, something that was symbolized by the knighthood bestowed upon Alf Ramsey in 1967 for his role in England's World Cup victory. Yet, football management had been slow to modernize and the shift in the manager's role was gradual. It not only echoed football's unwillingness to embrace reform but also a reluctance within society generally.

During this period, the development of 'British modernity was always a balancing act between innovation and tradition'. The continuity of English traditions acted as a buffer against modern American culture and ideas in many areas of life, including business.[3] Initially, due to an increase in post-war economic production and mechanization, a demand for managers had arisen. Furthermore, the welfare state became a haven for professional administrators. Following the nationalization of certain industries, the 1945 Labour Government promoted a new 'managerial class', something that was continued by Conservative administrations. As a result, Britain underwent something of a managerial revolution, with the numbers of managers, administrators and higher professionals increasing from 1.96 million in 1951 to 3.36 million by 1971, more than one in five of the working male population. British society became more meritocratic but instead of a professional structure based on career hierarchies, professional interests became entangled with the class system.[4] Middle managers, for example, were organized into ranks with differentiation based on privileges and badges of position as opposed to expertise. In addition, post-war attempts to utilize American ideas, such as personnel management, floundered because they 'conflicted with long-standing indigenous methods and traditions within British industry'.[5] Whereas many Americans felt that British firms were run on autocratic and unscientific lines, the British believed that management was about leadership of people in the same way that the army was led by generals, and in this respect football management was little different.

The overall management of football clubs changed little. In 1964, a director's average age was 58 with 38 per cent aged over 60. Boardrooms were riddled with complacency and characterized by staleness and immobility, with shares generally passed on to relatives and friends. Little attempt was made to embrace new management ideas. In 1965, a survey of seventy-six clubs found that in seventy-three, one manager was responsible for all spheres of the club's activities – playing, administrative and financial – with only three employing a general manager.[6] Attitudes to management were partly shaped by the prevailing parochial nature of English football that held little regard for the rapid progress of European football. As League Champions in 1955, Chelsea had been invited to be England's representatives in the inaugural European Cup but the Football League would not sanction their participation for fear of fixture congestion. Before competitions were instituted, some English clubs did play foreign opposition in friendlies under floodlights, an innovation that was at an embryonic stage. Wolverhampton Wanderers victory over Honved in 1954 created great interest, particularly as the second half was televised live. Wolves played a number of friendlies against top continental opposition, and other clubs recognized that European football was an important source of revenue. It also demanded improved playing standards but the widespread acceptance of this was a slow process.

The management of the England team epitomized English insularity and the reluctance to change. In 1945, it was taken for granted by many people, both inside and outside the game, that England was still the premier footballing nation. Even the shock defeat by the USA in the 1950 World Cup was written off as a one-off. English football, however, received a major jolt in 1953 when Hungary's 6–3 victory at Wembley made them the first European team to defeat England on home soil. It got an even bigger shock the following year when England lost 7–1 in Budapest.[7] Before the Wembley game, the press had disregarded the Hungarians but defeat created a demand from the same newspapers that English players should be subjected to the same modern, pre-match preparation as their opponents. There were mounting anxieties about the performance of British sport in general (cricket being an exception) during the 1950s, due to the rise in international competition and the Cold War.

In 1946, Walter Winterbottom had been appointed England team manager as well as director of coaching. His role, however, was an advisory one, and the International Selection Committee picked the team, with members nominating and then voting on players for particular positions.[8] Some European countries had different ideas. Although Sweden and France employed selection committees, others, including Austria and Spain, employed a team manager.[9] In West Germany, Sepp Herberger had been the *de facto* national coach since 1936. In 1950, it was written into his contract that the German Football Federation's playing committee would have no say in the running of the team.[10] Winterbottom gradually gained more influence over selection but it was never total. In 1954, he was allowed more time to prepare the international team but was still instructed to keep reports of players that members of the committee had brought to his attention.[11] Alf Ramsey's appointment as Winterbottom's successor in 1962 had followed meetings between the FA and prominent club managers. Apart from recommendations concerning the co-operation between clubs and the England manager in the preparation of players for the 1966 World Cup, it was the unanimous feeling among all the managers canvassed that the England manager should have full responsibility in selecting the team.[12]

The FA, especially its secretary, Stanley Rous, had actually been aware of the rise in playing standards in Europe and that also, by the early 1960s, most European clubs and national teams only employed qualified coaches. In Italy, for example, the first football management course was introduced in 1946 with a diploma initiated two years later.[13] In addition to providing formal qualifications for coaches and physiotherapists, in conjunction with a growing concern for sports medicine, the FA endeavoured to establish similar courses for managers during the 1960s. However, it was frustrated in its efforts.[14] The FA's concern for improvements in the training of managers was linked to the high rate of managerial turnover where many new appointees proved unsuitable for the job. Between 1945 and 1965, it had been estimated that over 600 managers had parted from their clubs and that the annual turnover of football managers was a quarter, probably the highest turnover for any industry.[15] The FA's overall aim was to establish a formal appointments procedure for football management, similar to other professions. This was perhaps a reason for the rejection of their proposals. Directors of Football League clubs, for instance, would have been loath to forgo their prerogative of employing who they wanted as manager, while managers without qualifications would not have been in favour of a system that decreased their chances of finding work. Like their counterparts in industry, football managers continued to learn their job 'on the job'.

Despite this lack of professionalization, there had been a significant increase in new managers entering football between 1945 and 1970 – about 350. Nearly all were former professional players, and a large proportion – between 30 and 50 per cent – had been internationals, although this figure declined steadily over the period. Like their counterparts in industry, directors believed that leadership qualities were important and a high percentage of managers had also been captains. Of the twenty-three captains who lifted the 'Cup' between 1946 and 1970, seventeen 'made the move upstairs'. In addition, former England captains, Stan Cullis, Eddie Hapgood, George Hardwick and Billy Wright, became managers during this period, but of this group only Cullis enjoyed managerial success.

Although not a prerequisite for the job, some directors did look for evidence of qualifications, and an increasing number of managers, like Bill Nicholson and Jimmy Adamson, had acquired FA coaching badges. The coaching schemes initiated by the FA during the 1930s were expanded after the war. Supervised by Walter Winterbottom, they were attempts by the Football Association to modernize, and were the beginning, albeit slowly, of the game's move towards a technocracy. Initially, there was much resistance to the idea of coaching. Not only did working-class players distrust anything theoretical, but coaching challenged firmly held beliefs that English football was based on individual skill and masculine toughness. Senior England players like Tommy Lawton and Raich Carter, for instance, were critical of Walter Winterbottom's early team meetings.[16] Stan Cullis regarded most coaching as too theoretical and academic, and worried if some of his players came back from England games with new ideas. Once, in exasperation, he (allegedly) said to his international half-back Bill Slater, 'Bill, Bill, you're playing . . . like an England player!'[17]

Because of their working-class background, most managers had left school at 14. Others, some of whom had successful careers, did enjoy a better education. Alan Brown, for example, attended Hexham Grammar School, while Bill Nicholson won a scholarship to the prestigious Scarborough Boys' High School.[18] Stan Cullis won a scholarship to Chester Grammar School but his father refused to let him go. He later attended French and Esperanto evening classes and had knowledge of shorthand and bookkeeping.[19] Matt Busby's headmaster had initially advised him to train as a schoolteacher, while Walter Winterbottom had actually been a PE lecturer at Carnegie College in Leeds before he was appointed England manager. Before 1960, there was no formalized apprenticeship scheme for footballers and many managers had work experience, usually in typical working-class occupations. Some, like Bill Shankly, Matt Busby and Jimmy Adamson, had worked at collieries.[20] Before joining Sunderland, Raich Carter was an apprentice artificer in a forge, but never served his time. Don Revie left school at 14 and was apprenticed as a bricklayer.[21] George Hardwick gained an apprenticeship as a draughtsman at Dorman Long.[22] After failing to get a job at the newly built Ford plant in his home town of Dagenham, Alf Ramsey decided to become a grocer and was apprenticed to the local Co-op store.[23]

Because of the generation gap the everyday values of some managers had more in common with earlier times than the permissiveness of the post-war period. Despite a downward trend in religious observance, for example, a number of prominent managers held strong religious beliefs. Raich Carter was a Primitive Methodist who, when at Hull City, read the lessons for Sportsmen's services in local churches. During his spell at Sunderland (1957–64), Alan Brown joined 'Moral Rearmament', a Christian evangelical movement based in Switzerland.[24] Matt Busby was a devout Catholic and received a papal knighthood in 1968. He was known to 'kneel quite unselfconsciously inside his own boardroom to kiss the hand of a visiting bishop'.[25] Stan Cullis was a regular church-goer, and his son, Andrew, later became a vicar. Dubbed the 'Passionate Puritan' by John Arlott, Cullis never swore – probably one of the few managers who didn't. The nearest he got was to spice any outbursts with the word 'flopping'.[26] In the early 1950s, Britain was still a class-conscious society in which accent was a significant indicator of class. Before becoming a manager, Alf Ramsey took elocution lessons in order to eliminate his Dagenham accent and increase his self-confidence.[27]

In addition to their football experience, life in the military, either during the war or through National Service until it ended in 1962, continued to have a significant influence on managers. Some professional footballers had served as physical training instructors, giving a number of future managers a feel for handling men, albeit in a less intense environment than military life. Matt Busby had initially served in the 9th Battalion of the King's Liverpool Regiment but was later transferred to the Army Physical Training Corps. He also managed the Army football team which included internationals like Bert Sprotson and Frank Swift. Future Spurs manager, Arthur Rowe, was attached to various units and was also put in charge of service sides.[28] Stan Cullis actually joined the South Staffordshire Territorials in May 1939. He was called up when war broke out and became a company sergeant-major instructor in an anti-tank regiment. In July 1944, he took charge of sport at an Eighth Army military rest camp in Italy.[29] Of course, football managers developed their own styles despite exposure to military management methods, but nevertheless, notions of authority, embodied by life in the forces, helped to shape their outlook.

As standards of living rose during this period, clubs were forced to compete in an ever-expanding leisure market. Between 1950 and 1966, there was approximately a 1 per cent fall in attendances for every 1 per cent increase in consumer spending: from a post-war peak of 41.3 million in 1948–9, Football League attendances had dropped to 27.6 million by 1964–5. Fans were becoming more discerning and the poor condition and lack of seats in many stadiums were cited as contributory factors to their staying away. People now expected higher standards of comfort.[30] Moreover, the home became the family's chief leisure centre as gardening, DIY and, especially, watching television became alternatives to going to a match.[31] By 1969, television occupied nearly a quarter of the leisure time of both men and women in England and Wales.[32]

The most significant impact on the management of football clubs during this period, though, was the abolition of the maximum wage in 1961 and the modification of the retain and transfer system two years later. It signalled the start of the decline of mutuality amongst Football League clubs as well as a change in club–player relations. The financial risks of running a football club also grew as the footballing competition intensified. Because of these new pressures, directors and chairmen would ultimately place more power and trust in the hands of the manager. The process towards this change, however, was an uneven one and varied from club to club.

Until the 1960s, clubs had strongly resisted abolishing the 'maximum' and reforming the transfer system, despite a growing militancy amongst the players. Their stance was hypocritical as clubs continued to lure players with under-the-counter payments. In 1957, Sunderland were heavily fined and several directors banned for life after it was found that they had made illegal payments to players that stretched back many years.[33] Despite playing in front of large crowds, footballers, who increasingly thought that they were part of the entertainment industry, actually saw their earnings fall in comparison with those of skilled manual workers. Under the threat of a strike by the Professional Footballers' Association, the Football League abolished the 'maximum'. Following the 'Eastham Case' in 1963, the High Court found the retain and transfer system to be in restraint of trade, although it was modified rather than abolished. Arthur Marwick has argued that the removal of these restrictions symbolized the period's prevailing mood which resulted in an 'end of Victorianism', where 'British society seemed to have broken out of the straitjacket of dullness and conformity which had pinioned it since Victorian times'.[34]

The changes in football's industrial relations, together with the fall in demand for professional football and the changing habits of fans, saw the emergence of a process of economic rationalization. This had begun in the mid-1950s and accelerated during the 1960s. First division clubs were less affected by the fall in crowds than teams in the lower divisions and, in terms of income, first division clubs steadily increased their share. By 1964–5, first division clubs accounted for 50.4 per cent of the game's gross receipts. In 1950–1, this figure had been 44.4 per cent. The other divisions experienced a concomitant decrease in their gate receipts.[35] Not only were fans supporting the bigger teams but the best playing talent became steadily concentrated in fewer clubs.

Management pressures, therefore, were building up within clubs to confront these changing economic and social circumstances. How did they affect the relationship between a manager and his directors? In essence, the growing tensions between them redefined their relationship without changing its basic structure. The directors were still the bosses who traditionally disliked delegating, did not like spending money and were reluctant to cede power to managers. In addition, some directors may not have wanted them to be too well qualified because that would have made them more difficult to manipulate. Managers, on the other hand, wanted to manage their own way and were increasingly assertive, reflecting the overall decline in deference. Initially, however, the directors held the upper hand. Indicative of this was how West Ham picked its team. In 1952, manager Ted Fenton claimed that, a more appropriate name for a Manager is a Technical Adviser, for every Tuesday throughout the season a meeting is held at which I recommend to the Directors the teams which should represent the Club at the following Saturday's matches and explain my reasons for any proposed changes. The Directors are always ready to accept those changes which I consider necessary, and whilst occasions do occur when my recommendations are criticised, I am happy to say that they show confidence in my selection. Many times, however, I have had reason to thank a Director for making a useful suggestion about the composition of the team.[36]

Even in 1962, West Bromwich Albion manager, Archie Macaulay, could only recommend the team he wanted to his directors.[37] A number of managers left, grumbling of interference from the boardroom, a problem that perhaps partly stemmed from the terms of a manager's actual contract. For example, the details of Raich Carter's contract with Leeds United in 1955 left his role open to the interpretation of the directors. It was stated that the 'manager shall *subject to any orders or directions given to him by the Board of Directors* [author's italics] during his employment hereunder be responsible for and have the control of the training and management of all the football players'. In other words, directors reserved the right to interfere.

At smaller clubs, directors probably had a greater say in the running of the club, particularly as money was tighter compared to first division clubs. Darlington were a perennial lowly club during the 1950s, none of its managers had money to buy new players and the club's management had changed very little from the 1930s. In March 1952, the club appointed Bob Gurney, a centre-forward for Sunderland when they won the League in 1936 and the Cup the following year. Despite his playing reputation, the directors continually questioned Gurney's team selections and the players he wanted to sign. On one occasion, it was recorded that, 'the manager submitted his team. . . . Certain suggestions were made by us as to the constitution of the team and it was agreed that the manager would consider them in the light of playing conditions.' In 1957, Gurney was replaced by Dick Duckworth, Sheffield United's chief scout. One of the terms of his contract was that as manager he would have full control of the playing and training staff, and scouts, and to be responsible for all team selections. However, a few months later it was recorded that the manager had put forward his 'suggested' teams for Saturday's game.[38]

How a manager gained autonomy in team matters was an almost imperceptible process. Much depended on an individual club's management culture, something which could be shaped by powerful personalities, and, during this period, an increasing number of managers fell into this category. Early in his stewardship at Manchester United, Matt Busby used the force of his personality and argument to establish control over team affairs, following disagreements with some of the directors. On one occasion in 1947–8, club chairman Jimmy Gibson had insisted that Busby should sign a player but Busby refused and stood his ground. He claimed that from then on his autonomy as manager was never questioned again.[39]

When Bill Shankly was recruited by Liverpool in 1959, it was because of his reputation for running small clubs on shoestring budgets rather than for the dominant personality he became. Then in the second division, Liverpool's average gates were under 30,000. Shankly subsequently encountered directorial interference similar to that which he had experienced at his other clubs, Carlisle United, Grimsby Town, Workington Town and Huddersfield Town. When he was manager at Workington the board had selected the team and signed new players. The club had a large number of directors who were continually involved in power struggles and at one chaotic meeting some nearly came to blows.[40] Initially, the Liverpool directors were unwilling to provide him with any money to buy players. However, help was literally round the corner in the form of near neighbours Everton.

In 1960, John Moores, owner of the Littlewoods football pools company, became chairman of Everton. Everton themselves had had a tradition of directors running the team stretching back to William Cuff who had dominated the club for many years.[41] The club's first manager, Theo Kelly, was not appointed until 1939. Kelly had been the secretary and the directors continued to run team affairs. Cliff Britton, a former Everton player, replaced him in 1948, while Kelly resumed his secretarial duties.[42] In 1956, Britton resigned citing directorial interference but, rather than appoint a successor, team matters were delegated to a sub-committee with Ian Buchan as chief coach.[43] In 1961, however, Moores installed his own choice as manager, Harry Catterick.[44]

Moores was also the major shareholder in Liverpool and a bridge-playing friend of its chairman, Tom Williams. He decided to place his own nominee on the Liverpool board, Eric Sawyer, who was in charge of the accounts at Littlewoods.[45] In 1961, Sawyer, now Liverpool's financial director, persuaded his board members to release the money for Shankly to buy Ron Yeats and Ian St John, two players who were pivotal to Liverpool's promotion to division one in 1962. Liverpool's later success was in no small way due to Shankly, although he could perhaps be considered fortuitous to have come to the club under the right circumstances. Not only was it a 'fallen giant' with potential to exploit football's changing climate, but these conditions eventually allowed him more freedom to manage.

Shankly's influence over the running of the club continued to grow, including negotiating players' salaries.[46] Yet, his relationship with the directors remained strained right up until his mysterious departure in 1974. He had perhaps begun to alienate the directors, feeling that the club could not do without him. Shankly had threatened to resign on a number of occasions as a way of getting the directors to accept his views on a specific issue. In 1966, for example, he applied for the vacant job at Manchester City.[47] Perhaps Liverpool's directors felt that the club was in such a healthy financial position that Shankly was now dispensable, or the growth in commercial activity meant that they felt they needed to control the club's finances.

Despite any changes in their relationship with the board, the recruitment and buying and selling of players remained the most important aspect of the manager's job. The abolition of the maximum wage, however, now forced clubs to concentrate their resources, in particular trimming massive squads that could number up to eighty players. During the 1960s, wages and transfer fees began to escalate, although even in the era of the maximum wage, the bigger clubs could still attract the best players. Matt Busby was never afraid to pay out large transfer fees, and in eighteen seasons between 1950 and 1967 United made a loss on transfers on eleven occasions.[48] Managers also had to satisfy directors who had an eye on the balance sheet. Even after the Liverpool directors allowed Shankly to spend money on building up the team, he still had to sell other players. By 1964, he had invested just over £150,000 in new players but had recouped just under the same figure.[49]

Stan Cullis, continuing the policy of Frank Buckley, was even more successful, and from 1948 to 1959 Wolves made an overall profit of £186,222.[50] During the 1950s, Wolves' success had been based on the production of homegrown talent, enabling the club to save on transfer fees. One of their nursery teams was based at Wath-on-Dearne in South Yorkshire. Run by a former Wolves player, Mark Crook, it had been instituted by Frank Buckley before the war. After 1945 it supplied the club with a number of players, such as Ron Flowers and Roy Swinbourne. Matt Busby also developed home-grown players at Manchester United. The 'Busby Babes', his most famous team, was virtually wiped out after the Munich air disaster in February 1958. It had been a product of United's youth system, and the team's average age when United won the League in 1955–6 had been 22. United's youth scheme had initially been set up in the form of Manchester United Junior Athletic Club by James Gibson when he first became chairman in 1931. The chief scout had been Louis Rocca who had many contacts all over Britain and Ireland. Rocca died in 1950 and was replaced by Joe Armstrong. His main asset was the ability to charm parents into letting their sons sign for United.[51]

Poaching talented schoolboy footballers, however, was a common, if shady, practice during this period. Dunphy has claimed that, originally, Busby would not agree to under-the-counter payments for schoolboy footballers but he later relented in the face of the competition from other clubs.[52] In 1959, Wolves were found to have contravened the FA's Rule 32(d), which stated that 'No approach of any description shall be made either directly or indirectly to a boy on the roll of a recognized school either to sign registration forms or to play for a Club affiliated to a County Football Association.'[53] A Wolves scout, Mr G. Cotterell, had denied trying to induce a young player but he admitted that he went to the player's house to help his father find employment when his son left school. Wolves were fined £250, with the commission taking previous offences into consideration.[54]

As the business of football clubs increased, managers delegated more responsibilities to a growing number of assistants. Backroom staff also provided some clubs with continuity when a new manager was appointed. At Manchester United, Matt Busby came to rely on Jimmy Murphy and Bert Whalley, who supervised the reserve and youth teams. Bill Nicholson's assistant, Eddie Baily, had been a playing colleague when Spurs won the League in 1951. Wolves maintained a strong link with its past. Stan Cullis, a former Wolves player under Buckley, had a short spell as assistant manager before his appointment as manager in 1948. Joe Gardiner, who as trainer acted as a foil to Stan Cullis, was another player under Buckley. Later, Wolves player Bill Shorthouse retired in 1957 and then became the club's coach. When he took over at Liverpool, Shankly's first task was to ensure the jobs of the club's coaching staff – Bob Paisley, Joe Fagan, Reuben Bennett and Albert Shelly. Known as the 'Boot Room', because the group would meet there to discuss tactics and the form of players, it oversaw the most successful period of any club in English football history. Each brought their own skills: Shankly was the leader who motivated the players, and Paisley was the tactical brains as well as keeping the manager informed of any dissension amongst the players, while Fagan was more of a psychologist. Paisley and Fagan later managed Liverpool, as did two future members, Ronnie Moran (briefly) and Roy Evans.

How was the relationship between the manager and his players affected by the changes in post-war football and society? Soon after the war, relations between the two parties were still distant. As a young player at Charlton, Malcolm Allison had questioned the value of the club's training. He was told to see Jimmy Seed the following day who informed him that he was being transferred to West Ham. His (apparent) response was to ask Seed if he could shake his hand. Allison said, 'I want to thank you for teaching me the art of communication, because you've just spoken to me for the third time in seven years.'[55]

With the decline in social barriers, footballers grew in confidence and became more independently minded, creating different challenges for managers. In the 1950s, a group of West Ham players, including Allison, became part of an 'Academy' that met in a local cafe, discussed tactics, and would then try to impose them on their manager, Ted Fenton. Danny Blanchflower regularly challenged convention. At Barnsley and Aston Villa, his ideas concerning tactics and preparation often ran contrary to those of the management. At Spurs he was dropped and stripped of the captaincy by Jimmy Anderson for changing formations during matches. When Bill Nicholson became Tottenham's manager in 1958, rather than seeing Blanchflower as a threat to his own authority, he decided to harness his footballing talents, allowing him to run the team during the game.[56]

However, there was no radical transformation of the relationship between manager and players. Managers still felt that young men needed discipline from an authoritarian figure. Nevertheless, subtle changes in the style of management did emerge that involved a closer rapport between the two parties.

Across all four divisions, many clubs now adopted pre-match team talks, although the team for the weekend was usually pinned up, in a cold fashion, on a noticeboard on a Friday. Some managers talked about a so-called 'family-like' atmosphere at their club but it usually revolved around the notion of the manager as the father-figure demanding obedience. This approach, though, did not always complement an increasingly permissive society, and in football clubs, as in any family, it did not prevent dysfunctional behaviour by some of its members. Some younger managers, though, were able to develop a better understanding of modern players. Stan Cullis, forced to retire early from football at 32 in 1947, regularly trained with the players when he became manager a year later. When Wolves won the Cup in his first season, Cullis put it down to the co-operation garnered from the Friday morning team talks he had initiated. In addition to planning tactics, the talks built up confidence and established trust between manager and players.[57] Conditioned by his experience as a player, Matt Busby wanted to adopt a more humane approach to management, similar to that of his manager at Liverpool, George Kay. Initially, Busby too trained with the players. He was also prepared to listen to a player's personal problems, although he was more concerned with their impact on his performance. In addition, Busby had his players vetted for any vices and domestic problems. His style of management was less confrontational than that of most of his peers but it did not preclude a streak of autocracy. Johnny Morris, for example, found his paternalistic style condescending. Following an argument with Busby on the training pitch, Morris walked off and was promptly placed on the transfer list.[58] However, when George Best started to dispute Busby's authority during the late 1960s, the manager was criticized for being too lenient towards him.

Some manager's motivational methods, however, still resonated with the past. Cullis was captain under Frank Buckley, and, despite a greater sympathy with his players, adopted a similar military-like persona. His son described him as a 'hard man'. Former player Dennis Wilshaw believed that their team spirit 'stemmed from the fact we all hated his guts'.[59] Bill Slater, however, another former player, described him as a 'very demanding manager' but one who the players liked. Slater said that they might 'complain a bit that he was never satisfied but I think they respected him, and liked him'. On one occasion, Cullis invited Slater, who was on his own, to his house for Christmas dinner. Cullis's methods of motivation were also more subtle then those of Buckley. After a victory he would pick up on some of their faults but after a defeat he would say very little.[60] On one occasion in 1953, he asked Roy Swinbourne, the club's leading goalscorer at the time, his age. Swinbourne said, 'Twenty-six.' 'Oh, I shall have to be looking for a replacement', Cullis replied, much to Swinbourne's astonishment.[61]

Sometimes the demands of management, however, resulted in an abuse of players. Ted Farmer discovered during half-time at one game that he was urinating blood after being elbowed in the stomach. Despite an examination by the medical officer, Cullis forced Farmer to play on. He told the doctor, 'Wait till it comes through his backside before you take him off.' His injury was later diagnosed as damage to the wall of his bladder, necessitating five days in hospital where no Wolves official visited him.[62]

The abolition of the maximum wage affected a provincial club like Wolves more than those from the big cities, and also created problems for Cullis as manager. Until then the club had prospered through a mixture of careful husbandry and nurturing home-grown players. Other clubs, however, were able to offer markedly better wages. Everton, for example, offered a lucrative bonus system linked to league position and crowd size, potentially earning some players over £100 per week. When Everton won the League in 1963 there was a 50 per cent increase in their wage bill.[63] Manchester United had a similar bonus scheme and it has been claimed that stars like Best, Denis Law and Bobby Charlton earned around £1,000 per week by the late 1960s.[64] By comparison, Wolves' wage structure was not radically altered after 1961. Initially, to maintain equality amongst the players, they were all paid the same. However, Cullis had problems coming to terms with the fact that players put money over their loyalty to the club. In 1961 and 1962, club captain Ron Flowers held out for more money before re-signing.[65] Previously, the imposition of the maximum wage had made moving not so attractive, making it easier for Cullis to motivate the players.

Bill Shankly motivated his players with his own peculiar brand of authoritarianism mixed with an enthusiasm and sense of humour that sometimes bordered on the eccentric. Despite his autocratic tendencies, though, he seems to have transcended any generation gap. At Huddersfield Town, for instance, the players preferred Shankly's openness to the more stuffy style of his predecessor, Andy Beattie.[66] If ever a player was injured, however, Shankly would ignore him. Ray Clemence described how 'if you were injured, you almost went round with a little bell'.[67] Ian St John claimed that Shankly was 'capable of exaggerating any situation to get the best out of his players'.[68] During team talks, Shankly would regularly dismiss Liverpool's opponents out of hand. Yet, there was method in his apparent madness because it had the effect of relaxing the players by banishing negative thoughts and filling them with confidence.

As the footballing competition intensified, there was a greater awareness by managers of the need to prepare players better. Wolves, for example, gained a reputation for being a very fit team and won many games during the final minutes. However, not only did Wolves pay more attention to training but they also concentrated on coaching and tactics. The club had acquired a special training centre at Castlecroft where on a Monday there would sometimes be an inquest on Saturday's game. Other days were given over to practice games and coaching plus some weight-training. For two days a week, Frank Morris, an international athlete and qualified coach, concentrated on the players' physical conditioning. The players would conclude the week with some light work at Molineux, including a spell in the shooting-pen, a legacy of Frank Buckley.[69]

For over thirty years, even after he retired, Liverpool's training was conducted under 'Shankly's Rules'. Training took place at Melwood over ninety minutes on a pitch the exact same size as Anfield. The day would begin with a long warming-up session, followed by ball exercises. (Surprisingly, Liverpool never practised any set-pieces like corners or free-kicks.) Stamina training was always done on grass, not on roads. To finish with there was a competitive five-a-side game. It was during these games that the basis of Liverpool's style of play – control, pass and move – was founded. Routine was important, particularly the 'cooling down' period after training. This served two purposes. First, the players changed at Anfield in order to make them familiar with their home ground; and second, it allowed the players' bodies to cool down, closing the pores and helping to avoid injuries. Shankly and Paisley both held qualifications in physiotherapy and earnestly believed in its advantages. It resulted in very few injuries and Liverpool would regularly field fewer players in a season than any other club.[70]

After 1961, some players, probably a minority, began to look upon coaching as something that was necessary to the extension and development of their own careers. Noel Cantwell, for example, who came from West Ham's 'Academy', was critical of Matt Busby's pre-match preparations and the lack of coaching at the club. When he left Manchester United for Leeds under Don Revie in 1963, Johnny Giles noticed a difference in attitude. Without the quality of players that United had at Old Trafford, Revie paid more attention to detail.[71] More people consciously thought about the game, would plan set-pieces and, in general, try not to leave things to chance. Alan Brown, for example, experimented with different free-kick routines.[72] Revie himself became famous for his dossiers on the opposition that would highlight their faults and strengths. He realized that managers, as well as inspiring players, needed to exploit the flaws of the opposition. Revie, however, was just as renowned for being superstitious. Despite his meticulous planning, this highlighted, if only in a small way, the insecurity managers felt, and ultimately how little control they had over events on the pitch. For the 1973 FA Cup final against Sunderland, Revie wore his 'lucky' mohair suit, but it was to no avail as Leeds lost 1–0.

After the war, and in light of the closer relationship between manager and players as well as their greater autonomy, managers increasingly made themselves responsible for the team's playing strategy. Despite the exposure of the limitations of the English style of play by Hungary's victory in 1953, the situation was not moribund as new tactical ideas emerged. There had been a fear that coaching would produce a uniformity of play but instead there was a variety of styles. Tottenham's manager, Arthur Rowe, instituted a continental 'push and run' method. He believed that the more a team retained possession, the greater its chances of scoring, and that this was best achieved through short passes.[73] Style, however, depended on the players a manager had at his disposal. Spurs won the League in 1951 but by the mid-1950s Rowe was unable to find replacements of a similar quality.

Stan Cullis, on the other hand, had a different philosophy. Under him, Wolves were characterized as a typically British 'kick and rush' team. However, it was more sophisticated than that. Cullis basically wanted to play the game in his opponent's half. Wolves employed a pressing game, harrying the opposition into mistakes, and a smothering defence so as not to let the other team enjoy easy possession. Wolves would then look to play long passes to their wingers, Johnny Hancocks and Jimmy Mullen. They would 'work the touchline' and be available for the clearance out of defence. It was also important that they were very good and they helped to create many chances for themselves and the other Wolves forwards. In every season from 1957–8 to 1960–1, Wolves scored over 100 league goals. Cullis followed the methods of Frank Buckley and was supported by Charles Reep, a football statistician who advocated a 'long ball' game. Although successful in England, Wolves were unable to reproduce their best form in European competition. In the 1960 European Cup, they were beaten 9–2 on aggregate by Barcelona.

As the game speeded up, and through greater contact with European teams, formations and tactics became more flexible. In 1962, Ipswich were surprise winners of the Football League playing a 4–3–3 formation. Their manager, then Alf Ramsey, played Jimmy Leadbetter, the left-winger, in a withdrawn role that allowed him to make runs into the penalty area unmarked, and score vital goals. England won the World Cup under Ramsey, it was said, with a team of 'wingless wonders'. However, Ramsey was more interested in how the team as a whole would function within a certain pattern, and found that none of the specialist wingers he tried conformed to his ideas. Alan Ball and Martin Peters were used during the competition, partly for their ability on the wing but also because they could 'tuck inside' and reinforce the midfield. The England team overall was built on a strong defence and an emphasis was placed on efficiency, with the team working as a unit. Clubs later copied Ramsey's methods, with lesser players bringing perhaps a blander form of football.

One of the most significant outcomes of these innovations was that by 1970, managers, in the form of their own tactics and beliefs, personified the style and identity of the teams that they managed. Because of this,

> the assumption that the managerial hand alone guided team performance, became more deeply woven into the popular football consciousness, gaining acceptance not only on the terraces and in the stands, but among directors and managers themselves.[74]

The media thought along similar lines. According to the press, not only were they responsible for their team's performance but managers, like Matt Busby and Bill Shankly, came to be regarded as figureheads for their clubs, an image promoted through the media's growing coverage of the game. This process was to be accentuated by the arrival of television, although football's relationship with television was still at an early stage. Images of managers were still formed mainly by the press. With falling attendances, football clubs became aware of the need to 'sell' themselves and to promote the right image, and by 1970, a flair for public relations was a requisite of the job. Advertising the club, therefore, became a function of the manager, and he came to be seen as 'the club'. Alec Stock, reflecting on a manager's increased media responsibilities, said,

> A manager is not granting a favour when he agrees to a newspaper, television or radio interview. He is doing an important part of his job. He is helping sell the game and his club to the public.[75]

No one understood this role better than Jimmy Hill. As manager of Coventry City between 1961 and 1967, he instigated the 'Sky Blue Revolution', changing the team's shirts to that colour, and inventing a song that the fans still sing today. Hill was very accommodating with the media generally and realized the benefits of a close relationship with the local community. It also helped that he was successful, winning promotion to the first division in 1967.

A manager's relationship with the media, though, was a two-way process. After the war, for example, local football personalities, like Blackpool's manager, Joe Smith, were sought by BBC radio for post-match summaries. Prophetically, with regard to the high media profile of today's managers, the BBC OBD S.J. de Lotbiniere remarked that, 'People's vanity can so easily be tickled by microphone appearances.'[76] During the 1950s, Stan Cullis appeared on a weekly local radio show, *Talking Football*, with Danny Blanchflower. Some managers developed their own post-match soundbites. Asked a question by Eamon Andrews on the BBC's *Sports Report*, Stan Cullis would invariably reply, 'I haven't got a crystal ball here to know the future.' Cullis, however, was aware of the importance of newspapers. He often spoke to journalists at work and he also took calls at home in the evening and on Sundays. Cullis claimed that 'the services of the newspapers are vital to the prosperity of football which could scarcely continue in its present position if the papers ignored it'.[77] However, this did not prevent him from banning David Jack, then a journalist, from the Molineux press box for a report that 'went beyond what might be expected from a Sportswriter of repute'.[78]

If Jimmy Hill was more media-savvy, Bill Shankly's relationship with the press highlighted the link between football and its mainly male, working-class fans. His instant quotability became a staple diet for tabloid reporters who were writing for a working-class audience themselves. Shankly's style of providing quick-witted one-liners established a template that other managers would try to follow. Shankly also had a flair for publicity. Before Carlisle home games, he addressed the fans through a loudspeaker. After buying Ron Yeats, he nicknamed him the 'Colossus' and invited the press to 'walk around him'.[79] Not only was he promoting the club by keeping Liverpool's name in the papers but he was also, perhaps unconsciously, enhancing his own image at the same time. Others, however, were still uncomfortable dealing with the press. Alf Ramsey always treated them with suspicion. The day after England won the World Cup, Ken Jones, a journalist who had supported Ramsey, requested an interview. Ramsey replied, 'Sorry, it's my day off.' When congratulated by reporters who had been less appreciative, his response was to ask, 'Are you taking the piss?' A year later on a tour to Canada, Ramsey was approached by a TV reporter who said: 'Sir Alf, we're going to give you five minutes of CBC time.' 'Oh no you're not', he responded, and continued to walk on.[80]

The relationship between football and television was at an early stage but the televising of the 1966 World Cup brought a number of innovations to the game's coverage. In addition to the extensive live exposure which brought huge viewing figures, a panel of experts was introduced (see Chapter 6) as well as slow-motion replays of incidents. Another innovation was a dedicated area set aside for managers for post-match interviews. It was during one of these interviews that Ramsey branded the Argentineans 'Animals' after England's victory over them in the quarter-final of the World Cup. His comments were soon relayed around the world. In South America, many British embassies became concerned over the possible impact of his inflammatory remarks on Anglo–Latin American relationships. It showed, if only in a small way, not only the potential power of television but also the importance of comments attributed to managers.[81]

Extra media duties further increased the demands made on football managers during this period. Yet they did not help themselves, as most were obsessives and workaholics, in line with some of their autocratic propensities. In 1967, it was calculated that the average business manager worked forty-two hours per week. It can be safely assumed that the total of the football manager was much greater. On top of administrative tasks, managers now spent more time coaching the players. Some managers had administrative duties written out of their contracts; others, though, were unwilling to delegate as they felt it would infringe on their own power base. Managers also spent a lot of time travelling up and down the country watching games. These trips were not only used for scouting purposes to improve their team's performance but also for gossiping with other managers, which reaffirmed their professional identity. Alec Stock claimed that he drove 25,000 miles per year on top of the travelling he did by rail and coach on club business such as scouting. During the season he worked seven days week and on some nights would get home at 11 p.m. or midnight. In addition to his training duties, he had to deal with some of the club's administrative matters. Before a home game on a Saturday, he even found time to support the club's youth team. On a Sunday, he would go to the ground to check on injured players as well as field questions from reporters over the telephone from his home. He allowed himself Friday afternoon off, spending two hours in a Turkish bath.[82]

There is no doubt that managing a football club was a stressful occupation, and probably became more stressful over this period. Tom Whittaker became ill with nervous exhaustion when secretary-manager at Arsenal and died in office in October 1956. Arthur Rowe suffered a nervous breakdown when manager of Spurs in 1954. After six months' recuperation he had a relapse and he had to step down in 1956. Bill Shankly's predecessor at Liverpool, Phil Taylor, retired on grounds of ill-health. He was only 42.[83] Yet, football management was perhaps also addictive. In 1964 Joe Mercer suffered a stroke when manager of Aston Villa but later admitted that he couldn't live without football. It has been speculated that Shankly died of a broken heart because his sudden retirement left him 'in the tormented frame of mind of one who had forfeited the power and responsibility of decision-making' in which he was centre-stage.[84]

Even when he was ill and confined to bed on doctor's orders, Stan Cullis would still conduct club business over the telephone such as negotiating transfers and picking the team.[85] Wolves sacked him in September 1964 two days after he came back from a week's recuperation in Eastbourne that his doctor had ordered. The directors later blamed Cullis's treatment of the players for their subsequent complaints and transfer requests, and claimed he had lost their confidence and respect.[86] Following a game during the club's 1964 tour to North America, Cullis was seen chasing the referee around the ground.[87] His son, Andrew, confirmed that he had not been well for a few months beforehand and that this may have been due to a mini-stroke. As a result, he became increasingly short-tempered with the players.

Despite their growing responsibilities, managers had little control over games, and referees were often the target of their frustrations. In one of his match reports, following a game at Cardiff that ended in a draw, Cullis described the performance of H.J. Husband as 'poor, a definite "homer"'. His appearance was described as unsatisfactory; his control of the game, poor; and regarding his fitness, he was insufficiently mobile. Another referee, K.A. Collinge, was blamed for inciting the misconduct of some Wolves supporters against Burnley. He was described as 'bad, incompetent, gave bad decision after bad decision . . . if he has one or two games like this he will be responsible for Grounds being closed'. Cullis concluded that, 'there is no doubt that the trouble was caused by the incompetence of the referee'.[88] It may also have had something to do with Wolves losing. The tensest part of the job, though, was still the game itself. Even for some successful managers like Cullis, it became a weekly torment. He said that 'the margin between success and failure is so small that every match in which Wolves play is something of an ordeal for me. Sitting in the directors' box or on the touchline, I make every pass, go into every tackle with every Wolves player.' Anyone sitting next to him would be kicked and elbowed throughout the game. Cullis wondered how other managers like Matt Busby could be so phlegmatic.[89]

But if the stresses of the job were mounting, so were its rewards. These not only included fixed salaries but managers' contracts also gave them some fringe benefits. Just after the war, for example, Jimmy Seed's salary rose from £1,500 to £2,000 while he was also given a Standard 12 car.[90] In 1955, Leeds United paid Raich Carter £1,850 per year plus 'reasonable' expenses. He was also entitled to twenty-one days annual holiday on full pay but this had to be taken during the close season. Furthermore, if Leeds reached the Cup final and became first division champions in 1958, he stood to earn a £1,000 bonus for each. By 1960, an industrial manager's average annual salary was £1,850. During the 1960s, many football managers earned considerably more, reflecting not only their importance but also the game's increasing commercialization, greater publicity and the demand for better management. When Matt Busby first became Manchester United manager in 1945 his salary had been £750 but this increased fourfold to £3,250 in 1949.[91] In 1963, while some of his players earned £25 per week, Busby's annual earnings had risen to approximately £6,000.[92] As manager of Ipswich Town, Alf Ramsey's salary in 1955 had been £1,500.[93] On becoming England manager in 1962, he earned £4,500.[94] After the victory in 1966, not only did his salary increase to £6,000 but he was also given a £6,000 bonus.[95] Interestingly, it was reckoned that Ramsey still earned less than a third of what first division managers earned in 1974.[96]

Football management was not as lucrative an occupation for those lower down the league but it still carried benefits. In 1952, Darlington offered Bob Gurney £15 per week. He also received 5 per cent on the profits made on transfers, highlighting how, if only in a limited way, managers had more freedom, compared to players, to negotiate the terms of their own contracts. By 1957, Gurney's annual salary had been increased to £1,000. His successor, Dick Duckworth, was later offered a three-year contract at £1,200 per year plus the same bonuses as the first team. He also received a car allowance for club business.[97]

With their growing status, managers began to augment their income from other sources. In 1959, following the example of several leading figures in entertainment and sport, Stan Cullis formed a private company, 'Stanwin Limited'. It centralized his various sources of income, which at the time included broadcasting, newspaper articles and book authorship. When Wolves sacked Cullis in 1964 he was paid £14,000 by a national newspaper for 'his story', probably twice his salary. It also highlighted the importance that tabloid newspapers had begun to attach to managers. They had now become personalities who could sell papers, reinforcing their relationship with the media. This figure was a record until 1974 when Alf Ramsey was paid £21,000 for three signed articles after his dismissal as England manager.[98] Following England's World Cup triumph, Ramsey was offered £10,000 by a Sunday paper for a few quotes but he refused. However, the salaries of even the top British managers paled in comparison with that of Inter Milan's Helenio Herrera who in 1966 was awarded a contract of £90,000, the equivalent of over £1 million in 2004.[99]

Despite more money, the increase in the pressures of the job meant that a football manager was rarely at home and his wife had to be selfless and understanding of the fickle nature of her husband's job. It probably helped that some, like Pat Carter, wife of Raich, enjoyed football. For those who attended matches, however, if the team was not playing well, they were sometimes forced to listen to cutting criticisms of their husband from frustrated spectators. Alex Stock's wife, Marjorie, also enjoyed football but she observed that,

> even if a manager's wife does not care deeply about the game I think she must understand his job. No woman could be happy otherwise. I must have spent more hours than anyone in Christendom looking out of a window with food ready and waiting in the kitchen. He never rings me to say he will be late, and if the team lose he slips into long silences or sleeps restlessly.[100]

Some wives would accompany their husbands on scouting trips just to spend some time together. Dave Bowen's wife, Audrey, saw such trips as a chance to catch up on conversation.[101] Stan Cullis sometimes took his son, Andrew, with him. It was one of the few opportunities for them to spend time together. Andrew recounted how the family rarely saw him. He was there at Christmas, but, because Cullis came from a large family, he would forget birthdays. When Andrew was born, however, he chose not to travel with Wolves to their game at Blackpool until the following day.[102] Following one scouting trip to Ewood Park, Cullis was driving home when he realized that he had left Andrew in the Blackburn boardroom.

Football managers began to enjoy a more middle-class lifestyle as the job's financial rewards gave more opportunities to enjoy a higher standard of living. The climb up the earnings ladder enabled some to send their children to private schools. Raich Carter, for example, paid for the primary education of his two children, Jane and Raich. Stan Cullis's son, Andrew, also went to preparatory school and then to Repton public school. His parents had chosen a boarding school because they felt that he should not be exposed to the pressures of living in a 'football home'. Cullis opted for Repton because it played football rather than rugby. His daughter was also sent to boarding school from the age of 7.

Although some managers like Shankly and Ramsey were content to live in modest semi-detached houses, where managers lived was another indication of social mobility. Stan Cullis had lived in a small house when he was a player but as manager he moved to the middle-class area of Tettenhall. Many managers during this period lived in houses owned by the club. Raich Carter always lived in club houses but they were in keeping with a more comfortable lifestyle. When he went to Leeds his wife, Pat, commented that 'it was a fabulous house, very beautiful house. We had a car. The standard of living was wonderful.' When he was manager at Middlesbrough, they were able to choose their own house. Pat recalled that, 'They let you choose it and they would buy it. They would pay for your choice in wallpaper. They'd pay for the decorating and your removal expenses. It was quite exciting because it meant we could have a new carpet.'

Managers also began to move in different social circles compared to their working-class origins. Some mixed with showbusiness personalities, while others were invited to sportsmen's dinners and to join various societies. Jackie Milburn and Jock Stein, for example, became freemasons.[103] Stan Cullis, on one occasion, was invited to speak at a meeting of the South Staffordshire branch of the Institute of Marketing and Sales Management in Wolverhampton where he pontificated on the challenge to football from changing social habits.[104] In any spare time that they had, managers usually found some form of relaxation. Stan Cullis liked to play a bit of golf but he particularly liked to tend to his garden. He would also take his family to church on a Sunday. Cullis was unable to spend much time on holiday with his family due to his football commitments. In the summer, Wolves would often tour so the rest of the family went to places like the Channel Islands and Tenby without him. For Bill Shankly, however, relaxation proved near impossible. He liked to listen to records of hymns and drink lots of tea, but mostly he liked to talk about football. On Sunday afternoons at Huddersfield he regularly met a bunch of boys and their dads for a kick-about. His one concession to his wife was that he cleaned the oven before he went out.[105]

Similar stories about Shankly would eventually establish him as a cult figure on Merseyside. Yet the way in which he made this transformation between different eras to earn this status demonstrated how football management itself had developed. By 1970, the public's idea of a football manager was an all-powerful, charismatic figurehead – something the growing media were willing not only to accept but also to perpetuate. Through football's commercialization, managers were the specialists who ran the club: they were the professionals; the directors were regarded as amateurs. Yet, football management's development was as much shaped by the forces of tradition as by social change: managers were still supposed to be leaders rather than technocrats, and experience counted more than learning. As with British modernity generally, both processes complemented as well as reinforced one another.

Chapter 6

Managers in the television age, 1970–92

Following the 1960s, football's place in English life over the next two decades became a set of contradictions. On the one hand, the game's image was blighted by hooliganism. On the other, it ushered in a new, more glamorous era as by 1970, most households had a colour television, bringing the game to a wider audience and implanting it more deeply into the national consciousness. Managers, as a result, became more visible, with some more colourful than others. It was an era of 'Big' men like 'Big Ron', 'Big Mal' or 'Big Jack'. Not only did they become renowned for their successes (and failures) but also, through their charisma and personality, some became household names due to their frequent appearances on 'the box' and the outspoken comments which usually accompanied them.

After the optimism and general permissiveness of the 1960s, the next two decades were marked by a reactionary backlash. Moreover, Britain, a member of the European Economic Community by 1973, moved into a harsher post-industrial age that changed both the political and economic landscape. The post-war political consensus of 'Butskellism' came to an end and, partly because of the 1973 oil crisis, there was a steady erosion of Keynesian macroeconomics. By the 1980s, this policy had been replaced by Thatcherite free market ideology. Nationalized industries were privatized, while neo-liberal attitudes also displayed contempt for the professions as most areas of public life became subject to market forces. Football-style league tables, for example, were drawn up for schools and hospitals. There was a wave of rationalization throughout the economy with most city high streets possessing the same chain stores and four major banks. However, manufacturing industry was badly hit, resulting in unemployment levels not seen since the Depression. In 1981, the jobless total reached 3 million for the first time since the 1930s and remained at that level until June 1983. A further slump between 1990 and 1992 again resulted in unemployment topping the 3 million mark. Yet the effects were not evenly spread. In general, southern England prospered. A north–south divide became more noticeable as former centres of heavy industry, like the north-east, became unemployment blackspots. Alan Bleasdale's *The Boys from the Blackstuff*, set in Liverpool, epitomized the misery of life on the dole. Furthermore, despite the introduction of comprehensive schools and the abolition of the socially divisive 11 plus entrance examination for grammar schools, the legacy of Britain's class system persisted. Public schools continued to flourish during this period, perpetuating the creation of social elites. In 1972, a survey of 'top people' by *The Economist* found that 67 per cent had been to public schools; in 1992 this figure was still 66 per cent.[1]

The economy's shift from a dependency on primary industries towards the service sector was accompanied by an increase in UK managers, whose numbers were estimated at 2.5 to 3 million by 1987, about 10 per cent of the total labour force. But if managerial numbers were increasing in general, there was little change in the management culture of British industry. As a result, the quality of management was a factor in Britain's relatively poor economic performance when compared to its competitors. In a survey carried out in 1976, it was found that managers, in both large and small firms, were only marginally better qualified than the population as a whole. Over half the managers had no qualifications at all, with only 3 per cent holding a degree. The picture for training was no less bleak, and in-house training programmes for managers of big companies were exceptions to a general rule. In 1992, for example, it was reported that half of managers had received too little training, with 12 per cent having none at all.[2] Tiratsoo has argued that during the 'Winter of Discontent' of 1978–9, the employers and managers were more culpable than the unions. Their aloof attitude had not been conducive to harmonious relations with the shopfloor, and many managers believed that there were only two options in industrial relations: to be a 'bastard' or a 'hard bastard'.[3]

Football, of all British sports since the war, had been characterized by a shift away from amateur values and controls to a far more commercialized structure. But within the game there had been much resistance and a reluctance to change. Although the FA finally abolished the amateur–professional distinction in 1974, the governing bodies were still dominated by men steeped in the traditions of voluntarism. In 1970, the FA's chairman was Dr Andrew Stephen, a retired 64-year-old Scottish GP. He had originally been Sheffield Wednesday's club doctor before becoming a director and later its chairmen. Stephen also served on the Football League Management Committee. He was succeeded as FA chairman in 1976 by an Oxford academic, Professor Sir Harold Thompson, who had founded the famous amateur club, Pegasus. The Football League was run by men like Len Shipman and Bob Lord who strongly believed in the sanctity of their organization. Both were self-made businessmen who regarded football as a hobby, and both played important roles on FA committees. Lord, chairman of Burnley, ran a butchery and advocated that visiting clubs should receive more than 20 per cent of the gate in order to equalize the competition. He said that, 'In my butcher's business I don't want competitors: in football you can't do without them.'[4]

The image of the game itself during this period was of a sport in decline. 'A slum sport, played in slum stadiums and watched by slum people', was one observation. It reached its nadir in 1985 when in the space of a few weeks fifty people were killed in a fire at Bradford's ground, and thirty-nine spectators died at the European Cup final between Liverpool and Juventus in the Heysel stadium in Brussels.[5] Hooliganism, or perhaps more accurately the perception and threat of it, had been highly damaging to football and its economy since the early 1970s. Between 1968 and 1985 Football League attendances fell from 30 million to 16.5 million with the greatest fall occurring in the lower divisions.[6] In the mid-1980s three relatively big clubs, Middlesbrough, Wolverhampton Wanderers and Bristol City, were all forced into liquidation due to crippling debts before subsequently reforming. Later, Aldershot and Maidstone would go out of business and the League altogether. Other clubs also suffered, although mismanagement was as much to blame as the economic recession.

Football, however, was not unique among leisure industries in experiencing a decline in public interest. The leisure market generally continued to grow and diversify due to increases in disposable incomes, leisure time and personal mobility. As a result, there was an increase in spending on, and the use of, in-home entertainment like the video cassette recorder. There was also a growth in active sports participation, compared to a relative decline in spectator sports generally. Yet, whereas other industries experienced corporate growth and mergers, and a high degree of concentration, the Football League retained almost the same number of clubs throughout the entire period.[7] Having been built on the notion of mutuality, however, the League now became subject to market forces. In 1972, Chelsea had pointed to a more commercially driven future, revealing plans to turn Stamford Bridge into a modern 60,000 all-seater stadium, designed to cater for the corporate sector.[8] The scheme would not be realized but other people in football were thinking on similar lines. Big clubs increasingly sought ways to extricate themselves from what they perceived as restrictions on making money, widening the gap between the rich clubs and their poor relations. The host of cross-subsidizing mechanisms that had been in place to maintain a semblance of equality, in terms of both playing talent and finance, had mostly disappeared by the early 1980s. The principle of sharing gate receipts, for example, was abolished in 1983 and meant that clubs kept all their gate takings. As a result, Manchester United saw its revenue increase from just over £500,000 to £11.5 million between 1970 and 1990. The revenue of West Ham, a club that was mainly a first division club during this period, went up from £400,000 in 1974 to £6.6 million by 1991. Over the same period, Wrexham, a typical lower division club, saw its revenue rise from £155,000 to only £734,000.

Another key event was when professional footballers were finally awarded freedom of contract in 1978. Whereas the outcome of the Eastham Case had modified the retain and transfer system, players were now free to move at the end of their contract, with a transfer fee set by an independent tribunal. It marked another shift in power away from the clubs to the players. They could demand higher wages and, inevitably, there was a greater concentration of the best talent within the bigger clubs. In 1985, the League's ten most powerful clubs had threatened to break away to form a 'Super League'. This was only averted when the 'rebels' were placated by substantial changes in who controlled Football League policy and its income-sharing arrangements. Bigger clubs gained more voting rights and a larger share of television and sponsorship incomes, further undermining the League's fraternity.[9]

All clubs, however, needed to find new forms of income to make up for the loss of revenue through the gate. The League Cup, inaugurated in 1960, was continually renamed after various sponsors from 1982. For the top clubs, playing in Europe was even more important. Clubs had also begun to seek sponsors as a new form of income, many associated with the drinks trade. By the early 1980s, virtually all clubs had signed deals that allowed companies to emblazon their name on the club's shirts. In the lower divisions many individual supporters sponsored a single player's kit. Executive boxes also became a feature of a growing number of grounds as clubs embraced corporate hospitality.

Although television would eventually be the most lucrative form of income, football was initially ambivalent towards the potential of this relationship. It would not be until the mid-1980s that its importance would be fully realized, deepening further the schism between the rich clubs and their poorer relations. Along with the 'soaps' and royal events, England World Cup games have dominated the listings for most watched television programmes, illustrating the potential for live football. Although commercial television had begun in 1955, successive governments had chosen not to open up sports broadcasting rights to the free market. Instead, in an attempt to preserve a national culture, a list was drawn up of ten sporting events, including the FA Cup final, that had to be shown by at least one of the channels. Initially, televised coverage of football had been restricted to the Cup final, a few internationals and the odd European game. Although live Football League games were not listed events, the arrival of commercial television did not initiate a bidding war for the simple reason that the League decided firmly against it, mainly because they feared a drop in crowds. In 1964, *Match of the Day* was launched on BBC 2, in black and white, as a compromise to the pressure to allow televised football and the need to protect live attendances. Its first showing attracted only 75,000 viewers but by the 1970s not only was coverage of the game increasing, but so were the viewing figures. *Match of the Day*, now in colour and with an eye-catching style of presentation developed by Jimmy Hill, was averaging audiences of 12 to 13 million, and ITV's *Big Match*, launched in 1965 and shown on Sunday afternoons, attracted 9 to 10 million. More people, therefore, experienced the game through television than through attending matches.

With hooliganism making an indent in the game's coffers as well as its image, the clubs were grateful for television's money. 'Live' football began tentatively in 1983–4 as clubs still had anxieties over the impact of television, particularly on attendances. In 1988, though, with the advent of satellite broadcasting and the stirrings of competition for sports broadcasting rights, football was becoming as important to the television companies as money from television was to the clubs. That year ITV won exclusive rights to Football League games in a £44 million four-year deal, a figure that the BBC could not match.[10] However, both broadcasters had effectively formed a cartel regarding the rights, up until 1992 when BSkyB broke it.

The potential of the relationship between sport and television had been realized earlier in other countries. In 1977, the Australian media baron, Kerry Packer, after failing to gain exclusive access to Australian test cricket, had set up his own cricket 'circus', World Series Cricket. Packer's Channel 9 eventually gained the rights to cover test matches in Australia as well as establishing a made-for-TV one-day series.[11] The relationship between US sports and television was even more intimate and lucrative. Live transmission of baseball and American football games had generated huge sums of money from television companies, and in 1964, CBS had actually bought an 80 per cent stake in the New York Yankees.[12]

By the early 1980s, due to changes in FA regulations and attitudes, directors, potentially at least, were able to make money out of football. Foremost amongst this new group emboldened by the prevailing neo-liberal philosophy was Irving Scholar, a 35-year-old multi-millionaire property developer. Partnered by Paul Bobroff, aged 31, they staged a takeover of Tottenham Hotspur in 1982, and the following year Spurs became the first football club to float on the Stock Exchange. Rule 34 of the FA's constitution had limited shareholder dividends to 7.5 per cent but Spurs simply by-passed this regulation, without any protest from the FA, by making the football club a subsidiary to a holding company, Tottenham Hotspur plc. Football was the 'core' business but it also diversified – for example, by setting up the leisurewear company, Hummel. On leaving the club in 1984, the outgoing manager, Keith Burkinshaw, made a thinly veiled attack on the club's new corporate direction, saying that 'There used to be a football club over there.'

In addition, Rule 34 had also forbidden club directors from drawing a salary but this was overturned in 1981.[13] It meant that managers were under greater pressure as this new breed of director now demanded better results in a shorter space of time. In 1982, Martin Edwards, the chairman of Manchester United, had been the first to award himself a salary. Initially it was £30,000; by 1989, it had increased to £80,000. In 1980, Edwards, aged 34, had succeeded his father, Louis, as club chairman. Two years earlier, the Edwards family had devised a shares scheme not only to increase their control over the club but also, it was planned, to make money out of it. At the time, though, there was no market for football shares and, instead of selling off their shares, the Edwards family became stuck with them. Later, in 1989, Edwards tried to sell his 50.2 per cent stake to Michael Knighton for £10 million but Knighton was unable to come up with the money.[14]

At Newcastle United, a boardroom power struggle in the late 1980s symbolized the shift in directors' motivations. John Hall, a former miner who had founded the Gateshead Metro Centre, then Europe's largest shopping centre, was one of Mrs Thatcher's favourite businessmen. His Magpie Group was trying to take over the club. By contrast, his opponent, club chairman Gordon McKeag, represented an earlier age. He was an alderman of the city and his father, William, had also been a chairman. Hall eventually won the battle and in 1991 he launched a share flotation scheme, although this flopped.[15]

Perhaps the clearest example of the impact of Thatcherism on football during the 1980s came not in England but in Scotland at Rangers. Previously, medium-rank businessmen, who identified with the Church of Scotland, the Orange Order, the Freemasons and the Tory Party, had run the club. But in 1986, the club recruited a new manager, Graeme Souness, someone who had distinct Thatcherite leanings. He broke the club's wage structure and reversed a long tradition of not buying English players. The chairman, John Lawrence, had intended to use the club as a flagship for his company, Lawrence Industries, and financial experts such as Freddie Fletcher were brought in to make Rangers more commercial by exploiting the club's brand. In 1988, Lawrence sold up to David Murray, a friend of Souness's, for £6 million. In 1997, the club was valued at £160 million.[16]

Football's *nouveau riche*, however, were an exception to the general rule. Most directors still did not receive any financial benefit from football. The majority were still part of the voluntary tradition, content with the 'warm feeling inside' and the publicity that they gained from being in charge of their local team. The distribution of shares within football clubs, however, meant that there was little chance of change in most boardrooms, and in 1976, more than half were in a position where it was unlikely that they would be out-voted. Because of the small size of football clubs, it was almost inevitable that directors would interfere, and some chairmen also considered the club as their own private fiefdom. On one occasion, Aston Villa chairman, Doug Ellis, demanded that Ron Atkinson put in his programme notes how helpful he had been in forming the manager's tactics and team selections.[17]

Football's commercialization and higher profile meant that chairmen and directors came under more pressure to take action when results were going badly. The number of managers who were sacked consequently escalated. Clubs frantically searched for fresh managerial talent and the number of new managers who entered football increased to an average of seventeen every year between 1971 and 1993, while average tenure per club fell from 2.5 to 1.5 years. One in three football managers, on average, lost their jobs every year. Some long-serving chairmen, like Ellis at Aston Villa and Peter Swales at Manchester City, gained notoriety not only for interference but also for sacking managers, especially after the board had earlier given them the dreaded 'vote of confidence'. In 1974, after publicly declaring him the best man for the job, Swales sacked Ron Saunders, subsequent to canvassing the opinions of players on his management methods.[18]

Unsurprisingly, directors continued to believe that practical experience was the best form of preparation for managers. In contrast, the Football Association placed a great emphasis on management training, probably more than most other industries. However, attempts during the 1970s and 1980s to implement a European-style licensing system faltered at the feet of club directors and were met with apathy amongst former players. The FA was acutely aware of how England lagged behind its European competitors in terms of its provision for managers and coaches. In West Germany, for example, candidates for the highest coaching diploma, without which it was not possible to gain employment with a first division club, had to undertake a six-month course at Cologne's Sports High School. This highlighted an overall lag in attitudes towards coaching, from senior to youth levels, compared to most of the continent. The FA's Annual Coaching Report for 1972 claimed that,

> Our coaching courses are not long enough or professional enough in content nor are they likely to be until football recognizes the need for highly professional training and gives evidence of this recognition in providing opportunities for employment in the game for those who have been prepared to study and to serve sensible apprenticeships at all levels.[19]

Nevertheless, in partnership with the Football League and with the co-operation of the PFA, the FA initiated the first ever course in professional club management, which took place at Loughborough University's College of Management Studies in 1969.[20] But in 1973, after only two intakes, the Football League withdrew its support for the programme.[21] Efforts, though, to implement a licensing system for managers continued. In 1977, the FA Instructional Committee agreed that 'advanced training for men who aspire to become professional football coaches or managers should have a high priority'. After much deliberation, an Advanced Coaching Diploma was scheduled to begin in May 1982, but by the end of the year it had to be discontinued due to lack of numbers. The attitude of club directors was again a major stumbling block because they did not want to be forced to choose managers from a list of qualified candidates.[22] They not only demanded the freedom to choose who they wanted but probably did not regard professional qualifications for management as necessary. It probably also conflicted with their ideas of a football manager's station since directors felt that a manager should be someone they could dominate. It would be nearly twenty years before the FA contemplated introducing another licensing scheme for managers.

The background of managers, therefore, because of the continued resistance to the professionalization of the job by directors, remained similar to that of their predecessors. There was no screening process and initial entry into football management was still based on the assumption that playing experience was the main qualification. Directors, however, were spreading their net wider and not just looking for former internationals, although this group continued to be a popular source of managers. Some managers, like Lawrie McMenemy and Dave Bassett, had just played non-league football, while others, such as Jim Smith and Graham Taylor, had not played at the highest level. In some ways it was a paradoxical situation. Directors sought the best available managerial talent but refused to endorse any official screening process, in terms of mandatory qualifications.

Most managers still came from working-class backgrounds and, unsurprisingly, this was reflected in their education, although, of course, this did not prevent some from becoming successful. Jack Charlton's background, for example, was typical. Both he and brother Bobby came from the mining village of Ashington in Northumberland. Whereas Bobby passed his 11 plus and attended Bedlington Grammar School, Jack failed and instead went to Hirst Park Secondary Modern. Other managers did pass the 11 plus, at least showing a degree of educational aptitude. Jim Smith, for example, went to Sheffield's Firth Park Grammar School in the early 1950s but left with only a history O level. Graham Taylor, whose father was a sports journalist for a Scunthorpe newspaper, also attended grammar school but left before finishing his A levels to take up a career as a professional footballer. Bobby Robson, whose father had been a miner, failed his 11 plus and went to a local County Durham secondary modern. Brian Clough had also attended a secondary modern school in Middlesbrough and left with no qualifications. His father was a sugar boiler at a local sweet factory before becoming one of its managers.[23]

Although their background was mainly in football, most managers had experience of working in industry, perhaps making them more rounded individuals. Bobby Robson, for example, had initially been unsure about a career in football and started an apprenticeship as an electrical engineer before deciding to make a go of it as a player.[24] On leaving school Brian Clough worked as a fitter and turner at ICI but failed his apprenticeship and later became a junior clerk. Jim Smith gained some management experience when he joined 'Tinsley Wire Industries' as a trainee manager. Smith later left to pursue his playing career when they insisted he worked on Saturdays. While playing part-time in non-league football, Dave Bassett worked for a large insurance company before becoming an independent broker. He later admitted that the administrative experience he had gained had been 'a big help' in his career as a football manager.[25] Ron Atkinson worked for five years as a sales representative for a construction firm. They offered him a position as sales manager but he turned it down to manage Kettering Town. Similar to Bassett, Atkinson believed that the 'experience in the building game had prepared me well to understand the business world and how to deal with people on various levels'.[26] Bertie Mee's preparation for management was more unusual than most and a total contrast to his predecessor, Billy Wright. A brief, injury-interrupted football career was followed by a stint in the Royal Army Medical Corps where he qualified as a physiotherapist. He joined Arsenal in this capacity in 1960 before being appointed manager six years later.[27] Despite the abolition of national service in 1962, there were still some managers born before 1940 who had been called up. Jack Charlton's playing days at Leeds, for example, were interrupted by two years of national service with the Royal Horse Guards, while Clough became a Leading Aircraftsman in the RAF.[28]

Scottish-born managers had similar backgrounds to their English counterparts. Alex Ferguson, for example, was brought up near the Govan shipyards where his father worked as a toolmaker. Ferguson does not seem to have excelled at school, Govan High, and served a five-year apprenticeship as a toolmaker with a local company. This included one day a week at technical college studying engineering. Yet while serving his time he was to show examples of leadership when he represented the other apprentices as their shop steward. He would later lead them out on strike in sympathy with the engineering apprentices in the local shipyards. Furthermore, he once ran his own pub, 'Fergies'.[29] Kenny Dalglish's family had been typically Scottish working-class. His father was a diesel engineer while his mother looked after the house. While on Celtic's books, he had been an apprentice joiner and would shovel shavings and run errands, which included requests for left-handed screwdrivers. He discontinued the job after signing full-time a year later.[30]

Despite the shortcomings of England's coaching culture, a growing number of managers did acquire coaching qualifications, and it did provide a means of preparation for management. A kind of informal technocracy slowly emerged where, if not the clubs, then prospective managers realized that their coaching badges held some worth. Jack Charlton, for example, believed that attending the FA's coaching course at Lilleshall opened him up to thinking about football in a completely different way.[31] He eventually gained his full badge and felt it made a vital difference when it came to management. He compared his attitude to that of his brother, Bobby, who briefly managed Preston North End. Bobby was not a coach. Instead, he shared Matt Busby's philosophy of playing the game the players wanted and ignored the Lilleshall way. Dave Bassett was another future manager who held a full FA coaching badge, although when first offered the position of Wimbledon manager he refused it on the grounds that he was completely unprepared.[32] Managers may have thought coaching was important but there was still much resistance within the professional game to the idea of qualified coaches from the amateur game. On attending a course in the early 1960s, Brian Clough made a point of trying to belittle his instructor, Charles Hughes, later the FA's Director of Coaching.[33]

Notwithstanding the increasing precariousness of their job, this was the heyday of the 'Boss Class'. Throughout the 1970s and 1980s, aided by television exposure, football managers enjoyed more autonomy than ever before or since. Since the war, and in light of the changes that promoted a more egalitarian society, managers had generally become less deferential towards directors. As their professional credentials increased so also did their desire for greater autonomy and their contempt for directors who they believed to be amateurs with no knowledge of football who should keep out of matters they knew nothing about.

'There are 92 club chairmen for a start', Brian Clough once replied when asked about the problem of football hooligans. This comment was only semi-ironic and epitomized his attitude towards directors. At his first club, Hartlepools United, the chairman had been Ernie Ord, a credit draper who had sold up his business and devoted himself to the club. Clough complained that he always interfered, and, as a result, personality clashes emerged. 'He would come in every day, demanding to know what I was up to and not happy at being told it was none of his business. I took exception to his interference in my job.' At Derby, Clough initially enjoyed a very close relationship with the chairman, Sam Longson, who regarded him as a 'surrogate son' and showered gifts on him. Clough, however, believed that Longson basked in the reflected glory that he was bringing to the club. He also thought Longson was weak, whereas Clough was brash and believed that he should run the club from top to bottom. Clough's success made him more autonomous and he signed players without gaining the chairman's assent. Longson lost patience, however, and called his manager's bluff. Clough tendered his resignation and to his surprise the other directors accepted it. His later success at Nottingham Forest, between 1975 and 1993, can partly be attributed to the independence he enjoyed there. Forest were unique, however. Whereas every other Football League club was a limited liability company, Forest was a members' club with comparatively much weaker financial powers. Clough's success and the money it brought in made the club more dependent on his management and this allowed him greater control. However, his then chairman, Maurice Roworth, once refused Clough permission to manage Wales on a part-time basis.[34]

Because football clubs were small, at the heart of the director–manager relationship remained its personal element. This, however, had become more potentially combustible due to managers being more prominent and less subservient. The nature of the relations Alex Ferguson enjoyed with the directors of his clubs in Scotland varied. In his first job at East Stirlingshire, he was continually in dispute with the individual directors despite being there for only three months. Later, at Aberdeen, he enjoyed a more cordial relationship with the chairman, Dick Donald.[35] However, in between these clubs he had been sacked by St Mirren in 1978. Ferguson took the club to an industrial tribunal but the case was dismissed. He had enjoyed footballing success, winning the first division in 1977, but the tribunal found that St Mirren were justified in sacking him for 'the arrogant and overbearing way he tried to run the club'. Ferguson had wanted to run the club from top to bottom and this included the boardroom. At one meeting, a director, John Corson, confessed that he knew nothing about football. Ferguson was quick to agree with him and suggested that as he knew nothing about football he should shut up.[36] The tribunal decision described Ferguson, at the time, 'as one possessing neither, by experience or talent, any managerial ability at all'. To a certain extent, his behaviour reflected the continuing assertiveness of managers in an increasingly professionalized society where, in doing a job, merit was becoming more important than one's social origins: football was their professional domain and not to be encroached upon by amateurs. Moreover, managers were charismatic and forceful people and, even if they did not always get it, they certainly wanted things done their own way. Many directors (reluctantly) agreed with this and were prepared to place greater trust in their manager's judgement.

This situation peaked, symbolically at least, in 1981 when directors were able to draw a salary for the first time. It not only meant that directors became more involved in the day-to-day running of football clubs but also that many were able to keep a closer eye on their investment which they increasingly wanted a return on – which differed from the aspirations of their predecessors. It was not an overnight transformation but rather a very gradual, piecemeal process, initially affecting only a few big clubs. It also marked the start of a more formal change in the manager's role as it gradually became more specialized. With less control over club finances, they became more concerned with the playing side. Yet each football club had a different approach. When Ron Atkinson, for example, became manager of Manchester United in 1981 he found that the chairman, Martin Edwards, in his role as chief executive, was at the ground on a daily basis. The club's activities had also been split into four separate departments – playing, administration, commercial and catering. The manager of each division was given his own budget and told to report directly to Edwards. Before, Atkinson had run all aspects of his other clubs, even first division West Bromwich Albion, but now it was Edwards who, significantly, dealt with players over their contracts.[37]

Following the departure of Bill Shankly, Liverpool had taken the opportunity of changing their management structure. Liverpool put the club's business such as players' contracts and shirt sponsorship in the hands of Peter Robinson, the club secretary, and later chief executive. Successive managers managed only the team. Robinson consulted the manager about transfer targets, and together they would draw up a wish list. Robinson and the chairman, John Smith, then signed the players. These methods established a managerial practice for Liverpool that lasted throughout the entire period.[38]

With the business of clubs growing, there was a corresponding rise in the work of the manager. But because of the lack of a job description for football managers, the nature of the work differed at each club. In general, most managers had responsibility for virtually all aspects of the club's business. As we have seen with Ron Atkinson, though, this was mainly dependent on the size of the club. At lowly Hartlepools, Brian Clough learned how to drive the club bus. When manager at St Mirren, Alex Ferguson not only managed the players but also the club's day-to-day administrative affairs.[39] Tony Waiters's remit at Plymouth Argyle was: 'the overall responsibility for team affairs including the preparation, selection and recruitment/termination of all staff'. He regarded, in order of importance, his three main duties as: preparation and selection of first team; recruitment and development of senior professional players; and, perhaps revealingly, press and TV relations. Other responsibilities included looking after the reserve and youth teams as well as the development of the club's youth structure. Yet he also had tedious administrative duties like travel arrangements and responsibility for the maintenance of the pitch and dressing rooms. Ron Tindall's job at Portsmouth in the early 1970s was very wide-ranging. Not only did he have responsibility for improving the first team but his job also entailed the development of Waterlooville as a nursery club and the improvement of Portsmouth's youth policy. Other duties included making Portsmouth a more integral part of the community and improving its financial position.[40]

The main facet of the job still remained team-building, and because of their greater freedom, some managers spent more heavily in the transfer market than ever. As they were now increasingly perceived as professionals who knew best, more managers were able to resort to 'cheque-book management' to try to 'buy success'. With competition more intense and players gaining freedom of contract, wage demands and transfer fees escalated. In 1979, there was a spate of million-pound transfers. Trevor Francis was the first, signed by Nottingham Forest. Manchester City was perhaps the most profligate club as Malcolm Allison invested huge sums in relatively ordinary players. During the 1980s, there were periodic 'booms' in the transfer market, although it was usually clubs like Manchester United and Liverpool who ignited it as they were rich enough to pay out record sums on players like Bryan Robson and Peter Beardsley respectively. Increasingly, clubs sought the best playing talent available, and in spite of racism on the terraces and in the boardroom, this included black players like Laurie Cunningham and Viv Anderson. In this sense, commercialization was breaking down barriers. Glasgow's sectarian divide was breached when Graeme Souness signed Maurice Johnston, Rangers' first Catholic player, in 1989. Despite Britain's growing multiculturalism, however, residual attitudes to race persisted in football. For example, when Newcastle manager, it was alleged that Gordon Lee refused to sign black players.[41] Furthermore, an England manager of this period claimed that when he was in charge, two senior FA officials had told him not to pick too many black players.[42]

As the business of a football club grew, more managers employed assistants to divide up some of their duties. Not only did they need someone to lean on but, like Liverpool's 'Boot Room', they used assistants to bounce ideas off. In some cases the management of clubs was undertaken, de facto, by a partnership. When Terry Neill was first appointed Arsenal's manager he dealt with all club matters. But in 1977, Don Howe was appointed chief coach. He concentrated on coaching while Neill was responsible for personal matters like contract negotiations.[43] The most notable partnership was that between Brian Clough and Peter Taylor. Clough was the manager but it was Taylor who scouted for players. He advised Clough on who to buy and Clough was then responsible for looking after them. The combination of their talents was highly successful. They had been players together at Middlesbrough, and when Clough became manager of Hartlepools in 1965 he asked Taylor to join him. Taylor, however, did not have a formal role. The chairman did not think he needed a partner so, instead, Clough made him trainer. Together they won the League with Derby and then Nottingham Forest plus two consecutive European Cups.

With many managers gaining coaching qualifications, it meant that they spent more time on the training ground, thus generating a greater affinity with their players. The term 'tracksuit manager' was commonly used to refer to practitioners of this type. At the 1973 FA Cup final, in order to symbolize his identity with the Sunderland players, Bob Stokoe wore a tracksuit rather than the traditional suit. This trend also complemented football management's traditional masculine qualities of toughness and hardness in the quest to maintain discipline. As Arsenal manager, George Graham preferred to be on the training ground coaching the players. Yet he also brought a 'new intensity' to the club. He issued rule-books, kept a distance between him and the players, and the dominant feeling around him was one of fear. He wanted the players to call him 'boss': behind his back, they nicknamed him 'Gadaffi'.[44] Some managers, like Jack Charlton and Alf Ramsey, encouraged their players to refer to them on a first-name basis. Before the start of a game, Charlton would even collect the players' tracksuits. Most players, though, still referred to the manager as either 'Boss' or 'Gaffer'. The word 'Gaffer' itself echoes traditional workplace relations as it refers to a foreman of a gang of workmen, and football remained one of the few industries where the term was used. At Hartlepools, Brian Clough insisted (very forcefully) that the players called him 'Boss' in order to reaffirm his and the players' status.[45] On becoming player-manager at Liverpool in 1985, Kenny Dalglish actually held a discussion with the players about what they should call him. Eventually they decided on 'Boss'. He was forced to discipline Phil Neal, however, when he continually referred to him as Kenny.[46]

Player–management relations had continued to change following the greater freedoms players gained during the 1960s. Players were the club's main assets, and after 1978, when players gained freedom of contract together with spiralling transfer fees, they became more expensive, and needed careful handling. Some, like Francis Lee and Trevor Brooking, had business careers outside the game and became financially independent. Importantly, with the increase in media attention, players, like Kevin Keegan, were becoming more high-profile and confident generally. One result of this was a rise in so-called 'player power'. Dutch players were particularly noted for challenging the manager's authority but it was not absent in England. In 1977, for example, some Newcastle United players threatened to go on strike unless the club's coach, Richard Dinnis, succeeded Gordon Lee as manager. During the 1976–7 season, Alan Ball had openly challenged the authority of Terry Neill at Arsenal, leading to a situation where for half a season, half of the team supported Ball, the other half Neill. However, the overall relationship had not changed that much and, at the end of the season, Neill exercised his powers and transferred Ball to Southampton. George Graham was more pragmatic. While he disciplined younger players on the spot, he gave preferential treatment to his regular first team players, occasionally turning a blind eye to their antics. Graham realized that not only did they play for him on a Saturday but their success ultimately kept him in a job.

As with most things, some managers were better at man-management and motivating players than others. At West Ham, for example, Trevor Brooking felt that Ron Greenwood had a weakness in handling star players like Bobby Moore.[48] At Middlesbrough, Jack Charlton's initial strategy was to identify, then get rid of, the 'barrack room lawyers'. On the advice of Jock Stein, he also believed that 'you've got to shout at your players now and again, just to stir them up a bit and make them take notice'.[49] Some players expected nothing less. After a poor performance, Liam Brady reckoned that players knew when they deserved a 'telling-off', and that leadership and honesty were the two qualities that players rated in a manager higher than any other. Managers, however, did not set out to terrorize players for the sake of it: their aim was to get the best out of them.

Perhaps the best motivator of players during this period was Brian Clough, although he admitted that he was not sure about the secret of his success. He became a manager at a young age after an injury forced him to quit playing, thus bridging any generation gap. He was only 32 when he became Derby manager, and some players, like Dave Mackay, were older than him. He was an autocrat who demanded discipline from his players and almost made it his mission to convert players with troublesome reputations, like Larry Lloyd and Kenny Burns, to his way of thinking. He had no time for star players with egos, and thought that everyone should be treated equally. After signing Trevor Francis, Britain's first one-million-pound footballer, Clough gave him a debut in the third team, and for games that Francis was ineligible he had to make the tea.[50]

Such was the bond that Clough established with his players at Derby that when he resigned the players seriously contemplated the idea of going on strike. It illustrated – albeit an extreme example – a shift in the manager's sympathies away from the directors to the players. Perhaps their reaction was not so surprising as he had built up the side himself. He had improved them and this gave the players a belief in his ability. It was something he replicated at Forest. When he briefly managed Leeds, however, he generated the opposite reaction, highlighting the importance of gaining the co-operation of players who were becoming increasingly powerful and independent themselves. The Leeds players were a mature group who had grown up together under Don Revie and would have been suspicious of any new manager. Yet on a number of previous occasions Clough had criticized their 'professionalism': he called it cheating. He did so again at his first meeting with the players and inevitably there was friction between the two parties: Clough was sacked after forty-four days.[51]

One of the attributes of Clough's management was that he realized that the best way to get the maximum from the players was to keep them in a relaxed frame of mind so that they did not use up too much nervous energy. On the night before the 1979 League Cup final, for example, he made the players drink ten bottles of champagne before they went to bed.[52] Using alcohol as a way of relaxing players was seen as a way of relating to players as young working-class men, as this was one of their few outlets. Some felt that it built up team spirit. During this period, Liverpool adopted the motto: 'the team that drinks together, sticks together'. Manchester United manager, Ron Atkinson, seemed to indulge his players regarding their drinking habits but he argued that it was part of British culture and it would have a retrograde effect on team morale if all players were forced to abstain.[53] Other managers felt differently. When he succeeded Atkinson at Old Trafford, Alex Ferguson had been alarmed by stories of excessive drinking amongst the players, and even more so by a ban on drinking less than two days before a game. Ferguson immediately replaced this with a ban on drinking during training.

Following on from the advances made during the early post-war period, the development of tactical thinking and strategies continued during the 1970s and 1980s. With greater pressure to win, it became even more incumbent on managers to develop strategies of their own. It not only highlighted their greater tactical responsibilities but, with many having acquired coaching qualifications, managers now felt that this was an important, if not the most important, part of their job. Directors began to realize this only slowly and despite the increase in their workload managers were expected, but were not unhappy, to juggle their coaching duties with administrative duties.

European coaches had been exploring various avenues in order to improve performance during this period. In the mid-1980s, for example, Dynamo Kiev's tactics, under Valeri Lobanovsky, had been based on a computer programme that dictated particular positions for their players when they were in possession in certain areas of the field.[54] Perhaps the most famous innovation of the period was 'total football'. It was pioneered by Ajax and the Dutch national teams of the early 1970s where both forwards and defenders inter-changed positions frequently, placing an emphasis on speed and the exploitation of space. Both teams were managed by Rinus Michels but essentially built around the talents of Johan Cruyff as well as a strong defence. Ajax won three consecutive European Cups between 1971 and 1973, the second against an ultra-defensive Inter Milan, the third against Juventus.

It emphasized a power shift in Europe's football landscape. Following the domination of Spanish, Italian and Portuguese clubs, it was now the turn of northern Europe. It had begun in 1967 with Celtic's symbolic victory over Inter Milan where it was shown that attacking flair could overcome the negativity of 'catenaccio'. After Ajax, Bayern Munich won three consecutive titles and this was followed by English clubs winning seven out of the next eight finals. In football generally, there was an increasing emphasis on pace and fitness, which probably favoured the northern Europeans. A 'pressing' game emerged which entailed the harassing of opponents with the ball and squeezing the 'space' by defenders pushing up to the halfway line. AC Milan's domination in the early 1990s was based on a similar strategy as well as on the talents of three Dutchmen, Van Basten, Gullit and Rijkaard.

People in Britain also began to think about football in more theoretical terms. Yet what emerged was 'direct play', more popularly known as 'the long ball', harnessing traditional British values of speed, strength and power. Where did this style emerge from? We have seen earlier how Stan Cullis at Wolverhampton Wanderers was supported by the statistical analyses of Charles Reep. Building on Reep's work, Charles Hughes, in his capacity as FA Director of Coaching (1982–97), promoted the benefits of direct play to a whole generation of coaches. In 1990 his book, *The Winning Formula*, was, like Reep's work, based on performance analysis. And like Reep, Hughes, and another football analyst, Neil Lanham, came to the same conclusions. First, as most goals originated in the final third of the pitch as a result of either defensive mistakes or attacking movements, teams should get the ball forward into that area as quickly and as much as possible. It could be exciting, and tended to create much goal-mouth action, but at its worst it dehumanized football, making it devoid of creativity. It was a percentages game, reflecting the growing fear of losing that was prevalent within the game.

Yet this development showed how managers and coaches were bringing a more methodical outlook to football. Direct play itself required coaching as teams had to be told what to do and players were only allowed to express themselves in certain areas of the field. One of its earliest exponents was Jack Charlton at Middlesbrough in the 1970s. He claimed that it was a response to the offside trap defenders were then employing. Charlton's plan was to by-pass the congested midfield area by delivering the ball from further out and to employ a fast midfield runner, in Middlesbrough's case Alan Foggon, to get behind the defence into the space it was leaving as it pushed up to play offside. It was derided as old-fashioned kick and rush but Charlton claimed it required great skill to match the pass to the midfielder's run.[55] He later enjoyed success with a similar pattern of play as manager of the Republic of Ireland.

By the 1980s a growing number of managers had adopted the long ball game. One of the most successful was Graham Taylor, first at Lincoln City, then Watford and Aston Villa. His teams also placed an accent on strong running as the game was played at a high tempo to keep the opposition under pressure. As a result, fitness levels in players improved, along with the pace in the game generally. Other managers who gained a reputation for these tactics included Howard Wilkinson, John Beck at Cambridge and Dave Bassett at Wimbledon. Much of their thinking was dictated by a pragmatism born out of the increasing gap between the rich and poor clubs, and consequently the gap in the ability of players available to these clubs. Wimbledon constantly defied the odds by retaining their position in the top flight. Dave Bassett argued that 'limited talent means limited skills and I have to plan the strategy accordingly'. Similarly, Steve Coppell believed that this particular tactic could bridge the gap.

I wanted to win football matches and I felt given the kind of players I had and the financial resources I had available, the style of play that I was adopting was the best way for me . . . I felt that, looking at my problems, the solution, being pragmatic, was to adopt a more direct style and please my chairman who was employing me to win games.[56]

Despite the spread of the long ball game and the way in which it incorporated the virtues of pace, power and perseverance, it was not employed across the board. Because of the increased contact with European football, some teams adopted a more continental style, in particular Liverpool, who won four European Cups between 1977 and 1984. Yet, it was only following a defeat by Red Star Belgrade in 1973 that they realized they needed to change their style if they were to win the competition. The following year Bob Paisley, a more astute tactician than Shankly, became manager. Liverpool then began to combine the best of the English game with that of the continentals: while opponents were still constantly pressurized, Liverpool's players were able to control and pass the ball as well as European teams. Nottingham Forest, adopting similar tactics based on retaining possession, won the European Cup in 1979 and 1980. The success of the clubs, however, was not matched by the performance of the English national team which had declined from the heights of 1966. This was put into perspective when Holland defeated England 2–0 at Wembley in 1977, a result so comprehensive that Kevin Keegan claimed it was the equivalent of the Hungary defeat in 1953. Overall, English players continued to be deficient in the skills of ball control and passing while the national style continued to be based around notions of masculinity.

The image of the manager as the 'Boss' who devised tactics, spent big in the transfer market, and dominated players and directors alike was cultivated further by his relationship with the media. With the arrival of television, managers became more visible and as a result more of a focal point for the clubs that they managed. Throughout the 1980s especially, managers were becoming more central to the coverage of football, and this furthered their professional identity as the person in charge. It was they who the cameras would increasingly focus on before and after games for interviews, and during the match itself as the camera tried to catch their reactions to on-field incidents. Football managers not only developed their own media personas but were becoming part of an emerging celebrity culture.

The growing attention that they were attracting, however, needs to be seen in the light of developments within the media industry and how football itself was being presented. This can be partly traced back to Rupert Murdoch's takeover of the *Sun* in 1969 and the introduction of a racier tabloid style of presentation. Other tabloids followed and a circulation war developed between the 'red tops' as the press sought ever more salacious stories and controversial articles. Managers were a major source regarding football. The BBC and ITV were also involved in a competition for ratings and aimed to attract a mass football audience. In 1966, the BBC had inaugurated a World Cup panel of 'experts' including Johnny Haynes, Billy Wright and Walter Winterbottom. For the next World Cup in Mexico, ITV followed, but with experts like Malcolm Allison and Derek Dougan who were prepared to be more outspoken and, with the added attraction of colour television, more 'colourful' and entertaining. Panels helped to legitimize managers not only as experts, reaffirming their professional identity, but also turning them into TV personalities. On Saturday lunchtimes both channels also screened football magazine shows that featured interviews with managers. While the BBC showed *Football Focus*, ITV had *On The Ball* and later *Saint and Greavsie* which made much of the presenters' on-screen banter: a sop to football's mainly tabloid-reading audience.

A manager's relationship with the media came to be seen as an important part of his job. Some even used it as a forum to manage their players by either praising or criticizing them in public. Directors increasingly felt that, in a more media-friendly society, managers should be able to transmit a certain image of the club, and by keeping it in the news, through generating publicity, managers were now 'selling' football clubs. In 1981, Manchester United replaced Dave Sexton, a highly skilled coach, with Ron Atkinson, a more flamboyant character who made good 'copy' and came across better on television. The change in manager was partly induced by the employment of publicity-conscious managers, like Malcolm Allison and John Bond, at rivals City. Sexton, on the other hand, had been referred to by one of his former players as 'Whispering Dave'.[57]

The boundaries between sport and entertainment were becoming increasingly blurred and, with the rise in their profile, managers were not only perceived as important football figures but some were becoming media personalities in their own right. Mike Yarwood would regularly impersonate Brian Clough, for example, while Jack Charlton had his own programme on field sports. Such was his celebrity status that Clough's views – he publicly supported the Labour Party – were sought on non-football matters. On one occasion in 1980, he appeared on a Friday night chat show and became engaged in a discussion with a Soviet diplomat about the USA's abortive attempt to free hostages from its Tehran embassy that day. Clough, typically wagging his finger at the official, opined that if the hostages had been from the USSR, the Red Army would have invaded Iran to liberate them.

With British society becoming more meritocratic, the rewards for football managers matched their increasing profile and importance, something which had a commensurate impact on their lifestyle. During the 1980s especially, their salaries reflected the fact that, due to football's commercialization, more importance was being attached to management. As a consequence, from being former players who became managers because they knew little else, by the early 1990s, some were paid executive-level salaries, making them financially independent. In 1976, it was estimated that their salaries ranged from £5,000 to over £15,000, dependent on the status of the club and the reputation of the manager, and that the average was £6,500.[58] With freedom of contract in 1978, the wages of star players also rose steeply. By 1986, for example, Manchester United's Bryan Robson was earning £98,000 a year.[59] This salary, along with those of other players, as well as the £80,000 Martin Edwards awarded himself every year, was considerably more than that of the manager, Alex Ferguson. When he took the job in 1986, Ferguson actually took a pay cut from the £60,000 salary he earned at Aberdeen. But he had started at the bottom and worked his way up in a meritocratic fashion. In 1974, he had earned £40 per week working as East Stirlingshire's part-time boss.[60]

Managers were now more inclined to go to another club if they were offered more money. In 1977, for example, Gordon Lee joined Everton from Newcastle, in the process doubling his salary to £24,000. One of the better paid managers was, inevitably perhaps, Brian Clough. At Derby, in addition to his £20,000 salary, he earned money from his TV work. Later, at Leeds, his salary was £25,000 and when they sacked him he was given £98,000 in compensation. This gave him financial independence, enabling him to pay off his existing mortgage and to purchase a big new house. Rising salaries had important consequences for some managers. With their future secure, managers could look at a job differently and not feel obliged to accept it unless the conditions suited them. Clough was wealthy enough to sign a cheque for the Inland Revenue for £35,000 that enabled Forest to keep operating. He later claimed he lent his chairman, Maurice Roworth, £108,000, but did not get his money back.[61]

More and more, managers moved away from their working-class roots – not only because of their salaries but also because of their upwardly mobile aspirations. Some, like Bill Nicholson and George Graham, put their children through university (although Nicholson insisted his children went to state secondary schools). Graham's affluence enabled him to live in an apartment in fashionable and expensive Hampstead.[62] Others, emboldened by their new wealth and status, tried to extend their influence into the boardroom. Terry Venables, for example, attempted to take over QPR in the early 1980s. This failed, but in 1991, with computer tycoon Alan Sugar as chairman, Venables moved from manager to chief executive at Spurs. In Scotland, Graeme Souness became a club director of Rangers after buying a stake in the club worth £600,000, while during the 1980s, both Jim McLean and Walter Smith served on the board of Dundee United. During his five years at Rangers, Souness earned nearly £1.5 million, some of which he invested in homes for the elderly, and later made a £1.5 million profit on the venture.[63]

Any monetary rewards were offset, however, by the demands of the job. To a large extent, it was something that managers had brought upon themselves. They had sought greater control and responsibilities as well as exposure, and this meant longer hours, little social life and a detrimental effect on their families. Tony Waddington, for example, resigned as Stoke manager in 1977 because of the pressures the job was putting not only on him but also on his family.[64] There is a perception that football managers have a high divorce rate because of the time-consuming nature of the job. George Graham's first wife left him because he was hardly at home.[65] Graeme Souness's first wife made him choose between his job at Rangers and his family. After they split, Souness travelled to England straight after weekend games in order to see his children. And when they were at home football managers could be bad company. Kenny Dalglish, due to the pressures of the job, shouted at his children and needed a drink to relax him. Of course, not only did the job affect a manager's family. With the game coming under ever more scrutiny from television and the greater stress he was under to get results, it could also have a deleterious impact on the manager's health. At the relatively young age of 39 Graeme Souness underwent a triple heart by-pass operation in 1992, caused partly by his hereditary factors but also by his job.[66] Most famously, Jock Stein suffered a heart attack and died after a vital Wales versus Scotland World Cup game in 1985. Kenny Dalglish came under enormous strain following the Hillsborough disaster in 1989. As manager, he was the club's figurehead, the public face who had to communicate with the media. In this role he also attended the funerals of many of the fans who had died and performed other duties not usually within his remit as manager. On top of this, his main job was still to win football matches. Unsurprisingly, perhaps, the mounting pressure on top of the responsibilities he carried made him resign in February 1991. Before then the stress had caused blotches to break out all over his body.[67]

Following his heart operation Souness sold an exclusive story about it to the *Sun*. His actions were condemned as insensitive yet they were also indicative of how the manager's job had developed by the end of this period. First, managers were becoming celebrities and their actions and lives off the pitch were just as newsworthy as events on it. Second, it perhaps demonstrated how football in general and managers in particular had moved away from and lost touch with their working-class roots. In the week following Hillsborough, the *Sun* had published a story about the alleged behaviour of Liverpool fans headlined 'The Truth'. Many Liverpool fans were (and continue to be) outraged by the story and therefore felt insulted that *their* manager should show such a lack of awareness of their anger towards the newspaper. The new identity managers formed as professionals gradually began to replace a manager's association with his roots. Not that football managers were actually part of a true profession. Many clubs still chose managers on their playing record. Others, however, believed that, in the media age, someone who kept their club in the headlines was important.

Chapter 7

The 'postmodern' football manager?

After its slump in the 1980s, professional football had undergone a renaissance by the new millennium. Following the Hillsborough disaster in 1989, the Taylor Report became the catalyst for football to appeal to a more affluent and middle-class audience with some clubs moving to new stadiums as seats replaced terraced standing areas. England's performance in the 1990 World Cup also sparked a cultural transformation: of the 30 million viewers who watched the semi-final against West Germany half were female. Inspired by Nick Hornby's *Fever Pitch*, a 'soccer literati' emerged and helped to spawn a new type of fan. A relatively successful Euro 96 saw the appeal of the English game cross most social divisions as footballers became part of the growing cult of celebrity. This all took place amidst the most profound changes in the game's history in the twentieth century. Foremost among these was the formation of the Premier League in 1992, which saw the first division of the Football League break away from the rest. In the previous year, in its *Blueprint for the Future of Football*, the FA had advocated a smaller first division of eighteen clubs which, it argued, would 'produce an improved product in commercial terms', as well as enhance the performance of the national team. Instead, a footballing version of Frankenstein's monster emerged as the big clubs began to control the FA. The Premier League was bankrolled by Rupert Murdoch's BSkyB, signalling a much closer relationship between football and the media. The structure of professional football in England was subsequently transformed as the gap, both in terms of wealth and ability, between an elite of twenty clubs and the other seventy-two, widened every season.

At the heart of the transformation of football's image was the manager. In 2000, David Lacey had argued, with only mild irony, that,

> It is becoming increasingly difficult to define precisely what a football manager is for, apart from slagging off referees and doing Marcel Marceau impressions in his little rectangle of rage by the touchline.[1]

Certainly, with the intense media spotlight that football now came under, managers became more visible. This was mirrored in their growing status within public life generally. Not only did Alex Ferguson receive a knighthood for Manchester United's 'treble' in 1999, but he also had close links with the New Labour administration. Sven Goran Eriksson, on the other hand, became the focus of lurid tabloid headlines concerning his private life. The extent of media intrusion turned football into a soap opera, in which managers played the central roles. Yet, this was also a paradox. Despite the perceived increase in a manager's importance, the influx of money into the game coincided with a decline in managers' overall powers and their role became more narrowly defined. At the top end of football, this saw English clubs move, if somewhat reluctantly and not without some cultural resistance, towards a more European style of management. It was something that Bobby Robson had noticed during his management career,

> At Ipswich [1969–82], I was the first person there in the morning and the last to leave. So it was a big shock to me when I first went abroad [1990] and found that my responsibilities only went as far as the first team. Now that's happening more and more in England, although only a few years ago, when I phoned managers in England and told them I was finished for the day at 1 pm, they could not believe it. While I was off to the beach, they were just starting paperwork, contract talks, the whole caboodle.[2]

Like football, Britain had also changed by 2000. After eighteen years of Conservative government, Tony Blair was elected Prime Minister in 1997 as Labour metamorphosed into New Labour. Through its obsession with presentation and media management, New Labour projected a more youthful and modern image as it moved away from its socialist and trade union roots. Blair even exploited football's new popularity by incorporating lyrics from 'Three Lions' into one of his speeches after the success of the song during Euro 96. British society generally became more technocratic and professionalized as the number of people entering university rose dramatically. However, the legacy of Thatcherism still loomed large. Manufacturing industry and union membership continued to decline, reflecting a fragmentation of working-class culture. The government was also reluctant to raise direct taxation to improve social institutions and services for fear of not being re-elected. Instead, the values of consumerism infected much of society. People wanted to choose where to send their children to school as well as which supermarket to shop at. Yet not all sections of society benefited as a disaffected and growing 'underclass' became cut off from the rest.

For the majority, however, the 1990s was a period of long-term economic growth in which standards of living increased while unemployment levels fell and stabilized. One of the decade's buzzwords was 'globalization'. In economic terms, the power of multinational corporations expanded through an intensification of the 'branding' (another buzzword) of their products. Advances in media technology like the internet and satellite television, which made the world seem a smaller place, also accelerated this process. And to give an idea of football's popularity, to the list of global brand names like Coca-Cola, Nike, Pepsi and Shell, Manchester United was added. Nevertheless, globalization was as much about cultural resistance and the reaffirmation of traditions within a changing world as it was about inclusiveness. In adapting to this new world, football branded itself by exploiting the game's cultural cachet, and through the use of modern marketing techniques it embraced commercialism more fully than ever before.

Television underpinned the game's new confidence and wealth. In 1992, BSkyB and the BBC signed a landmark deal with the Premier League worth £304 million over five years. For the next contract Murdoch's company agreed to pay £670 million. Murdoch used the acquisition of television sports rights as a 'battering ram' in his quest to monopolize the satellite broadcasting market. In addition to its vast coverage of football, BSkyB bought up a host of sporting events like the Ryder Cup, England's overseas cricket tests and rugby internationals. The peak of football's relationship with television was reached in 2000 when a new contract worth £1.1 billion was signed between BSkyB and the Premier League.

By the late 1990s, it had become a cliché to say that football had become a business, but it was true nonetheless. With little regulation, the game was almost an exemplary model of capitalism, and at the top of football's pyramid, a 'consolidation' process emerged with a small number of clubs dominating the market. The Premier League became the richest league in Europe: its growing economic power was underlined by the world record transfer fee for Alan Shearer who moved from Blackburn to Newcastle in 1996 for £15 million. In addition, Manchester United regularly topped the list of football's wealthiest clubs. With the rise in football's popularity, major corporations like Nike and Vodafone increasingly coveted association with the game. The bigger clubs also had the opportunity to increase their funds through the lucrative Champions' League. As a direct result of English football's new-found riches, the gap between the Premiership and the Football League widened exponentially. By 2002, the average turnover of a Premier League club was estimated at £75 million while the average for a Football League club was £7.2 million.[3]

Football's boom and wider cultural appeal was reflected in an increase in attendances. Partly due to the building of new stadiums and the modernization of old ones, gates rose virtually every year after 1985. By 2002–3, Premiership attendances totalled 13.5 million, an average of 35,000 per game: the best figures since 1976–7. Moreover, despite the growing financial gap between the rest of the Football League and the Premiership, crowds for three lower divisions also rose: nearly 15 million in 2002–3 (an average of nearly 9,000), the highest since 1964–5. The combined total of over 28 million was the best since 1972. Conference clubs also prospered, several turning professional on a full-time basis. By exploiting its brand and new popularity, football attracted a new, affluent 'consumer' from a wider cross-section of society (although not from the ethnic minorities). In 2001, 14 per cent of Premiership season ticket holders were women, who also made up the largest number of new fans, while 11 per cent of fans earned over £50,000 per year.[4] Supporters from lower income groups, however, were progressively priced out of the new craze.

The increased wealth of the Premier League was matched by a steep rise in expenditure, most of it going on players' wages and ever escalating transfer fees. In 1999–2000, although the total revenue of all professional clubs rose by 13 per cent to £1.1 billion, from the previous season, expenditure increased by 21 per cent with salaries accounting for 68 per cent (£747 million) of all spending.[5] While a smaller group aimed for the Champions' League, most Premiership clubs more than ever were gambling on buying the best talent available in order to retain their place in the League. Unsurprisingly, football was unable to sustain this growth. The collapse of ITV Digital's deal with the Football League in 2001 showed that the football market was saturated. Several League clubs later went into administration while others came close. Relegation from the Premier League also had serious consequences. Despite 'parachute payments' to soften their fall, the incomes of relegated clubs dropped dramatically although they were still paying Premiership wages. Sheffield Wednesday, Bradford, Barnsley and Queen's Park Rangers all dropped into the second division during this period as a result of the economic fallout and instability that followed their demotion from the top division. After ITV Digital's collapse even the Premier League had to face up to a new realism. Its next contract was still worth over £1 billion but the number of games to be televised was doubled thus halving the value of its product. However, predictions of a meltdown with up to thirty clubs going out of business did not materialize.

But there have been spectacular declines. In 2004, Leeds United were relegated to the Football League, three years after appearing in the semi-final of the European Cup. Leeds, in its quest, as former chairman Peter Ridsdale said, to 'live the dream', exemplified the new financial risks. By 2004 the club was over £130 million in debt. Financed through complex loan agreements, Leeds had spent heavily on new players and wages. But because of their failure to qualify for the Champions' League in 2002, the club's debts began to mount. To relieve them, players were sold and, inevitably perhaps, relegation followed.[6] Ridsdale, a former retail executive at Top Man, was in many ways typical of the new breed of football director that emerged during the 1990s. Instead of local businessmen, directors and chairmen were increasingly successful executives in multinational companies. Many entered the game smugly thinking that they knew how to run the football business because they had been successful as businessmen in industry and business was, well, business. One director at Manchester United, epitomizing the priorities of this new type of football executive, apparently said of Alex Ferguson that he may be a good manager but he didn't sell many shirts.[7]

In addition to the new celebrity status that owning a club brought with it, many football directors now wanted to make a profit. During the previous decade, a few clubs had demonstrated entrepreneurial tendencies, but it was not until the 1990s that more clubs fully embraced the market. Spurs had been the first in 1983 and, by 1997, twenty clubs were listed either on the Stock Exchange or the Alternative Investment Market.[8] Some directors made vast personal fortunes from their clubs. When BSkyB launched its (abortive) takeover of Manchester United in 1998, the club was valued at £623 million. Martin Edwards held a 14 per cent stake then worth £88 million.[9] In 1997, Newcastle United was worth about £200 million, with John Hall and his family holding a 57 per cent stake.[10] Ken Bates bought Chelsea in 1982 for £1 (he also took on the club's debts). In 2003, he sold his share for £17.5 million to Russian oil billionaire, Roman Abramovich. The total cost of the purchase was £140 million. (It remains to be seen what Abramovich's overall intentions are.) A number of directors at smaller clubs, like Brighton, also tried to profit from selling a club's ground as real estate. In 2001, at lowly Carlisle United, its then chairman and chief executive, Michael Knighton, collected a salary of £120,000.[11]

The commercial imperative inevitably brought with it greater pressures for football managers, and not just on the field. Newcastle United's planned flotation, for example, caused the resignation of Kevin Keegan in 1997. To satisfy City rules, the club had to publish a prospectus for stock market flotation, and to expedite the venture Mark Corbridge had been recruited from the City as chief executive. He put pressure on Keegan to sign a new contract so that the certainty of his position could be included in the prospectus, as the football manager was deemed an important part of the company's management team. Keegan, however, who was unsure of his future, refused to sign a new two-year deal and resigned.[12]

Despite the emergence of these new directors, the motivations of most have remained complex, and for many, their reasons for getting involved in football have changed little since the 1880s. During the 2002–3 season, for example, Rob Bradley, the chairman of third division Lincoln City, took out a £50,000 mortgage on his home to help save the club.[13] A number of chairmen, including the late Jack Walker at Blackburn Rovers, Jack Hayward at Wolverhampton Wanderers and Middlesbrough's Steve Gibson, have claimed lifelong support for their clubs and spent a lot of money in pursuing these allegiances.

Because there were greater risks, unsurprisingly perhaps, football's new commercialization went hand-in-hand with a rise in managerial turnover. Between 1981 and 1985, there had been an average of thirty-eight managerial changes every year.[14] From 1996 to 2001, over 230 managers were either dismissed or left their clubs, an average of forty-six every year, while only twenty-eight from 1996 were still in a job by 2001.[15] This trend continued. Between May 2001 and May 2002 alone, seventy managers from the ninety-two league clubs had lost or left their jobs. Managerial change was not confined to the big clubs and turnover was actually higher in the lower divisions. Out of the seventy-two Football League clubs, forty parted company with their manager in the 2000–1 season. Moreover, managers who lost their jobs had little chance of being reappointed elsewhere. By the start of the 2002–3 season only eleven managers had been in charge of their clubs for five years or more.[16]

Clubs also began to spread their net wider in their search for managers, mirroring changes in the wider world during the 1990s. Through the Maastricht Treaty and Single European Act, Britain's links with Europe became closer and there was greater movement not only in trade but also among workers. European football's pivotal moment was the Bosman ruling in 1995. It enabled footballers to leave a club at the end of their contract without being subject to a transfer fee, and, as a result, the cost of the transfer was passed on to the player in terms of higher wages. In addition, footballers who were citizens of a European Union nation could ply their trade in any country of the EU, causing a rapid increase in the number of non-nationals in English football. In 1992–3, there had been eleven overseas players employed in the Premiership; by 1998–9, this figure had increased to 166.[17]

'Bosman' also hastened the quest for better managerial talent. The appointment of a foreign manager made sense not only because they had experience of managing foreign players but also because, as the pool of potential players expanded, they usually had better contacts for signing foreign footballers than British managers. It could be argued that it was just a trend, yet in the new commercial climate, some football clubs probably felt that European managers were just better at the job than their British counterparts. An early pioneer had been Josef Venglos, a doctor of physical education and the former manager of the Czech national team, whom Aston Villa appointed manager in 1990. He left a year later, however, as it was thought his educated approach clashed with the attitudes of the mainly British squad. Initially, foreign managers remained exotic, partly due to cultural differences such as language but also due to a deep-rooted British distrust of anything foreign. When, in 1996, Arsenal appointed the Frenchman Arsene Wenger as its new manager, the football world was taken by surprise. An economics graduate, he had enjoyed success with Monaco and Grampus Eight in Japan. Yet, because he did not have much of a playing pedigree, his appointment was greeted with scepticism, partly based on ignorance by sections of the media. It is arguable that Wenger has since become the most influential manager in the English game since Herbert Chapman. Others soon followed him. Gerard Houllier, who had actually been a student teacher in the city, went to Liverpool, originally as joint manager with Roy Evans but later as the sole person in charge when Evans resigned in 1998–9. Houllier, a former manager of the French national team, had been responsible for the establishment of France's national scheme for developing young players.[18] Spurs tried (unsuccessfully) to emulate their north London rivals by recruiting the Swiss, Christian Gross, in 1997. The former French international and Monaco manager, Jean Tigana, managed Fulham from 2000 to 2003. In 1999, Chelsea fielded a team without an English-born player, and have only appointed foreign managers since 1996. During the close season of 2004, there was a flurry of foreigners appointed. The Spaniard, Rafael Benitez, succeeded Houllier at Liverpool, while the manager of the French national team, Jacques Santini, moved to Tottenham. A Dutchman, Martin Jol, succeeded him a few months later. Following months of speculation over who was to take over from Claudio Ranieri at Chelsea, Jose Mourinho, the head coach of Porto, the new European champions, was appointed.

Ruud Gullit at Chelsea and then Tigana at Fulham were the Premier League's first black managers. The number of British black managers, however, seems to have been disproportionately low compared to the number who have played professionally since the 1980s, and none have managed in the top flight. Ed Stein was the first black boss (he was also foreign, being born in Cape Town) when Barnet appointed him in 1993, but there has only been a sprinkling since. In 2003, there were three black managers, all managing lower league clubs: Leroy Rosenior at Torquay, Mansfield's Keith Curle, and Keith Alexander at Lincoln City.[19]

The FA's decision to make Sven Goran Eriksson England manager in 2000 was perhaps the most salient appointment during this period. His recruitment, and that of Bertie Vogts as Scotland's coach, mirrored developments in other sports. During the 1990s, global migration accelerated and the movement of coaching talent was part of this process. In 2000, for example, not one of the twelve Rugby League Super League clubs had a British coach. Instead, there were nine Australians and three New Zealanders.[20] In 1999, England appointed Duncan Fletcher, a Zimbabwean, as its cricket coach, and the year before the Welsh Rugby Union recruited Graham Henry from New Zealand. Henry also coached the British Lions during their 2001 tour of Australia. In 2000, the Australian, Bill Sweetman, was charged with changing the fortunes of the British swimming squad. Eriksson's appointment caused much resentment and no little controversy in the tabloids and the game itself. It highlighted, however, differences in how British managers have been produced compared to those in Europe. Richard Williams identified deeper reasons for employing the Swede, and by implication the appointment of other foreign managers,

> The biggest indictment of all must be directed at the English educational system, divisively structured and carelessly administered. All the necessary evidence is to be found in the styles of the candidates to whom the FA looked when it concluded that there was no suitable English-born applicant.[21]

In terms of preparing prospective managers for a career in football, England continued to lag behind its continental competitors. In Germany, for example, any aspiring manager – technically a head coach – required not only a qualification to gain a licence to work in the Bundesliga but also a mandatory two years' experience in the lower divisions. Another manifestation of this lag was that, by 2000, whereas in France there were 17,000 UEFA qualified coaches and in

Germany, 53,000, there were only 1,000 in England.[22] It has probably been no coincidence that Britain's overall record in industrial training has been echoed in football. The British virtually abandoned the education and training of non-academic teenagers during the later years of the last century, creating a skills shortage amongst the workforce from which the country continues to suffer. In 1990, for example, 49 per cent of manufacturing companies had problems in recruiting staff.[23]

Within the English game there continued to be resistance to the idea of qualifications for managers. Qualified coaches were regularly stigmatized as 'schoolteachers', and for many in the game, experience of professional football remained the key quality. Kenny Hibbitt, a former player and the manager of Hednesford Town, put the common view: 'It doesn't matter what qualifications you have got, you have to have been in situations to know what it's about. . . . Players respect ex-players and they find out if you've never played.'[24] The mistrust of the intellectual is rooted in the history of Britain's social relations. In football, it has formed a self-justification for players' own careers, lives and identities as professionals who generally emerged from working-class backgrounds with few educational qualifications. What they have achieved has been built on old-fashioned, working-class values like hard work. This has formed the basis of their outlook on work and engendered a distrust of people with professional qualifications from the middle classes who have enjoyed a more privileged education and upbringing.

In contrast to England, managers from Europe are less likely to have had a playing career because the screening process for managers has been more thorough and includes compulsory qualifications.[25] At Auxerre, in France, Guy Roux, who ran the club for over thirty years until his retirement in 2005, never played professionally. Similarly, neither did Arrigo Sacchi, manager of AC Milan, and later the Italian national team, in the late 1980s and early 1990s. Jose Mourinho combined a brief playing career with studying physical education at the Sports University of Lisbon where he specialized in football methodology. He later became assistant to Bobby Robson at Sporting Lisbon, Porto and Barcelona.[26] The German, Ottmar Hitzfeld, who won the European Cup with both Borussia Dortmund and Bayern Munich, had trained as a teacher in both PE and maths.[27] German coaches invariably have little experience as professional players, and, like Uli Hoeness at Bayern Munich, it is more common for the general manager to be a former player. In England more people were becoming aware of how these trends had permeated English football. The football writer, David Lacey, for example, recognized that,

> The lingering belief that outstanding deeds on the field automatically confer on a retired player the gifts of motivation, inspiration and a deep understanding of the human psyche gets less credible as the financial side of the game becomes increasingly tied up with big business.[28]

However, moves were afoot in England to 'professionalize' the manager's role, similar to the rest of Europe. In 2001, for example, the first eleven English managers enrolled on the UEFA Professional Licence course, qualifying successful graduates to work in any of Europe's top leagues. Before the 2003–4 season, each manager had to acquire either a Football Association Coaching Diploma or a UEFA Professional Licence, and it was stipulated that no club could employ anyone who did not hold these qualifications after that season.[29] Interestingly, by 2003, forty-two coaches from north of the border had acquired the UEFA 'Pro-Licence' but only eleven in England. Coaches from other countries, including Mourinho, had also taken the Scottish route. Nevertheless, a professional class of English football managers and coaches slowly emerged. In 2002, sixty of the seventy-two managers in the Football League had gained an advanced coaching licence. In 2002, the League Managers' Association also launched its own business management course for football managers, the Certificate of Applied Management, run in conjunction with the University of Warwick's Business School. Its objective was to give its students a more rounded view of their job and it incorporated aspects of man-management, marketing and business planning.[30] The League Managers' Association (LMA), after removing itself from the Football League umbrella, had been formed in the same year as the Premier League. One of its main aims has been to campaign for the introduction of mandatory qualifications for managers. LMA chief executive, former manager John Barnwell, has argued that, 'You're giving the chairman a kite mark to look at, a standard to reach.'[31]

Of course, mandatory qualifications only narrow the field down to those competent enough to pass them and management culture is probably still more important in how football managers in England are chosen. English attitudes to recruiting managers have been rooted in the past and the implementation of a licensing system will not dramatically alter that culture or the mindset of people within the game. For example, David Platt's fast-tracking by the FA into the position of coach of England's under-21 team highlighted the thinking that it was players, and those with international reputations, who were thought to be best suited for management positions.[32]

Despite some modernization, football management still had much in common with its past. Football clubs, Manchester United excepted, were still relatively small organizations, with the personal relationship between the chairman and his manager the most important one in the club. But the game's rampant commercialization during this period clearly affected the manager's role. Football management underwent a new division of labour during the 1990s, and many clubs followed Liverpool's model of the 1970s and 1980s where the manager managed the players while a skilled administrator, like Peter Robinson, ran the club. People with some real financial training and experience now handled the financial management of several clubs. As a result, clubs from Manchester United to Hartlepool United employed a chief executive to run their day-to-day affairs. Even high-profile managers like Ferguson and Wenger were excluded from high-level boardroom decisions, with their responsibilities limited to team matters as their role became increasingly narrowly defined. In particular, it was chief executives, like Peter Kenyon, who usually dealt with transfer and wages negotiations with either the players or their agents. Not only can this be a time-consuming process, but perhaps because of the sums involved, and for their own sake, the clubs wanted to make the whole process more transparent. During the 'bung' scandal of the early 1990s it was alleged that a number of managers were taking a percentage of the transfer fee and 'gifts' from agents without the clubs being aware of what was happening.[33]

The manager of a top club, therefore, has increasingly been removed from the club's financial management. As a result, his role has generally become more specialized, akin to a head coach, and similar to that in top European clubs as well as in American sports. At some clubs, like Chelsea, managers have devoted their energies entirely to the first team. Responsibilities for youth development and scouting for players have been given over to other people, such as a general manager or director of football. Spurs have followed this model. In 2004, David Pleat was replaced as director of football by the former Danish international, Frank Arnesen, before the appointment of Jacques Santini as head coach. At Liverpool, former player Steve Heighway has been responsible for overseeing the emergence of such players as Michael Owen and Steven Gerrard. This division of duties is essentially designed to lighten the manager's workload and give priority to the first team. However, most British practitioners still prefer to be known as the 'manager'. On his appointment at Spurs, George Graham insisted in his contract that he was called manager rather than head coach like the previous incumbent, Christian Gross. How this affected his role, though, is unclear.[34]

Not that this new management structure was a guarantee for success. In June 1999, Celtic had appointed Kenny Dalglish as its general manager with John Barnes as coach. Barnes was solely responsible for the first team while Dalglish's role covered the buying of players and youth development. Celtic's then chief executive, Allan MacDonald, formerly an executive at British Aerospace, had endorsed Barnes's appointment. By the following February, though, Barnes had been sacked. Perhaps this was unsurprising as Celtic was his first managerial position and what little coaching experience he had included helping out at Eton when he played for Watford.[35]

The steady dilution of the manager's powers was not a linear process, however. A number of managers resisted the reduction in their powers, highlighting the ongoing tensions between commercialization and traditional attitudes towards football management. At both Leicester and Celtic, Martin O'Neill insisted on being given full control of the playing side while not brooking any interference from directors. On one occasion at Leicester, he stormed into the commercial director's office and emptied a sack of mobile phones onto his desk following complaints about their overuse by O'Neill's staff. On his arrival at Celtic he insisted that he not only brought his own staff but that there would be no general manager.

Following a breakdown in his professional relationship with Kevin Keegan, Manchester City's chairman, David Bernstein, resigned in March 2003. Keegan had accused Bernstein of being too cautious and not matching his ambition: refusing to spend money on players, in other words. Other directors had agreed with Keegan, causing a rift in the boardroom, forcing Bernstein's departure.[36]

After West Bromwich Albion gained promotion to the Premier League in 2002, a power struggle developed between the manager, Gary Megson, and the chairman, Paul Thompson. Unusually, the manager won. Megson had threatened to resign, complaining that Thompson had wanted to take charge of the club's scouting system and transfers, roles that Megson considered to be his. Thompson had countered that Megson, because of his success, was now too powerful and would not accede to any of the board's decisions. Megson had refused to discuss team affairs with him for two years. The chairman pointed out that Megson had no financial training and greater expertise with money was needed now that they had gained promotion.[37] However, because of their promotion other directors felt that Megson was more important to the club and Thompson was forced to step down. Power is tenuous, however, and for a football manager it is dependent on success: both Keegan and Megson left their clubs in 2004–5.

Despite these internal struggles, the powers of a manager of an English club were not as diluted as those of managers at big European clubs like AC Milan and Barcelona, where chairmen and general managers made the decisions over transfers. In 2004, for example, Real Madrid's coach queried why the club had bought Michael Owen from Liverpool, implying that he had nothing to do with the transfer.[38] In England, with the odd exception, the manager still had influence over the composition of the playing staff. Indeed, Wenger has claimed that he prefers to work in England because 'it is the only big football country in which a manager can work with freedom. In other countries there is too much confusion about the definition of the job.'[39] Of course, this 'freedom' is still dependent on the resources available. At some clubs it has been suggested that the chairman, rather than the manager, has been proactive in the transfer market. It was claimed, for example, that Newcastle's chairman, Freddie Shepherd, instigated a number of transfers, such as that of Patrick Kluivert from Barcelona, when Bobby Robson was in charge.[40]

Admittedly, managers like Ferguson, Wenger and Keegan have been given the opportunity to build teams and this perhaps highlights that a manager's most important asset is still his ability to judge a player. But if managers get it wrong they can find themselves out of a job. It was claimed that a reason for Gerard Houllier's departure from Liverpool in 2004 was that he had 'bought badly': a reference to the £20 million he spent on players like Diouf, Daio and Cheyrou in 2002.

At Manchester United, Ferguson was fortunate to have a number of home-grown players like Ryan Giggs, David Beckham and Paul Scholes who formed the nucleus of the highly successful Manchester United team of the late 1990s. This then enabled him to make key signings like Eric Cantona, Roy Keane and later Ruud Van Nistelrooy. However, even Ferguson's record in the transfer market was not infallible. In 1999, he paid £4.5 million for the Venezia goal-keeper Massimo Taibi, but due to his errors Taibi only played four games and was sold back to Italy for £2.5 million. In 2002, Ferguson spent £28 million on Juan Sebastian Veron who, a year later, was sold to Chelsea at a loss of £12 million. Every manager makes bad buys though; it is just that Ferguson's can be partly obscured because of the money at his disposal.

While Ferguson relied on an English backbone to his team, at Highbury, under Arsene Wenger, Arsenal went cosmopolitan, building the team around French players like Patrick Viera, Nicolas Anelka, Robert Pires and Thierry Henry, all of whom had trained at the French national coaching centre in Clarefontaine. Wenger also scoured other countries for players. He bought the Spaniard, Juan Antonio Reyes, for £20 million, but because Arsenal were unable to match United's buying power, Wenger was also forced to look for bargains such as Kolo Toure of the Ivory Coast. Buying players is one thing, but Wenger has also built a reputation for developing and improving the players under his charge.

Clubs like Charlton and Blackburn, though, had different aspirations from the elite clubs, namely staying in the Premier League, and they had to plan accordingly. Because of the potential reduction in income, Bolton Wanderers were determined not to be burdened with debts similar to those of relegated clubs like Sheffield Wednesday and Bradford. Bolton's manager, Sam Allardyce, consequently bought foreign stars on short-term contracts with the proviso that if they were relegated, they could be released at the end of the season. Other clubs followed similarly cautious policies. West Bromwich Albion, for example, were promoted to the Premier League in 2002 and kept mainly the same group of players for the following season. Despite relegation in 2003, the club had taken a more long-term and realistic view of its expectations, and this paid off with promotion back to the Premier League the following season.

As transfer fees escalated, clubs went to greater and more sophisticated lengths to research a prospective player. The availability of satellite television and video footage, for example, allowed managers to see more players. In addition, clubs expanded their scouting networks to Europe. Before Ruud Van Nistelrooy signed for Manchester United, Ferguson and his scouts had watched him play on forty occasions. Initially, his transfer was cancelled because a medical examination revealed damage to his knee and, indicative of the new commercial climate, the club's insurance company was unwilling to cover him.[41] Some clubs have not been as diligent in their research, however. In 1996, Graeme Souness, then manager of Southampton, tried out a Senegalese player, Ali Dia, who had been recommended by someone claiming to be George

Weah, the former World Footballer of the Year. Souness gave the player a month's trial and for one game brought him on as a substitute, but he was so awful that Souness substituted the substitute. He got rid of him after fourteen days.[42]

Football's changing landscape brought different challenges for managers regarding their relationship with the players. Throughout industry generally, there had been a change in the structure of organizations during the post-industrial age. Instead of clearly defined hierarchical bureaucracies, organizations became flatter and more fluid and the lines of authority less clear.[43] Football clubs, though, not only remained small companies but also hierarchical in nature with a clear demarcation between workers and management. Nevertheless, even football had to adapt. Players were becoming richer as well as celebrities in their own right, and were also more independently minded. The balance of power in the relationship between managers and players consequently shifted more towards the players – although not in their favour. In addition, the influx of foreign players post-Bosman brought with it cultural and language problems for both players and managers. Shortly after signing for Middlesbrough in 1996, for example, Emerson went back to Brazil claiming that his wife liked neither the area nor the weather. He later returned.

Many foreign players were characterized as mercenaries. Much blame was placed at the feet of agents whose numbers and activities proliferated after the Bosman ruling. Not recognized officially by FIFA until 1994, agents were also employed by some clubs to find foreign players or to act as intermediaries in negotiations with foreign clubs. Many saw them as the scourge of football, as they stood to profit from their clients regularly moving between clubs. Moreover, foreign players were generally more liberal in their comments to the media and ready to criticize more frequently than their British counterparts. Nevertheless, many foreign players also wanted to develop their own careers. Emerson's former teammate, Juninho, for example, played for Middlesbrough in three different spells, and, although money was an important factor, it indicated an affinity with the club. At Scunthorpe, the Spaniard Alex Calvo-Garcia was similarly popular during his stay between 1996 and 2003.

Domestic players also become more assertive and outspoken. In October 2003, England players threatened not to play against Turkey in the final Euro 2004 qualifier in protest at the omission of Rio Ferdinand from the squad because of his missed drugs test. The players also carried power through the PFA. In 1991, the union's threat to strike over its share of television revenue was backed by 95 per cent of its membership. A similar dispute in 2001 received a 99 per cent mandate.[44] Management also viewed players differently. In 2004, for example, apprehensive about losing some of their best players, Liverpool almost felt compelled to confer with the likes of Steven Gerrard over the club's choice of its new manager. This was something unheard of even five years previously.

Perhaps more importantly, with the increase in transfer fees, the players' value to clubs as assets also increased. A greater onus was placed on managers to extract the best from them. As dressing rooms became more cosmopolitan and the egos of players matched their salaries, managers needed to use different methods for handling them. Gordon Strachan commented on the 'ever-growing power wielded by players' during his time as a manager, and observed that the 'staggering amount of money in football has certainly had a negative effect on the mentalities of a lot of players'. Perhaps as an unconscious insight into his own management skills, Strachan wished he had been,

> fully aware of the problems of getting the best out of players who are earn-ing massive salaries, without needing to win something or even be in the first team . . . I must admit the pampering I've had to do at times, when I have had to control the temptation to get stuck into a player, has not made me feel very good about myself.[45]

Similarly, in 1998, Derby manager, Jim Smith, who began his management career with non-league Boston United in 1968, remarked that,

> you have to treat players a bit differently to when I started out. . . . Then, if the manager said 'jump' you jumped. If not you were out of the team. These days, particularly once they get a bit of a name in the first team, they can't handle a bollocking too well. My method used to be to use a bit of sarcasm, but they're too fragile for that now. You need real man-management these days.[46]

In some respects, the influx of foreign managers, like Wenger and Eriksson, has signified a move away from a sergeant-major type model to the officer class in terms of managing players. To a certain extent, these changing attitudes have mirrored those not only in today's 'relationship economy' where there is much less 'command and control' type management, but also in society in general where there has been a decline in respect for authority figures like school-teachers and policemen. Instead, 'managers have to build consensus, persuade and influence people'.[47] Despite the unique nature of the football industry, some of these attitudes have permeated its management. Managers like Eriksson have urged players to look at themselves and their own performance to get the best from them. At Arsenal, Wenger changed the culture within the dressing room by 'intellectualizing' the players, reminding them that it said professional footballer on their passports, and inviting them to 'behave like professionals'.[48]

Yet football managers the world over still require the personality to put across their ideas, and in England it helps if they have a good grasp of the language. Not all players can be kept contented all the time and harsh decisions still have to be taken, such as leaving players out of the team or putting them on the transfer list. Players still have to be motivated and kept reasonably happy.

The stereotypical image of a manager 'throwing tea cups' has begun to fade but on occasions some English players expect their manager to 'lift them'. Eriksson has made a point that he is not one for shouting. However, during the half-time interval in England's 2002 World Cup quarter-final against Brazil, one member of the squad remarked that, after conceding an equalizer, the players needed a speech of Churchillian proportions to inspire them but what they got instead was one that could have come from Iain Duncan-Smith (the then beleaguered Conservative party leader).

Partly through a decline in respect for authority, but also, perhaps, better management, the relationship between manager and players grew closer. Consultation on tactics, for example, took place on a regular basis. After a particularly heated dressing room discussion in December 1997, Arsenal's defenders argued that they needed more protection from their midfield. Wenger later instructed Petit and Viera to carry out this task but at the same time he was able to maintain his own authority and retain the respect of the players.[49] During Euro 2004, Eriksson dropped the 'diamond' formation for a flat four in midfield after consultation with some of the players. A rise in concern for the self also meant that players relied more on managers to help develop their careers. Some, like Ferguson and Wenger, cultivated closer relations with their players not only because of the longevity of their tenure but also because they had helped to improve them as footballers. Ferguson's relationship with his players has been regarded as patriarchal in its nature. Despite an acrimonious falling out, David Beckham recognized the role that Ferguson had played in his career. Ryan Giggs believed that Ferguson had not only helped him to develop as a player but also as a man.[50] When George Weah was voted FIFA World Player of the year in 1995 he insisted that Wenger, his manager at Monaco when he first came to European football, accepted the trophy. Weah acknowledged that it was Wenger's constant encouragement that gave him the confidence to develop. Weah said, 'What can I pay him? I can't give him cash because he makes money. And money can go but the trophy will stay, to remind him what he did for a player.'[51]

Of course, all managers still want and strive for discipline from their players. At Arsenal, Wenger has delegated disciplinary matters to his assistant, Pat Rice, enabling him to remain the players' friend. On his appointment as Tottenham's manager, George Graham banned mobile phones on the team coach and ordered the players to wear blazers. He also introduced fines for players who were late for training. He said that it was in order to inculcate them with a sense of professionalism. 'By turning up late, you are showing a lack of respect for me, for the coaching staff and also for your fellow players,' was his rationale.[52] These attitudes were perhaps more prevalent further down the footballing pyramid. On meeting his players for the first time, Steve Claridge, the new player-manager of Weymouth, said to them, 'Right, I want you to call me "Gaffer", and him, Mr Chairman.'[53]

Alex Ferguson remained in the old school of management. His temper is well known and in many ways he manages by imposing his authority on players through fear. Players underperforming have been given the 'hair dryer' treatment and on one occasion he kicked a boot into the face of David Beckham. Yet Ferguson has not been successful without learning to adapt. He recognized that Eric Cantona was a special player, for example. As the key to the team's performance, he did not want to upset him. Ferguson exempted Cantona from some of the more petty fines handed out to the other Manchester United players and he is one of only three players that Ferguson has never shouted at. Cantona later repaid Ferguson by abiding by the club's rules because he felt he owed it to the manager.[54] Ferguson, like Wenger, also saw marriage or long-term relationships as essential for discipline on and off the pitch. Ferguson used a network of 'spies' to check up on his players and their behaviour, and once ordered Lee Sharpe to return to living in lodgings, under the supervision of a landlady, after he was found partying at his own house. Similarly, when he was at Aberdeen, he interviewed Neale Cooper, and asked him to explain why he had been seen leaving the same house every day for the last five weeks. A flabbergasted Cooper replied that it was his own place. Ferguson ordered him to get rid of it, saying that he was too young to be living on his own, and to return to his mother's, which he did.[55]

Complementing changing man-management techniques as well as the game's commercialization and greater competitiveness, football became more scientific in its preparation of players, precipitating a further process of specialization within its management. People's previous idea of football and sports science was of the trainer running onto the pitch with his bucket and 'magic' sponge. Perhaps unsurprisingly, compared to other sports like cricket and both rugby codes, there was an initial reluctance to embrace new and innovative ideas.[56] However, younger managers were keen to experiment with enhancing their players' preparation. At Crystal Palace, Iain Dowie brought in a rugby league coach to improve the fitness of his players. In 2004, after being in the relegation zone at Christmas just before he took over as manager, they won promotion to the Premier League. Managers took on a host of specialists in areas like nutrition and physical conditioning as clubs tried to 'extract' the maximum from their players. No longer, for example, was it incumbent on the manager to take coaching sessions. Instead, many employed specialist coaches. Jim Smith noted how the job had changed since he first started,

> I used to be completely 'hands on', but that's not really possible in the Premiership. I've got a good coach [Steve McClaren] and then there are people like your masseurs and your fitness coaches. At one time, your players just ran around a pitch, had a pie and chips and played. But because of the money involved in staying in the Premiership, we have to do everything possible to prepare players properly.[57]

Unsurprisingly, Arsene Wenger has been at the forefront of this new scientific approach. On taking up his job at Arsenal, he hired a number of French health and fitness experts to assist the players. He insisted that they stretched for thirty minutes after every game and training session, something foreign to British players. Nutrition was another area he changed at Arsenal. Learning from his experience in Japan, he preferred his players' staple diet to consist of boiled vegetables, rice and fish. Although Wenger did not insist on what players ate, he frowned upon the stereotypical British diet of red meat, eggs, chips and baked beans. He also offered players the choice of vitamin injections and dietary supplements, in particular creatine, which was designed to boost energy and reduce fatigue. Training was run by a stopwatch and was very organized and detailed. One of the major benefits for Arsenal of this new regime has been 'periodizing,' the ability to peak at the right moment, namely at the end of the season.

Manchester United also became adept at this particular technique, although perhaps more importantly their big squad allowed them to rest and rotate players to ensure they were fresher come the run-in. Nevertheless, United also went down the sports science route. When Steve McClaren was Ferguson's assistant he introduced a number of innovations to the club, including computers to log the performance of every United player. He also borrowed ideas from American basketball coaches on how to keep highly paid players motivated, although he admitted that the threat of being dropped was still the best form of stimulation.[58] After becoming manager at Middlesbrough, McClaren appointed a psychologist, Bill Beswick, as his assistant, indicating another avenue that was being explored. For the England team, Eriksson used Willi Railo, a Norwegian who was regarded as Europe's most eminent sports psychologist.[59] By contrast, his predecessor, Glenn Hoddle, employed a faith healer, Eileen Drury. The overall aim of these developments was for clubs to get the best from the players. When he was at Newcastle, Kevin Keegan went as far as using Dave Aldred, a kicking coach from rugby union who later assisted Jonny Wilkinson. Keegan felt that if Newcastle scored two extra goals because of Aldred's sessions, it would have been worth the expense.

The flirtation with sports science unquestionably improved the players' fitness levels, and in turn affected how the game itself was played. It also shaped the extent to which a manager could influence a team's style. With players bigger, fitter and faster, the games themselves became 'battles' where there was little space to play and more challenges were made. This had been exacerbated when, from 1992, it became illegal for goalkeepers to handle an intentional pass from a teammate. The new law speeded up the game and playing was also made easier for forwards by the outlawing of the tackle from behind. Another consequence of the changes was that rather than teams from different countries being noted for a distinctive style, there was instead a convergence of styles creating a kind of football globalization. This was unsurprising given the regularity with which the top teams and players now met each other, due largely to the expansion of the Champions' League. In addition, because of 'Bosman', teams were largely composed of players from different nationalities, thus accelerating the exchange and aping of styles and new ideas. All clubs demanded versatility from their players and everyone needed to be able to attack and defend, although an overriding caution infected much of football. Most teams played a counter-attacking game to exploit those fleeting moments when the opposition was disorganized and allowed space to appear between and behind their midfield and defence. Greater emphasis was placed on efficiency and defensive organization, with games decided by small details such as defensive mistakes, individual brilliance or a piece of tactical ingenuity by the manager.

Despite a growing conformity, managers and coaches still needed to be flexible in changing the team's formation to suit the players at their disposal – or at least that is what the best tacticians seemed to do. During the last ten years, a proliferation of formations has emerged: 4–3–3, 3–5–2, 4–4–2, 4–4–1–1 or 4–5–1. A new terminology regarding the players' positions was also invented. There were now 'holding players' in midfield, like Dunga of Brazil; the one 'in the hole' who plays between midfield and attack, such as Dennis Bergkamp; and 'wing-backs' also emerged with a dual purpose to defend like full-backs and attack like wingers, although the emphasis was on running. Managers could still influence games by the use of substitutes as well as use half-time to give further instruction. The introduction of technical areas gave managers and coaches the opportunity to give orders from the touchline, but to what extent players carry these out during the excitement of the game is unclear.

With the range of their responsibilities more narrowly defined, it is perhaps the role of tactician that will form the main part of the manager's job in the future. By being excluded from the overall strategy making, and with general managers becoming more involved in the transfer of players, plus clubs now employing specialists to take on tasks that the manager once undertook, managers will be expected to use their tactical acumen to influence the outcome of games. Some managers of English clubs, though, have still been able to stamp their own ideas and style on teams. Wenger changed the image of Arsenal from a side that under George Graham was renowned for its defence and ability to win games 1–0, to one that has been described as having played the most attractive football in the history of the English game. At Liverpool, Gerard Houllier did the opposite (although not without some success). Liverpool had been famous for their attacking passing game but under Houllier they developed a counter-attacking style, which led to accusations that the team was boring and negative.

After 1992, the coverage of football in the media, particularly on television, expanded to such an extent that the game almost turned into a 'male soap opera', something that was parodied by the ITV show, *Footballers' Wives*. The figure of the manager reached other areas of popular culture. The *Fast Show* character 'Ron Manager', a parody of Alec Stock, the former QPR and Fulham manager, satirized those managers who became football pundits. In *Mike Bassett:*

England Manager, the eponymous manager is caricatured as typical of previous hapless incumbents, while the film uses many footballing clichés, like throwing tea cups at half-time. Because of their historical relationship with the media, managers became more visible as the coverage of the game increased. It reinforced the perception not only that they were important but also that they were emblematic figures for the clubs they managed. Unlikely as it sounds, some, like Kevin Keegan, were even tagged a 'Messiah'. He had earlier been a player at Newcastle and when he returned as manager it was called the 'Second Coming'.

Because of a greater individualism and exhibitionism within society generally, the coverage of football reflected shifts within the media, especially its obsession with celebrity. As a result, sensationalism, speculation and gossip became the main fodder of much of the media – television and newspapers alike. Continuous sports news channels, for example, were inevitably dominated by the latest football happenings. BSkyB, with its numerous sports channels and the need to fill air-time, packaged and marketed the game as another form of entertainment, although one which mainly appealed to young men. Not only were matches broadcast live but there was endless build-up to games with 'expert' analysis before, during and after they finished. Football's symbiotic relationship with the media almost produced its ideal union in 1997 when Everton's chairman, Peter Johnson, offered the manager's job to Andy Gray. Gray had been an Everton player but had no management experience, although he had briefly been a coach at Aston Villa. The main factor behind the offer seemed to have been that because of his job as an expert summarizer with BSkyB not only was Gray knowledgeable about football but he was now a high-profile figure within the game and amongst fans. A week later, however, Gray rejected the job and opted to remain in television.

Accompanying the dramatic rise in its coverage, there was a distinct increase in the hyperbole surrounding football. While broadsheet newspapers devoted more serious comment and analysis to the game, the tone of tabloid newspapers, which gave 20 per cent of their space to sport, became increasingly chauvinistic and intrusive. Because of his celebrity status, Eriksson's private life regularly made the front pages. No one suffered more from a glut of distasteful headlines than he and his predecessors. A combination of a circulation war between the tabloids and powerful editors unafraid of letting objectivity get in the way of a good story has seen a number of England managers feel the wrath of the 'red tops', usually for the national team's shortcomings. After Euro 92, Graham Taylor was pictured as a turnip, while Glenn Hoddle was later hounded out of the post due to his comments about disabled people and reincarnation. Radio football phone-ins supplemented the press and television, providing supporters with the opportunity to rant and give their instant reactions to the latest results. Inevitably perhaps, many disillusioned callers saw or demanded a change of manager as the answer to their team's poor form. Although all this could be dismissed as hyperbole, it may not have been a coincidence that the rate of managerial turnover increased over the same period. Nervous chairmen perhaps felt that, with the game having such a high profile, they themselves needed to be seen to be doing something when their team's results slumped.

Managers, however, continued to play the central role in football's soap opera. As his media responsibilities grew, it reinforced and authenticated the perception of the manager as an all-powerful figure. Managers' press conferences, for example, were hyped up as events in themselves with managers almost taking on a statesman-like presence such was the importance they were given. Journalists endlessly pored over their comments, and, because of the pressure to fill either air-time or column inches, deconstructed them for some extra meaning. It was felt, for example, that because they were the manager, their words gave a direct link to the state of mind of the players themselves, although it was perhaps the players' actions on the pitch that gave a better indication. Satellite television generally enhanced football's coverage by using more cameras and showing more angles and close-ups. Cameras were now fixed on both teams' dug-outs to capture a manager's reaction to on-the-field events – for example, goals or refereeing decisions that go against their team. At full-time, managers were expected to give a post-match interview in which they usually criticized the referee in between delivering well-rehearsed platitudes. Arsene Wenger, for instance, when asked about one of his players having been sent off, invariably 'did not see the incident'.

It would be wrong to think, though, that managers have been passive agents within this relationship. For instance, 'using the media' to praise and criticize their players in public has almost become a man-management technique in itself. Ferguson has vigorously defended his players in public. They are never wrong: instead the referee is usually at fault. Another Ferguson technique has been to bring up a different issue to deflect any criticism from the players. Even television analysts have felt the wrath of his temper. On one occasion, after Eric Cantona had committed a foul on a Norwich player that was unseen by the referee, Jimmy Hill described it as 'despicable and villainous'; Ferguson, in the post-match interview, responded by calling Hill a 'prat'. This type of defiance was intended to create a siege mentality amongst his players, a feeling that, apart from their own fans, everyone was against them. It is something that many other managers have copied. Some managers also resorted to playing so-called 'mind games'. By saying, for example, that 'it's their title to lose now', a manager tried to put extra pressure on a competitor. This use of the media, however, was a brand of 'pop' psychology. There was little evidence to suggest that it worked in a real sense, i.e. on the field, although that did not prevent managers from trying to use it. In 1996, Kevin Keegan famously 'cracked' under pressure during a television interview. Ferguson had commented that, in the title run-in, Manchester United's opponents were trying harder against them than against other teams and he hoped that they would put in the same effort against Newcastle. Manchester United eventually won the title but the main reason for

United's victory was surely because they had better players, rather than Keegan cracking.

Ferguson, himself, because of his success and the power of Manchester United, has wielded unique influence in the media. Many newspapers, both local and national, as well as television stations, have been frightened of offending him. This has not only been because of his infamous short temper but also the fear that these organizations would be denied access to Manchester United. Ferguson has fully manipulated this situation and has barred some reporters from Old Trafford because their questions have been regarded as too probing.

In an age where celebrity, together with income from television, brought significant financial rewards, players like David Beckham and Roy Keane earned around £100,000 per week by 2003. Some managers enjoyed a commensurate rise in their salaries which were similar to those of top businessmen. In 2000, over 110 executives received salaries in excess of £1 million, earning around twenty-four times more than the average manufacturing employee, although in football it is often the managers who are trying to maintain parity with the workers.[60] Football managers' salaries also compare favourably with those of senior politicians, reflecting how business has gained in importance compared to the public sector. In 2001, for example, the Prime Minister drew a salary of £163,418, while other members of the cabinet were paid between £99,793 and £117,979.[61] In 1998, Ferguson's salary was estimated to be over £1 million, while Arsene Wenger's, Ruud Gullit's and Kenny Dalglish's salaries at the time were between £800,000 and £1 million. When Ferguson decided not to retire in 2002, his salary was increased from £3 million to £3.5 million per year.[62] Eriksson's salary in 2004 was £4 million. Managers at smaller clubs naturally earned lesser salaries. At Nottingham Forest, Dave Bassett's salary was estimated at about £250,000, similar to Charlton's Alan Curbishley and Danny Wilson of Sheffield Wednesday. In 1998, lower league managers were paid on average between £40,000 and £100,000 a year, with the highest paid manager in the third division earning £40,000.[63] Because of their celebrity, multinational companies have also used managers to endorse some of their products. These have ranged from Kevin Keegan being used to promote a well-known cereal to Jose Mourinho advertising a credit card.

Yet there is more to it than money and some managers clearly gain a sense of satisfaction from their job. It is also very noticeable that some managers who have enough money not to have to work still want to. Being on the training ground, for example, helps to maintain a certain youthfulness for some managers who can join in a five-a-side game, as well as some banter with the players. The drug of success from winning matches and trophies is also very important to most managers, and perhaps explains why Alex Ferguson and Bobby Robson could well extend their careers beyond retirement, although Ferguson has said that for him the adrenalin rush that victory brings is only brief. Some managers gain satisfaction from other aspects of the job. At Crewe Alexandra, Dario

Gradi has developed a highly successful youth policy. He regards the most rewarding aspect of his job as coming 'to the training ground in the morning and see[ing] the facilities that the boys who have been developed here have paid for: the training area, the new stand, the sports hall, the weights room, all paid for by them'.[64]

As the rewards have increased, however, so have the stresses of the job. One visible symptom has been how quickly the hair of some managers, like Kevin Keegan's, has turned grey through stress. Yet, to a large extent, managers have been the source of their own health problems. By being workaholics, they continue to live up to the macho image of football management as any reduction in their duties is regarded as a sign of weakness. During 2001–2, Dario Gradi worked 70 to 80 hours a week and during the season he did not take a day off. In 2001, it was discovered that Gerard Houllier's aorta had been leaking during his gruelling work schedule. He had been worried about his health but had hidden it from his team. During West Ham's relegation battle in 2002–3, Glenn Roeder was rushed to hospital after a game complaining of chest pains. He was forced, temporarily, to stand down from the job.

Lots of people suffer from heart problems but football is unique in that the job revolves around ninety minutes every Saturday, so the week builds up to a climax on match days. And of course, once the game starts, there is very little managers can do to affect the outcome. So their own helplessness combined with the pressures they are under increases the tension. In 2002, two Premiership managers, Bolton's Sam Allardyce and Dave Bassett of Leicester, had their hearts monitored during a game. Allardyce's heartbeat rose from 46 per minute to 160, while, after a player was sent off, Bassett's heart muscles contracted.[65] It was the equivalent of being involved in a serious car accident. To try to counter these problems, the LMA established a programme at the Wellness Institute in Stockport to investigate its members' health. Of the forty league managers who took part in the research it was found that fourteen exhibited early stages of heart problems.[66]

If football management has become a more stressful job since 1990 then its practitioners have also become some of the most recognizable figures not only in football but also in public life. Television has been the key to this greater visibility and it has also been the catalyst for the game's economic revolution. It has also meant that football has become more competitive and the risks and rewards have become greater. Management has been identified as a crucial factor in determining a football club's fortunes. As clubs search to find this missing ingredient, managers have become more expendable as clubs seek the best talent available. And in a world that is becoming smaller, this search has extended beyond the British Isles. Foreign managers, like foreign players, have brought new styles and ideas to the British game. Management has also become more professionalized and specialized. This 'invasion' has found British managers wanting in the skills demanded to prosper in this new harsher environment. It has shown that the approach for preparing British managers, the practical tradition, is out-dated compared to that of other European countries. Some English clubs have decided that foreign managers, who have received some form of mandatory training as preparation for the job, are more suitable candidates than those that have not. And because of the greater stress placed on management, it has also became more specialized as more effort is put into getting more out of the players. The role of the manager, although still without a job description, is more rounded, more like a head coach, dedicated to managing the players. He surrounds himself with other specialists who pool their knowledge for the benefit of the players' performance. Yet the manager is still the focus of the media's attention, and in the age of cyberspace and presentation, the manager has remained the club's public face.

Chapter 8

What difference does the manager make?

Throughout this book we have seen how the manager's role has developed since the nineteenth century and how he has emerged as an important figure within the game. Because of this development there is a perception that the performance of the team is closely associated with the actions of its manager. The media, especially television, have reinforced this 'mystique' of the manager – the idea that managers, like witchdoctors, have the power to change games and transform teams. It is this notion that has been disseminated amongst fans, players, and importantly, directors. This process, however, begs important questions, most centrally, what difference does a manager actually make, what are they making a difference to, and do we really need them?

With reference to the modern era, Wagg has argued that,

> In plain terms it is simply wrong to equate the performance of a football team with the performance of its manager. It makes no more sense, in principle, to . . . blame the head teacher of an inner city secondary modern school for regularly poor exam results.[1]

Yet just as there are undoubtedly competent and incompetent head teachers, there are efficient and inefficient football managers. Russell has stressed how the ability of individual managers and coaching staff to get the best out of players remains the crucial ingredient: 'As any fan is aware, managers can literally make, re-make or break a club.'[2] It will be argued here that managers have made a difference but what difference and how this has been made has been dependent on the changing socio-economic and cultural context of football management.

Managers themselves seem to be realistic about their overall impact. Instead, they pinpoint (or perhaps blame) the players as the main element in a club's fortunes. Matt Busby recognized that 'players are as fallible and vulnerable as the rest of us. And it is the players and only the players, and how they play on match day, who make or break managers.'[3] Cesar Luis Menotti, Argentina's World Cup coach of 1978, has attempted to quantify a manager's impact. He has argued that 'a coach may be 60 per cent responsible for a team's performance in the build-up to a match', but, recognizing his own limitations, 'once the game has begun he is less than 10 per cent accountable for what happens on the field'.[4] Archie Knox, an assistant to both Alex Ferguson and Walter Smith, is even more forthright about the importance of what players do on the pitch,

> It's all about how [the players] approach games that dictates if you're going to win or lose, not the management or the coaches. That will always be the case, irrespective of what some people think. The idea that there is a magic tactic that can be adopted by putting a player in a different position or anything like that is the biggest heap of rubbish ever.[5]

Harry Redknapp, in his own colourful way, is equally adamant about a manager's overall contribution. He believed that, 'we get carried away with coaching and coaches. I have my coaching badges but they came out of a Cornflakes packet at the time.' He added that, 'I have yet to see a coach make a bad player into a good one . . . I got a full badge 15 or 16 years ago but you can't just wave a magic wand.' Talking about the importance of players, Redknapp said, 'I couldn't coach Paolo di Canio. These people are intelligent footballers. It's all a fallacy, this stuff about good coaching.' Instead, he believed that football management is 'all about players and picking winning teams'.[6]

So how can managers make a difference? Historically, coaching in sport has had a long tradition, dating back to the Ancient Greek Olympics. Boxing has provided an example in more recent times. Muhammad Ali, for example, built up a close partnership with Angelo Dundee. Through the Marylebone Cricket Club, cricket was one of the first sports to produce a coaching manual. Track and field athletes have also been noted for their close relationships with their coaches. The influence of Sam Mussabini was mentioned in Chapter 1. More recently, Sebastian Coe was coached by his father, Peter, while his rival during the early 1980s, Steve Ovett, was similarly successful under long-time coach, Harry Wilson. Other individual sports, like golf, have begun to place a premium on the value of coaching. From the mid-1980s, for example, Nick Faldo teamed up with David Leadbetter who helped him win six major titles. Because of the pressures of top-level sport, it is increasingly difficult for individuals to succeed by themselves. Instead, as in team sports, they need the support of experts such as agents, managers, coaches, dieticians and fitness trainers. Tiger Woods's entourage, for example, is known as 'Team Tiger'.[7] Yet, judging the value of managers and coaches is still problematic.

Measurements of the worth of football managers have traditionally been difficult to calculate. One 'common sense', if subjective, argument is to claim that, just as in Formula One the best drivers end up in the best cars, the best managers gravitate towards the biggest and most successful clubs. Some conventional observers have tended to make judgements about managers based on the number of trophies they win, taking no account of the socio-economic environment in which the work of the manager takes place. For example, King and

Kelly devised a graded scoring system that was predicated on teams finishing in first or second place in the League, plus cup wins, including European trophies, even though this was not applicable to some managers like Herbert Chapman.[8]

In recent years there has been a growing number of academic investigations into the value of football management and coaching. These have arrived at different conclusions. Dawson *et al.*, for example, have analyzed the worth of coaching by using the measurement of match outcomes as opposed to league rankings. Playing talent has been measured by a combination of the Opta Index that evaluates player performance based on a series of categories (*ex post*) and a player's start of season transfer value (*ex ante*) to predict coaching efficiency. Dawson *et al.* conclude that 'coaching efficiency is only partially correlated with team performance'. The most successful coaches are not necessarily the most efficient coaches as the measurement of coaching performance in terms of success is dependent on the playing talent available.[9] The most extensive work on the question of managerial contribution to the success of sports organizations has been on American major league baseball. A brief survey of the literature reveals that most studies conclude that managers can make a difference.[10] Porter and Scully, for example, state that 'managerial skill in baseball contributes very substantially to the production process'.[11]

Stefan Szymanski has brought a statistical approach to the question of managerial efficiency in English football. Concurring with Wagg's supposition, Szymanski states that managers 'have little impact on the performance of the clubs they manage'. Instead, it is the extent of a club's financial investment that is the main factor behind its success (or failure).[12] By using regression analysis, Szymanski and Kuypers have calculated that between 1978 and 1997 the relationship between wage expenditure and league performance was very tightly correlated. The money that a club spent on players' wages accounted for 92 per cent of its league position during this period. By contrast, the manager's contribution has been estimated at about 2 per cent.[13] In layman's terms, clubs got what they paid for: the best players cost the most wages. This 'goodness of fit' can be traced back to 1978 when footballers gained freedom of contract. There is, however, a greater variability when looking at just one particular year. For the 1996–7 season, for example, the correlation between wage expenditure and league position was 78 per cent, admittedly still a high figure. A comparison with the years 1950 to 1960 shows a regression of 50 per cent. Szymanski and Kuypers claim that wage expenditure did matter in the 1950s but the market was relatively inefficient. Because of the constraints of the maximum wage, wage expenditure was less important in terms of its relationship to league performance.[14] Football managers, therefore, worked under conditions that mainly revolved around a player's power in the market place. Before 1960, a player's power was restricted and the potential for management to influence performance was perhaps greater.

Despite this concentration on wage expenditure, Szymanski has produced a list ranking managers based on regression analysis over the 1982 to 1997 period, and Kenny Dalglish came top. It was argued that in winning championships with Liverpool and Blackburn Rovers, 'he achieved more at those clubs he managed than would have been expected given his spending on wages'. Other top ten entrants included Joe Kinnear, Lawrie McMenemy and Dave Bassett who appear due to their ability to extract the best from limited resources. Alex Ferguson is ranked only fifth and George Graham does not make the top ten despite their success at Manchester United and Arsenal respectively.[15]

On the face of it, Szymanski's work is convincing, arguing that in the bigger picture, managers are relatively peripheral figures in football's production process. However, in order to gain a more accurate picture of managerial efficiency, there needs to be a greater understanding of football's shifting historical context. Importantly, the aims and objectives of football clubs have been subject to football's changing commercialization process: changes which have had an impact on the game's economic and organizational characteristics, on the management of clubs and consequently on the role of the manager. Furthermore, football clubs were and are small organizations, giving more potential for individuals to influence their management and direction.

Early football clubs did not generally seek profits. Sloane has argued that football clubs were 'utility maximizers' where directors who had an urge for power, and shareholders who had a desire for group identification, invested not financially but emotionally. Even in 1966, the overall objective of a football club was 'to provide entertainment in the form of a football match. The objective was not to maximize profits, but to achieve playing success whilst remaining solvent.' Utility maximization, therefore, suggests that clubs would always strive to maximize their playing success.[16] Any profits were usually ploughed back into the club.[17] Furthermore, although virtually all clubs changed their status from members' club to limited liability company, the FA through its imposition of a 5 per cent dividend on football club shares in 1896 restricted commercialization.[18] And it was also not until 1981 that the FA allowed directors to be paid.

The policies and ethos of the Football League also had consequences for football management. In its capacity as a cartel, the League tried to equalize competition through the imposition of the maximum wage and the retain and transfer system. These measures enabled clubs to control their players and prevent the richer clubs buying up the best ones. To try and equalize competition, the League adopted cross-subsidization mechanisms. It regulated the quality of the competition by controlling entry into the League through a re-election process and by promotion and relegation so as to avoid unattractive one-sided contests. The offside rule had been changed in 1925 to improve the attraction of the game. In 1924 the Football League also approved a 20 per cent allocation of gate receipts to visiting teams. Furthermore, in 1890 the League set a minimum admission fee of 6d. There were few increases until the 1960s when football admission costs began to outpace inflation.[19] To prevent competition for spectators, the League decided in 1891 not to admit any club whose ground was within three miles of that of an existing member.[20] Arnold, like Sloane, has argued that as a result of the Football League's attempts to restrict competition, football clubs developed unusual business objectives: they were motivated by playing success not by maximizing profits.[21] Taylor has pointed out that the Football League's early policy makers, unpaid volunteers, were administrators not economists and had a different perspective on how the game should be run. Despite the importance of economic considerations such as increasing profits, they were just as interested in the notions of friendship and mutuality, and it was this which had permeated much of the League's early policy and which continued up until at least 1961.[22] Arnold and Benveniste also argue that 'individual sporting leagues reflect differences in the cultures in which they are grounded, in the aspirations of those who influence their activities, and in the historical development of their practices and rules'.[23]

The extent to which a sport was commercialized, as well as reflecting wider issues, had consequences for the way clubs were managed. Like their footballing counterparts, English county cricket clubs were not profit-oriented; unlike football, however, there was very little commercialization and county cricket was never viewed as a business in any form. Instead, the game's supporters were more concerned with notions of civic pride and county allegiance as the game was seen as an integral part of late nineteenth-century English culture.[24] Whereas football clubs turned themselves into limited liability companies during the 1890s, cricket clubs maintained their status as members' clubs. Their management, therefore, was based on traditional committee lines, the members democratically elected by the club membership. Committees picked the team and also looked after the club's finances. On the field, instead of a manager, it was the playing captain who was responsible for the team. This situation still basically exists today.

By comparison, ever since the nineteenth century, American baseball clubs have had few commercial restrictions placed upon them, mirroring how American society itself has been more business oriented than British society. Baseball has been organized for profit. It has allowed owners to move their club, or franchise, to different cities to exploit more favourable commercial opportunities such as access to large populations, most famously when the Brooklyn Dodgers moved to Los Angeles in 1958. In terms of a baseball club's organization, there was a more decisive division between ownership and control than in either football or cricket. Even early in its history, commercial forces had led to a manager replacing the captain as the architect of on-the-field tactics. The managerial hierarchy associated with major league baseball franchises hardly changed over the entire twentieth century. It consisted of the owner who provided the capital and took the risks; the general manager who had responsibility for acquiring and trading players plus salary negotiations; and then the manager who was responsible for the team.[25]

Partly because of the nature of the game's commercialism, football management has been a peculiar business. Initially, as we have seen, unpaid directors ran nascent football clubs rather than salaried managers as football management reflected the English traditions of amateurism and voluntarism. Not only did the absence of a profit motive temper the need for greater investment in managerial resources but club directors also became emotionally involved in clubs and devoted a lot of their spare time to running them. They were generally local business or professional men who had more interest in the indirect benefits that being a director of a local club could bring rather than any financial remuneration. Initially, the manager was usually the secretary who dealt with the club's administration, with the directors looking after team affairs. This situation gradually changed as football's competition intensified and the work involved in running a club increased. Directors usually had their own businesses to run as well. As a result, secretaries and managers gradually gained more responsibility for team affairs. This was not a linear process, however, with most clubs having different ideas on how they should be run. For example, following the split in 1892 of Everton Football Club's membership, and the subsequent formation of Liverpool, a different management culture emerged within each club. John Houlding, the chairman, had wanted the club to be run more on commercial lines, with him as the controlling figure, whereas the main bulk of the membership felt strongly that Everton should remain a members' club, and hence more democratic in nature. When Liverpool was formed after the split, it was run more for profit as well as being centrally controlled by Houlding. In 1896, Tom Watson was appointed secretary-manager, in line with Liverpool's more commercially driven policy. Despite becoming a limited liability company, Everton's management, on the other hand, continued to be run on more voluntary lines. This tradition persisted, and the club did not appoint a manager until the 1930s, with Will Cuff, an early member, remaining its dominant figure up to the 1940s.[26]

Football management's modernization was sluggish. Even the 1960s and 1970s were periods of transition as the old ways of management still dominated. Gradual change, and the decline of mutuality within football, began, however, with the end of the 'maximum' and the reform of the retain and transfer system in 1963 followed by further modification in 1978 when players were awarded freedom of contract.[27] During this time there was also a trend, reflecting movements in the consumption of leisure in general, towards the domination of football by a few big city clubs. A growing inequality in revenue within football emerged, allowing these clubs to afford the wages of the best players, resulting in a concentration of playing talent. This was further extended in 1995 by the Bosman ruling which not only allowed players to leave clubs at the end of their contracts without the need of a transfer fee, but also opened up the football labour market to all clubs within the European Union, prompting a drift of foreign players into British football.

During the 1990s, football embarked on a process of rampant commercialization. Following the establishment of the Premier League in 1992, the game enjoyed a closer and lucrative relationship with television. These developments were aided by a change in attitudes of football club directors towards their position. In effect, they were the new football entrepreneurs who were the first to realize that football was moving towards a more business-orientated future; and a number of clubs were listed on the stock market. Their attitudes contrasted sharply with the confused and still amateur ideals of those who occupied the corridors of power at the FA and the Football League. But because the boundaries have been blurred, it can still be argued that most clubs are still utility maximizers rather than profit seekers.

Even if clubs were or have continued to be utility maximizers they have still been dynamic and organic organizations. Within this largely non-profit-making context, their aspirations have been dictated by the changing nature of football's consumption. This raises the question, what are managers making a difference to? First, it may be beneficial to try to define football's production process and how football is actually consumed; and, as a result, how this has affected the manager's role. Football's production process is perhaps more difficult to disentangle than for other industries. Adam Smith stated that the 'sole end and purpose of all production' is consumption, defined as 'the process in which goods and services are bought and used to satisfy people's needs'.[28] Satisfying the needs of football supporters, however, has been irrational. The fans themselves may be football's consumers but it is difficult to define what is supply, demand or product. If, for example, someone bought a household appliance it would be replaced as soon as it stopped working rather than being kept for sentimental reasons. As a commodity, football does not conform to the forces of economic logic. For instance, the game needs competition or it would cease to exist. By comparison, in strict capitalist terms monopolization of the market is the aim.

Supporters themselves have 'consumed' the game in various ways. Some may have attended games because they saw football as a form of entertainment. Most fans, though, in the pre-television age, when local ties were stronger, traditionally identified themselves with the nearest team, usually staying with it for life. It has been said, and with more than a grain of truth, that the average male football fan will change his wife more often than his football team. Despite this captive audience, attendances have always fluctuated as supporters have never been a constant homogenous body. For example, before the 1990s and the advent of all-seater stadiums, one crucial element that dictated attendances was the weather. A cold, wet winter's day held little appeal, especially if it meant standing on the open terraces that were a common feature of the majority of grounds. Moreover, many supporters have drifted in and out of supporting their club in terms of actually going to games. A club's latent support, for example, could be stirred by a winning run in the FA Cup. Others perhaps would only go to certain games, such as those over the Christmas period, a local 'derby' or when the local team was playing against one of the big clubs. Most clubs have a hardcore of supporters who will attend almost every game. Fans will continue to support their team even if it has not been successful. Many fans are obsessives, something which the opening line in *Fever Pitch* illustrates: 'It's in there all the time, looking for a way out.' In terms of the nature of consumption this is irrational.

Post-war crowds became more heterogeneous, but only gradually, and there was little football on television to divert attention away from the local team. Only through the increasing exposure of the game through television, especially during the 1990s, has the nature of football's consumption diversified. Supporters can support whoever they want through television and other media or just by buying a team's replica shirt, although this usually applies only to the big clubs who now dominate the television screens. Because of changes in society, the twenty-first-century football supporter is probably less tolerant of failure than his or her counterpart fifty years ago. As a result, fans want success quickly. They are not interested in the bigger picture: it is the short term that counts.

Success has traditionally been the main attraction, although it has been relative to supporters throughout the game's history and dependent on the circumstances of the period. Moreover, some clubs from major conurbations have been inherently bigger and more ambitious than others due to the size of their potential spectator base. Thus, not only could the success achieved by a manager at one club be something entirely different to the success achieved by another at a different club but success has meant something different at different periods throughout the game's history. During the inter-war period, for example, Arsenal's ambition under Herbert Chapman was to win trophies. Other clubs, however, aspired to more modest targets. Lower division clubs, for example, had their ambitions stymied by the Football League's promotion and relegation system for a large part of this period. Despite the expansion of the Football League in the 1920s, promotion from the third divisions, north and south, was restricted to only one team per division.[29] A 'closed shop' emerged as there was little mobility within the league structure. Third division clubs, therefore, were forced into setting different targets. With promotion for the majority difficult to attain, financial stability became perhaps a more realistic aim – something that was aided by the League's rules on players' wages and mobility.

Yet there was still some pressure to succeed, and lower division managers continued to lose their jobs. One who kept his was Bob Jack, manager of Plymouth Argyle from 1910 to 1938. 'Argyle' were a founder member of the third division south in 1920, after previously winning the Southern League in 1913. Amazingly, in six consecutive seasons between 1922 and 1927 they finished second. Pressure mounted from the fans who believed it was a deliberate policy on the part of the board who did not want promotion.[30] Despite this 'failure', however, Jack continued as manager. In 1930, Plymouth finally won promotion, and maintained their second division status until 1938. Another manager who gave long service was Sam Allen at Swindon Town. Between 1902 and 1933, he was secretary-manager, when Swindon, who joined the Football League in 1920, were mainly a middling third division south team. From the perspective of their modern counterparts, it is difficult to believe that Allen or Jack kept their jobs for as long as they did. It highlights the different context in which football management operated, and how pressures, if not absent, were not as great as they are now. Not only did the Football League's policies cushion any inequalities but the media spotlight on the game was not as intensive. Directors, therefore, probably felt less pressure to take some action when results were poor. In later years, because of football's rising media profile, they believed that they ought to be seen to be doing something, and this invariably meant sacking the manager.

In the current era, for example, the motivations of a football club are influenced more by financial realities, especially the income Premier League clubs receive from television and commercial sponsorship. For example, every season since the 1990s, Manchester United has aimed to win the Premier League and usually the European Cup. During the same period, other Premier League clubs, however, have had different objectives and expectations. Newcastle's ambitions, for example, stretch towards qualification for European competition, whereas Portsmouth has been content just to stay in the Premier League. Most clubs in the Football League Championship aim for promotion to the Premier League. Crewe Alexandra, on the other hand, is a small club that has deliberately turned itself into something approaching a football nursery. By producing players and then selling them off to bigger clubs, Crewe have been able to achieve their more modest ambitions of maintaining their status and improving their ground. Furthermore, if they were to be relegated it would not be the financial disaster it would be for other league clubs. Because of Crewe's policy, the club's manager, Dario Gradi, is seen as integral to this long-term strategy and, as a result, he has been in the job since 1983. The example of Gradi highlights the different roles managers have to fulfil at different clubs. Gradi may have a skill for developing players and selling them on but perhaps his talents would not be suited to managing clubs such as Fulham or Aston Villa which have different objectives.

Thus, despite self-evident economic truths, like the importance of wage expenditure, football has generally operated outside this logic, and this is something that football managers have to contend with. Football fans are not really concerned with the fact that their club's performance is largely dictated by the amount they spend on wages. Only one team may be able to win the Premiership but supporters have adapted their expectations for their team and if this means, for example, a place in the Champions' League instead of one in the UEFA Cup or automatic promotion from League Two rather than a place in the play-offs, then supporters demand that their club fulfils these expectations. These 'demands' have been transmitted, via the terraces and the media, through to directors who then pass them on to the manager believing that he can make that difference. Of course, chairmen and directors have aspirations themselves no matter how unrealistic they might be, adding further pressure on the manager.

How has football management's development reflected the different aims of clubs? To a certain extent, the manager's role has been shaped by the changing nature of football's consumption. Initially, in the nineteenth century, management duties were carried out by a board of directors, and secretaries, the fore-runners of managers, were only administrative figures. Their powers gradually increased, however, and they gained some responsibilities for the players. Because of the game's increasing competition, the need for a scapegoat when results declined and the fact that directors needed to run their own businesses, secretaries or secretary-managers became more prominent. However, the development of their role was a gradual and uneven process as directors continued to take an active part in team matters. There were exceptions like Chapman as well as Buckley and Seed who enjoyed greater autonomy, but even by the 1950s only a few more managers, like Busby and Cullis, had similar powers. The management culture that emerged from this process has had long-term implications for the manager's role.

Football management has never carried with it a job description. Until 2003, no formal qualifications were required and the range of a manager's duties varied from club to club. This has highlighted British *laissez-faire* attitudes towards football management compared to those on the continent. In Britain, there has been a strong anti-coaching tradition throughout the game, and, unlike some European countries which have invoked a licensing policy, this has allowed clubs to choose anyone they like as manager.

The effects of the traditional relationship between a manager of an English football club and his directors can be seen when placed within Chandler's model of managerial capitalism. This model entails a complete divorce between control and ownership and allows for all forms of management to be undertaken by professionals.[31] There seems little difference between football's management hierarchy and that of American baseball's three-tiered structure for example. The division between ownership and control, however, is wider in baseball and therefore there has been more scope for professional management to undertake particular managerial tasks. In England, on the other hand, the potential for directorial interference is greater because the organizational structure of football clubs has caused power to be concentrated in the hands of directors.

Nevertheless, the 1960s marked a gradual change from the amateur tradition of management to a more professional approach. After the abolition of the maximum wage, there was an intensification in commercialism and competition. Despite the persistence of directorial interference, most directors probably felt that, after 1961, the direction of the team was best left to an expert. As a result, the manager's role gradually became more specialized. Because of football's organizational culture, it meant that managers themselves had greater potential to increase their influence within clubs through mini power struggles. This situation reached its peak in the 1970s and 1980s when managers were relatively powerful and ran most aspects of a club. During the 1990s, however, because of the new business ethos, this process seemed to reverse. It was recognized that experts were required in dealing with financial matters. Clubs began to employ chief executives, indicating a further reduction in the manager's powers, yet a greater clarification of his role. Importantly, with the exponential rise in transfer fees, players have come to be regarded as valuable assets and clubs now employ specialist coaches to cater for their personal and professional welfare. The specialization of coaching has long been a development in American sports. In American football, for example, in line with that game's shift towards specialist defence and offence teams, clubs have teams of coaches who are the ultimate responsibility of the head coach.

The position of a football manager, though, has involved more than merely being responsible for the team's results. In conjunction with developments in the media and changes in their role, managers have become emblematic figures for their clubs. Managers have traditionally been a reporter's link with a football club and a team's performance was increasingly reported through the actions of its manager. From the time of William Sudell and Tom Watson, a kind of footballing *ménage à trois* emerged between managers, the press and the fans; each one needed the other. To feed the rising interest in the game, newspapers required quotable comments and it was the manager who increasingly provided the copy. With fiercer competition, the media spotlight on the game increased. Directors, unwilling to take responsibility for poor runs, increasingly replaced their managers. At the same time, a fan's perception of a manager's powers increased through this heightened media interest. Whether real or imaginary, the stature of the manager was raised. It was Herbert Chapman who was the first to command such status and, after the war, this process developed further with Matt Busby. Following the Munich air disaster, and with the growth of television, Busby's stature became almost iconic. Since the mass ownership of television sets by 1970, the repeated media appearances of managers have not only turned them into the public face of their clubs, but also personalities in their own right. Through his witticisms, Bill Shankly was probably the first to build up his reputation in this manner. In a sense, a manager's role has also involved 'selling the club', necessitating good 'media skills'. In an age of media presentation, image has become ever more significant.

Occasionally, image can be deemed more important than results. During his tenure as manager of Scotland, Craig Brown was criticized for a lack of charisma by certain sections of the media. Instead, it was suggested that Scottish fans would have preferred a figure like Ally McLeod who was not averse to making extravagant claims. In 1978, when McLeod was the manager, he said that Scotland would win the World Cup. In contrast, Brown was much more conservative and pragmatic, but his record of achievement as Scotland manager was superior to McLeod's. Yet the criticism of Brown highlights an aspect of a manager's wider role, that of some kind of dream-maker, who 'gives hope' to fans. It was a function that McLeod, with his bold statements, was able to fulfil, even if they fell short of reality.[32] However, the extent to which being 'media-friendly' is important in improving team performance is not only problematic but difficult to quantify and perhaps inconsequential. Yet media skills are qualities that directors now look for in managers.

Overall, managers have come under much greater pressure from directors, as a consequence of the game's changing competitive nature and commercialization as well as the growing media spotlight. This was illustrated by an increase in the rate of managerial turnover during the twentieth century. Managerial terminations have usually been sparked by a recent run of poor form, although turnover has tended to be more rapid in the lower divisions despite the higher levels of interest in the top division. It has become a self-fulfilling prophecy within football that if you change the manager, your results will improve in the short term. Managers' image in the media has built up a mystique that they can quickly change things round, that a new manager will give the players and fans a 'lift'. However, the reality of a manager's impact does not always match the perception. Audas *et al.*, for example, have concluded that appointing a new manager does not tend to produce any short-term benefit. Teams tend to recover from a poor run of results more quickly by not changing their manager.[33]

A manager's length of tenure is usually a guide to his effectiveness. In theory, not only should effectiveness be based on how a manager has managed the particular resources at his disposal, but it should also be remembered that other managers are trying to do the same with their team. Sporting competition dictates that if one party is trying to win, another is trying to stop it. By what means then have managers been able to gain an edge over their rivals and improve a team's performance? In 'business speak', football clubs can be described as knowledge-based organizations where most of the value is generated by talent rather than capital equipment. The prima facie skills for football management are little different from those in other industries. Tom Cannon, a professor of business management, has stated that, 'Competition for talent is a battleground for all types of organizations. Leaders are judged by their ability to spot and get the best from talent.'[34] The modern-day football manager needs three basic qualities: an ability to judge a player, tactical acumen and motivational skills. Yet the extent to which managers have employed these skills has been dependent on the prevailing environment.

Managers have often said how powerless and helpless they feel once players 'cross the line' and the game starts. Good judgement of a player, therefore, is a manager's most important attribute as it is essentially players who win or lose matches; other management skills are secondary by comparison. Paradoxically, some clubs have been transformed due to the talents of certain players, making them more indispensable than the manager. Players like Derby's Steve Bloomer and Dixie Dean at Everton were deemed irreplaceable. Similarly, Tom Finney and Stanley Matthews were crucial to their clubs. Before the 1960s, however, it had been easier for football clubs to prevent players moving, due to the game's labour regulations. More recently, Diego Maradona, in addition to inspiring Argentina to victory in the 1986 World Cup, was also the force behind Napoli twice winning Serie A in 1987 and 1990, while in the 1990s Alan Shearer was the fulcrum of the Blackburn Rovers team that won the 1995 Premiership.

William Sudell and Tom Watson were the first two managers to reap the benefit of a good judgement of players. By obtaining players from Scotland and paying them substantial wages they established Preston North End and Sunderland, respectively, as the leading sides of the late 1880s and early 1890s. Where to look for the best players was soon apparent to other clubs and they also trod the path to Scotland, thus negating the advantage of Preston and Sunderland. The Football League's equalization measures, however, soon took effect and restrictions on player mobility and their earning potential made competition more even.

In the 1930s, however, Arsenal's managers were provided with the funds to back their judgement on players. First, Herbert Chapman spent record sums on players like David Jack and Alex James. In 1938, George Allison paid a world record fee of £14,000 for Bryn Jones of Wolverhampton Wanderers. Yet, because of its achievements, the club still made large profits. Wealth, however, was not a guarantee of success; it was the management of resources that was the crucial factor. Arsenal's policy of 'speculate to accumulate' compared favourably with the performance of some of London's other relatively prosperous clubs at the time. Tottenham Hotspur, for example, was thought to be as wealthy as Arsenal. It had assets worth £80,000 but the Spurs directors ran a very tight ship. They were unwilling to pay the same transfer fees as their North London rivals and, consequently, the club made a profit on transfers nearly every year during the inter-war period. Moreover, wage levels were only a third of the club's income. But in 1935, Spurs were relegated to the second division and its manager, Percy Smith, resigned, claiming that, because he had been unable to emulate Arsenal's success, he, instead of the directors, had been made the scapegoat.[35] West Ham's board was similarly parsimonious. It imposed strict financial constraints on its managers and for much of that period West Ham was a second division team.[36] Chelsea, on the other hand, as one of the best-supported teams in the Football League during the inter-war period, was much more ambitious. Unlike Spurs, the wages of Chelsea's players swallowed up over half of its income. Chelsea wanted to emulate Arsenal and in 1930 they paid Newcastle £10,000 for the Scottish centre-forward, Hughie Gallacher. Later, in 1933, they lured former Arsenal manager, Leslie Knighton, away from Birmingham City. Success was elusive, however, and Chelsea averaged only thirteenth place during the fifteen seasons they spent in the first division between the wars.[37]

It was not just a matter of managers selecting good players, however. Players needed to blend in with their teammates, and also fit into the manager's overall tactical plan. During the 1970s and 1980s Liverpool became the most successful club in the history of English football, dominating like no other before or since. In nineteen seasons between 1973 and 1991, they won the Championship eleven times and were runners-up on seven other occasions. In comparison, during this period Manchester United generated more income yet enjoyed little success. The managerial continuity of Liverpool was a major factor in the club's success but it was still dependent on the judgement of each manager. Consecutive managers at Anfield – Bill Shankly, Bob Paisley, Joe Fagan and Kenny Dalglish – displayed a proficiency in buying not only quality players but also ones who blended into Liverpool's style of play. Shankly had expounded the virtues of pass, control and move, and it was these tactics that, from the 1960s through until the 1990s, maintained a continuity on the pitch. And as a player retired or was transferred, his replacement appeared to make a seamless transition into his position. Perhaps Liverpool's most significant transfer was buying Kenny Dalglish from Celtic for a British record of £440,000 to replace Hamburg-bound Kevin Keegan in 1977. Other significant purchases included Ian Rush, Graeme Souness, John Barnes and Peter Beardsley.

Initially, it had been the players who devised team tactics but gradually managers took it upon themselves to make tactics their responsibility. Sudell had realized the importance of preparing for the opposition but other managers did not follow his early example. Herbert Chapman instead established the trend for pre-match team talks. It was through these that Arsenal devised the W/M formation to counter the change in the offside law in 1925. By gaining control over team matters, more managers began to impose their own tactical ideas on the players. In England this produced a variety of styles. At Wolves, for example, Buckley and Cullis favoured a direct style, a tradition later carried on by managers like Graham Taylor and Dave Bassett. Spurs, stemming from the 'push and run' days of Arthur Rowe's teams in the 1950s, had a style of football that was more pleasing on the eye. During the 1990s, though, this changed through managers who themselves favoured the direct style. Ironically one was former Arsenal boss George Graham. Under him the Highbury club had a dour reputation, something that was transformed by Arsene Wenger.

At international level, tactics are more important because coaches spend less time with the players and the pool of players they can select from is restricted by nationality. In 1966, England won the World Cup with the so-called 'Wingless Wonders', while in 1974 Holland played 'Total Football'. Greece's success in Euro 2004 owed much to their coach, Otto Rehhagel. In addition to creating an excellent team ethic, Greece's tactics focused on neutralizing more technically gifted opponents through man-marking and harrying them. They then looked to score on the break.[38]

Because of football's laws, however, a manager's ability to directly influence games has been limited, especially when contrasted with other sports. In basketball and American football, time-outs are available to coaches to devise plays in response to game situations. But the nature of association football poses different challenges for managers. For example, a game is played over two largely continuous forty-five-minute periods. Although the planning of taking and defending free-kicks and other set-pieces has become more sophisticated, a football match offers few opportunities to put them into practice. Instead, football is not only played mainly 'off the cuff', it is a 360-degree game where players frequently change positions. Furthermore, the game has steadily moved away from relatively static formations as the game's pace has increased. Footballers need to display all-round skills such as tackling, passing, heading, shooting. By contrast, a game of baseball is, in theory, timeless and revolves around the pitcher–hitter confrontation. As a stop–start game, it lends itself to frequent opportunities for coaching, if not by the manager then by other specialist coaches. Football managers need to juggle many variables, and usually in a short space of time, before making quick decisions.

Football managers have also had their sphere of influence curtailed in other ways. It was not until 1965–6, for example, that substitutes were first used in the Football League. There was a feeling amongst the rulers of English football that substitutions were somehow underhand and would be open to abuse. It was also felt that they would increase the use of tactics in the English game, just as they had done in Europe, something that was sneered at by English officials and players alike.[39] By contrast, American sports feature a constant turnover of players during games, reflecting their move towards specialization.

In soccer, coaching from the touchline was initially banned as it was regarded as a form of cheating, highlighting the conflict between football's amateur tradition and its burgeoning professionalism. In 1939, a law was introduced that stated, 'While the game is in progress . . . trainers or club officials must not coach players along the boundary lines.'[40] In 1955, Stan Cullis was asked by the referee to refrain from coaching during a game Wolverhampton Wanderers played at Grimsby Town. Cullis later said that it was essential for him to be able to shout instructions to a player during the game. He also claimed that most managers or trainers did the same, and, in exasperation, he asked, 'How else could they [managers] affect team positional changes if necessary?'[41]

It now seems to many fans that making tactical changes is the litmus test of a manager's competence. Since the 1960s, the importance of tactics or making changes to find that extra edge has increased as competition on the field has intensified. Defences have become better organized and, with the improvement in players' fitness, there is less space on the field. This has reduced the margins of victory thus making the need to find that extra advantage even more crucial. In addition to pre-match plans, such as detailing someone to man-mark a particular opponent, managers can now give tactical instructions or make changes, and substitutions, throughout the game. Sometimes, if the game is going well, the most prescient thing for a manager to do is do nothing and leave the side unchanged. Not only can managers make substitutions that have a positive impact but also ones that have a negative effect. In the 1970 World Cup quarter-final between England and West Germany, Alf Ramsey brought off Bobby Charlton twenty minutes from the end with England leading 2–1. Charlton had struggled with the heat but his departure freed Franz Beckenbauer who had been marking Charlton. The Germans came back to equalize and then win in extra time. Yet how culpable was Ramsey? England had been winning 2–0 and it could be argued that the team then became guilty of arrogance by dropping off into defence instead of going for a third goal. In contrast to Ramsey, Alex Ferguson enjoyed much greater fortune in the 1999 European Cup final. After trailing 1–0 and being outplayed by Bayern Munich for most of the game, Ferguson sent on two substitutes, Teddy Sheringham and Ole Gunnar Solskjaer, who both scored in injury time. To what extent making tactical decisions or substitutions is an art or a science is difficult to fathom, and how often substitutions like Ferguson's in 1999 actually work is unknown; instead, it perhaps owes more to luck than anything else.

Nevertheless, the figure of the manager shouting out instructions to players has now become a common sight at football grounds. A recent development has been the introduction of technical areas: a rectangle which now allows managers to pass on instructions without recrimination. In Euro 2004, Portugal coach Luiz Felipe Scolari passed on tactical changes to his players during breaks within games using a miniature board.[42] What input the manager can have, though, during the hurly-burly of a game, is again difficult to judge. The image of the manager coaching from the touchline, however, does put his role more firmly into focus regarding the crowd. It is something that opposing spectators do not like as it suggests that the other manager is all-powerful.

Players also need motivating and the personality of the manager is a key factor in managerial success. Team spirit is an important factor and without it teams can struggle. But how managers have achieved this has changed over the period. Initially, secretary-managers tried to keep their distance from the players. They were working-class whereas managers had middle-class aspirations and did not want to be associated with them. Apart from Chapman, most managers did not begin to develop closer relations with players until the 1950s. Later, successful managers, like Busby, Shankly and Cullis, gained reputations as leaders of men. They were charismatic personalities who had the capacity to dominate players. This authoritarian style has been a common trait amongst managers since. Cullis, along with Brian Clough, and latterly Alex Ferguson, gained a reputation for terrifying players. Many other managers have copied this style but have not been as successful. This may suggest that there were other ingredients that contributed to Cullis *et al.*'s accomplishments, or perhaps they were just better at terrifying players into playing well.

As a result of a decline in deference within society as well as the growing power of players, managers have adjusted their style. In the 1960s and 1970s, Don Revie built up a strong loyalty and team spirit within his Leeds team. He inherited a mostly young group of players, making it easier to impose his particular ideas. He gained an intense loyalty from them, and saw Leeds as a family club with him as its father figure. Revie placed great importance on the welfare of the players and their families, although in return they had to accept his strict code of discipline. More recently, managers like Wenger have relied less on dominating players and have given them more responsibility for their own actions. However, the aim has still been to develop a close bond between manager and players. Furthermore, the manager still requires the ability to get his message across, something made more problematic with the influx of foreign players and managers.

Perhaps the most successful example of the benefits of a strong team spirit was the club formerly known as Wimbledon FC. They did not measure success by trophies, although they did win the FA Cup in 1988, but by survival in the Premier League, due to the paucity of their resources. Wimbledon did not even enter the Football League until 1978 but had been promoted to the first division by 1986 and it was 2000 before they were relegated. They were consistently its worst supported team but always over-performed.[43] Wimbledon's success was based around its 'Crazy Gang' spirit, which was cultivated by its managers, first Dave Bassett, then Bobby Gould and Joe Kinnear. They tried to drum up a siege mentality amongst the players by, for example, frequently complaining about how they had been criticized in the press for their style of play. It helped to create an identity for the club, its fans and amongst the players, and maintaining this was crucial. This identity also complemented Wimbledon's direct, high-octane, pressing game that aimed to force teams into mistakes by creating pressure. It was very physical, earning them a reputation for roughness, which was embodied by players such as Vinnie Jones and John Fashanu. Egil Olsen was appointed manager in 1999 but seemed to be unaware of the club's unique characteristics. He tried to change the team's pattern which was at the heart of the club's identity. He was sacked just before the club's relegation in 2000, which precipitated a rapid decline. In 2003, Wimbledon left London for Buckinghamshire, transforming itself into the Milton Keynes Dons.

In addition to motivating players generally, managers also need to inspire their troops during the heat of battle. Before games, in an effort to relax them, Bill Shankly would tell tales to the Liverpool players of how the opposition already looked intimidated and beaten. Stan Cullis on the other hand would offer a few words of advice to his players before a game. Half-time histrionics are partly displays of temper but also to do with performance as managers try to inspire their players to greater efforts during the second half. The extent to which managers continue this ritual has diminished. With players becoming more assertive, just shouting at them can be counter-productive. During the half-time break in a Republic of Ireland international, Jack Charlton was berating his players one by one when Andy Townsend interrupted him by saying, 'This is not helping.' Charlton agreed. What the players expected was some constructive advice. Even Alex Ferguson is not all volcanic temper. In trying to inspire his players during half-time in the European Cup final he asked them what it would feel like to get so close to the trophy but not be able to touch it if they lost. Although their eventual victory owed more to luck, perhaps these words contributed in some small way to the United players' perseverance on the night. Alf Ramsey's famous line to the England players at the end of ninety minutes in the 1966 World Cup final has entered the game's folklore.

After conceding a late equalizer, he said, 'We've won the World Cup once, now go out and do it again.' However, to what extent these words made a difference is difficult to gauge. As Geoff Hurst said, 'He didn't need to lift us, he'd done his job by picking the right team.'[44]

Perhaps the main requirement of a manager, however – something which has already been alluded to – is luck. The fate of a manager is subject to many variables, mostly things over which he has little or no control. Luck can take a number of forms and in football the nature of the game can determine this. Games of football are generally low scoring which usually maintains an uncertainty throughout the contest. One team, therefore, can dominate the game in terms of possession without scoring and then concede a late goal. Furthermore, there are a variety of ways to score a goal, including own goals from lucky deflections that cannot be planned for. The referee can also influence a game's outcome by mistakenly awarding a penalty kick against a team. Of course, over a season luck should balance itself out but sometimes it may not and a team's bad luck may persist for longer. For instance, a club may be afflicted by a bad run of injuries, which unsettles the formation and morale of the team. Managers can also benefit from good fortune. For instance, it can be argued that Busby and Revie were fortunate to inherit a group of outstanding players when they first became managers at their respective clubs. Similarly, Ferguson was lucky that the youth team of the early 1990s comprised a number of players who would form the core of the side over that decade. Of course they needed developing but neither United, nor any other club, has produced such an outstanding crop of young players since.

There is no real secret formula to football management, and managers themselves don't really know how they have succeeded, because if they did they would keep on doing it. However, football managers, it can be concluded, can make a difference. Their contribution, though, needs to be assessed in various contexts, and the evidence used by Szymanski and Kuypers, for example, is only part of the equation for making this judgement. In recent years the manager's job has become more narrowly defined. But even so the culture of British football management means that there are still differences from club to club regarding a manager's job specification. In this sense, making an accurate quantitative judgement on a manager's contribution is difficult, and demonstrates a need for detailed case studies. In addition to examining managerial efficiency on a long-term basis, account must be taken of the short term. It is fans' short-term expectations that have largely determined the game as a product, something the projection of long-term economic forecasts cannot begin to explain. Questions about managerial efficiency are contingent on a definition of 'efficiency'. Yet managers have made an impact, and it has been all the more evident because football clubs, instead of resembling monolithic corporations, are really small organizations. And as such, the human factor becomes more important. The potential of an individual to influence outcomes is much greater but this potential is often constrained by football's management culture which, through the interference of directors, inhibits the role of the manager. Yet the perception of the manager as a powerful figure has continued to grow, and his success, or failure, has become increasingly public. Whatever their impact, directors, players and fans alike have deemed that managers matter.

Conclusion

It is the 2004–5 League Cup final and Chelsea have just scored a late equalizer against Liverpool. Soon after, the Chelsea manager, Jose Mourinho, is shown on the television putting his finger to his lips in a provocative shushing motion, allegedly aimed at the Liverpool supporters. He is then sent off for inciting the opposition fans. Much of the television coverage was then taken up with discussing where Mourinho was watching the rest of the match.

We began this book by asking, do we really need football managers? On this particular evidence, the answer would seem to be yes. The interest that Mourinho has aroused not only highlights the hyperbole that surrounds managers, it shows how they are part of the 'match' because it is perceived that they can make a difference. It is because of this perception that the history of football managers can give a number of insights into socio-economic and cultural changes in British life.

Since the Second World War, football has overtaken cricket as the national game of the English. Where previously cricket was the sport of the great and the good, football has now taken that position. One of the main agents in this process has been the media. In particular, the growth of television has both reflected and contributed to this change. And as the coverage of the game on the screen has expanded, so the profile of the manager has been given greater prominence. The popularity of football has also echoed social change more generally. A decline in deference has produced a brasher, more individualistic society, and whereas cricket represented the old class system, football had the mass appeal more in keeping with a consumerist age. Football managers have come to be seen as one of the symbols of these changes.

As we have seen, the relationship between managers and the press had become closer during the early part of the twentieth century, and had helped to embellish the status of the manager. But it is television that has turned him into an emblematic figure. Media interest has created a cult of personality around managers where the ability to deliver sharp one-liners, give 'good interviews' and play 'verbal tennis' with journalists is seen as at least as important as their tactical acumen. These media performances have not only provided something for fans to talk about but have also reinforced the notion of the manager as a powerful figure – something that has become deeply rooted within football's discourse. Moreover, because football has been largely a male business, it is male working-class fans who identify most with managers and their charismatic personalities.

How football managers have been portrayed has not been dissimilar to the representation of other public figures and celebrities. In politics, Tony Blair has been criticized for not working within his cabinet and for being too presidential. It is not clear how far this is a media invention, a tabloidization of both newspapers and television, but it does seem part of a 'dumbing down' process, through a need to fill a growing space with instantaneous news and gossip focused on personalities. It is a process which makes it easier for the general public to relate to the story but at the same time it distorts the bigger picture. Football managers have been treated in a similar manner, usually credited with any success but made scapegoats for any failure of their team.

The evolution of the football manager's role highlights how important management has become as both the economy and society have grown more complex. With the decline of Britain's industrial and manufacturing base, there has been a corresponding expansion of the service sector. As a result, the skills needed by the workforce have changed, with a greater stress placed on human capital, as Britain moves towards a knowledge-based economy. One result has been that the number of people graduating from university has risen dramatically since the 1980s.

In this respect, Mourinho symbolizes the professionalization of football management and its increasing division of labour. Rather than 'manager', he has the job title of 'head coach', underlining how the post has become more specialized. With the financial management of the club placed in the hands of a chief executive, Mourinho's main responsibility lies in the preparation of the first team and he is himself supported by a multitude of specialists in other areas.

Since the nineteenth century, the job of the football manager has become more narrowly defined and professionalized. This has not been a linear process but a rather slow and uneven one, dependent not only on the changing contemporary context but also on the management culture of individual clubs. Other external factors have framed these changes. The maximum wage and retain and transfer system, for example, maintained a kind of equality amongst clubs. Long-running tensions in the governance of the game between its amateur sector and emerging professionalism also created a resistance to wider managerial developments as there were no payments for directors and only limited share dividends. Overall, though, an intensity of competition, the growing commercialization of football and the accompanying media interest have been the driving factors behind the evolution of the manager's job.

Yet to talk of football management in terms of 'professionalization' is also a contradiction. Unlike law or medicine, you did not require qualifications to become a football manager, something that echoed a long tradition of British management. Like parenting (and until the 1990s, university lecturers), football managers learned by doing the job, rather than through any formal training or academic study. Experience of the game was thought to be the best form of preparation.

That Mourinho is from Portugal demonstrates how the training of British football managers has lagged behind the preparation received by their counterparts abroad. In responding to football's changing climate, in particular the commercialization of the 1990s, football clubs have widened their search for the best available managers. At some clubs, it has been felt that British candidates have lacked the necessary management skills. This is not to say that Britain can't produce quality managers. Instead, the system from which they have been created has been inefficient. It is noticeable that despite the influx of foreign managers, there have been few managerial exports abroad.

Arguments over the quality of management can be extended to the coaching culture within English football and its impact on the development of young players. The question of who coaches young players is an important one for the future of the game. As we have seen, coaches have largely been former players who, even if qualified, do not have much of an educational background themselves. English football has nurtured a coaching culture that has largely stymied the progress of young footballers with its mistrust of intelligence and its commitment to the macho attitudes of 'getting stuck in'. Many managers and other figures in the game have pointed to the lack of 'natural talent' coming through as the main reason behind the falling standards of British footballers. It has been suggested that one reason for this decline is the disappearance of street football.[1] This seems a fatuous and romanticized notion, mainly because even when street football was feasible and popular, England teams still underperformed. Questions instead need to be asked about why playing and coaching standards in Europe and other foreign countries have risen and there has not been a similar improvement in Britain.

France had cited the same problem of a lack of street football as being responsible for a decline in its fortunes. Unlike England, once identified, the French Football Federation established a scheme for selecting and educating talented young players who were then based at a chateau in Clairefontaine.[2] The apparent failure to raise standards in England has been supplemented by a historical resistance within the professional game itself that, perhaps partly due to the mainly working-class background of its players and managers, has displayed anti-intellectual tendencies together with a prejudice against the skilful player and a reluctance to practise improving technique and skills.

British insularity has meant that the tradition of managers learning on the job has had significant consequences for how they have managed footballers and the development of young players, something which has mirrored the attitudes to and methods of handling groups of young working-class men. Football managers have imposed their authority over players in a manner not dissimilar to that of early male role models like fathers and teachers and adult ones such as foremen and army NCOs. Former England cricket captain Mike Brearley stated that part of his job's make-up was epitomized by 'the image of a traditional Sergeant-Major' where at 'some point, consultation, delicacy of feeling, weighing-up of pros and cons need to give way to orders, bluntness, decisiveness'.[3]

Initially, football club directors, as well as picking the team, dealt with the players over disciplinary matters, leaving the trainer to keep an eye on them on a day-to-day basis, with the secretary looking after administrative matters. As more secretary-managers and managers were appointed, they became more responsible for the players' supervision and welfare but kept their distance from them and identified more with the directors. It was Herbert Chapman, long before any others, who realized that a closer relationship between manager and players could be beneficial, although he was still a disciplinarian. After 1945 the decline in deference helped to foster closer relations between the manager and his players. Because of their lack of training, however, ideas for handling footballers owed much to their own experience (many had been in the armed forces) and were grafted on to a quasi-military model. It has been a culture that has perpetuated itself, and been passed down through the generations as players who have gone on to become managers have known little else about the job save what they experienced as a player.

Football management has typified the division of workplace relations along class and hierarchical lines, a legacy of its Victorian origins. Yet changes have taken place, noticeably that of a closer relationship between management and players as the job of the manager evolved. Despite this, the relationship has remained an essentially authoritarian one where managers demand obedience from players, and generally rely on traditional ideas of masculinity to enforce it.

Away from their job, football managers have also been examples of twentieth-century social mobility, moving up from working-class backgrounds to living middle-class lifestyles. Initially, as secretaries in the nineteenth century, they tried to distinguish themselves from the workers. Later, they were in competition with other middle-class income groups and wanted to be seen as professionals in their own right. By the late twentieth century, in line with Thatcherite ideals and celebrity culture, a manager judged his status by the size of his salary.

Moreover, football management's development has highlighted the increasingly meritocratic tendencies of British society. In all probability, football has been more meritocratic than other areas of the economy. With family firms traditionally dominating the British business scene, it meant that factors like patronage and nepotism were important in shaping the make-up of management. In football, because of its competitive element, being judged on a weekly basis and the visible nature of the industry, directors have usually looked for the best man available to do the job.

So what of the future for football management? How will the role of the manager change? Because of the game's present rampant commercialization, it is probable that in terms of the structure of a club's organization, the role of the manager will become increasingly specialized. In this respect, a football manager in England will be comparable to a head coach in European football clubs and American sports franchises, although it is likely that even this process will be subject to British traditions and peculiarities. Since the recruitment of new players may be left in the hands of a director of football, and with clubs employing expert coaches, a manager's actual tasks may be reduced to not much more than picking the team, co-ordinating the staff attached to the players and using his powers of motivation to inspire them. Managers of English clubs will probably be better trained and qualified as clubs will demand candidates with evidence of proven pedigree. How many will actually be English remains to be seen. With a more specialized role, clubs may feel that in an ever more frenetic search for the vital ingredient that makes for either success in Europe or survival in the Premier League, managers are more expendable.

Appendix

Monetary conversion table

Year	Equivalent of £1 at 2004 prices	Year	Equivalent of £1 at 2004 prices
1880	£57.53	1945	£25.71
1885	£66.13	1950	£20.81
1890	£68.19	1955	£16.56
1895	£73.79	1960	£15.00
1900	£67.57	1965	£12.66
1905	£66.62	1970	£9.97
1910	£64.24	1975	£5.16
1915	£50.57	1980	£2.74
1920	£25.12	1985	£1.99
1925	£38.06	1990	£1.47
1930	£43.55	1995	£1.25
1935	£45.97	2000	£1.09
1940	£27.71	2004	£1.00

Source: Adapted from R. Roberts, *Schroders: Merchants and Bankers*, Macmillan, 1992, Appendix V (i).

Notes

Introduction

Note: all works cited are published in London unless otherwise indicated.

1 T. Mason, *Association Football and English Society 1863–1915*, Brighton: Harvester, 1980; N. Fishwick, *English Football and Society 1910–50*, Manchester: Manchester University Press, 1989; D. Russell, *Football and the English*, Preston: Carneigie, 1997.
2 S. Wagg, *The Football World: A Contemporary Social History*, Brighton: Harvester, 1984, p. xi.
3 C. Korr, *West Ham United*, Duckworth, 1986; A.J. Arnold, *A Game That Would Pay: A Business History of Professional Football in Bradford*, Duckworth, 1988.
4 S. Szymanski and T. Kuypers, *Winners and Losers: The Business Strategy of Football*, Viking, 1999.
5 C. Green, *The Sack Race: The Story of Football's Gaffers*, Edinburgh: Mainstream, 2002.
6 M. Crick, *The Boss: The Many Sides of Alex Ferguson*, Simon and Schuster, 2002. Other notable works include: S. Studd, *Herbert Chapman: Football Emperor*, Souvenir, 1998 (a first edition was published in 1981); S.F. Kelly, *Bill Shankly, It's Much More Important Than That: A Biography*, Virgin, 1996; E. Dunphy, *A Strange Kind of Glory: Sir Matt Busby and Manchester United*, Heinemann, 1991; D. Bowler, *Shanks: The Authorised Biography of Bill Shankly*, Orion 1996, *'Winning Isn't Everything . . .': A Biography of Alf Ramsey*, Orion, 1998.
7 Charles Handy quoted in D. Aldcroft, 'The Missing Dimension: Management Education and Training in Postwar Britain', in D. Aldcroft and A. Slaven (eds) *Enterprise and Management: Essays in Honour of Peter Payne*, Ashgate, 1995, p. 107.
8 J. Walvin, *Football and the Decline of Britain*, Macmillan, 1986, p. 28.
9 Ibid., p. 27.
10 Defining what constitutes a small firm is difficult but the European Commission has defined a small business as one with 10–99 employees while medium-sized firms have 100–499 employees. More than 95 per cent of firms in the EU are classified as small. See D.J. Storey, *Understanding the Small Business Sector*, Routledge, 1994, pp. 5–49. Until the late 1990s, most football clubs had fewer than 100 employees, and it is only recently that some, in terms of number of employees, have become medium-sized enterprises.
11 D. Coleman, 'Gentleman and Players', *Economic History Review*, February 1973, vol. 26, pp. 92–116; D. Jeremy, *A Business History of Britain, 1900–1990s*, Oxford: Oxford University Press, pp. 382–6.

12 N. Tiratsoo, 'Management Education in Postwar Britain', in L. Engwall and V. Zamagni (eds) *Management Education in Historical Perspective*, Manchester: Manchester University Press, 1998, p. 124.

13 Anon., 'A Yankee Boss in England', *World's Work*, December 1902, vol. 1, 1, pp. 53–7.

14 See, for example, S. Keeble, *The Ability to Manage: A Study of British Management 1890–1990*, Manchester: Manchester University Press, 1992, and Aldcroft, 'The Missing Dimension'.

15 Sports grounds, for example, at the Aston Lower Grounds and Lillie Bridge, had also been built as commercial propositions.

16 Jack Hobbs had actually stepped in as captain when the amateur, A.W. Carr, was taken ill during the fourth test against Australia in 1926, mainly because there was no amateur to take over. D. Birley, *A Social History of English Cricket*, Aurum, 1999, p. 230.

17 F.M.L. Thompson, *The Rise of Respectable Society: A Social History of Victorian Britain, 1830–1900*, Fontana, 1988, p. 47. By 1873 the permanent staff on Britain's railway companies numbered 275,000. F. McKenna, 'Victorian Railway Workers', *History Workshop Journal*, Spring, 1976, no. 1, p. 26.

18 C. Steedman, *Policing the Victorian Community: The Formation of English Provincial Police Forces, 1856–80*, Routledge, 1984, pp. 1–63.

19 For a vivid description of nursing during the Second World War see Ian McEwan's novel *Atonement*, Vintage, 2002, pp. 269–315.

20 A. Parker, 'Chasing the "Big-Time": Football Apprenticeship in the 1990s', unpublished PhD thesis, University of Warwick, 1996, pp. 72–4.

21 M. Taylor, 'Work and Play: The Professional Footballer in England c.1900—c.1950', *The Sports Historian*, May 2002, vol. 22, 1, p. 31; E. Levy, 'The Manager as Surrogate Mother', in J. King and J. Kelly (eds) *The Cult of the Manager: Do They Really Make A Difference?* Virgin, 1997, p. 100.

22 A. Hopcraft, *The Football Man: People and Passions in Soccer*, Penguin, 1971, pp. 84–5.

23 Quoted in J. Holden, *Stan Cullis: The Iron Manager*, Derby: Breedon, 2000, pp. 78–9.

24 *London Review of Books*, 6 January 2000, p. 32.

25 P. Willis, 'Shop Floor Culture, Masculinity and the Wage Form', in J. Clarke and C. Critcher (eds) *Working Class Culture: Studies in History and Theory*, Hutchinson, 1979, p. 194.

26 R. Holt, *Sport and the British: A Modern History*, Oxford: Oxford University Press, 1989, p. 173.

27 T. Mason, 'Kick and Rush or Revolt into Style? Football Playing Among the English Professionals: From Great Power to Image of Decline', unpublished paper, 1998.

1 The origins of football management

1 C. Lee, 'The Service Industries', in R. Floud and D. McCloskey (eds) *The Economic History of Britain since 1700: Volume 2: 1860 to the 1970s*, 2nd edn, Cambridge: Cambridge University Press, 1981, p. 143.

2 W. Vamplew, *Pay Up and Play the Game: Professional Sport in Britain 1875–1914*, Cambridge: Cambridge University Press, 1988, pp. 52–68.

3 Mason, *Association Football*, pp. 2–3, 150; Russell, *Football*, p. 13; G. Williams, *The Code War*, Harefield: Yore, 1994, p. 50; Vamplew, *Pay Up*, table 6.2, pp. 63, 53.

4 R.J. Morris, 'Clubs, Societies and Associations', in F.M.L. Thompson (ed.) *The Cambridge Social History of Britain, 1750–1950*, vol. 3, Cambridge: Cambridge University Press, 1990, pp. 412–18.

5 See Holt, *Sport and the British*, ch. 2.

6   P.M. Young, *Bolton Wanderers*, Sportsman's Book Club, 1965, pp. 18–19; *Football on Merseyside*, Stanley Paul, 1963, pp. 13–15.
7   A. Appleton, *Hotbed of Soccer*, Sportsman's Book Club, 1961, p. 164.
8   Williams, *Code War*, p. 71.
9   Korr, *West Ham*, pp. 1–3.
10 J. Catton, *The Rise of the Leaguers*, Manchester, 1897, p. 105.
11 Mason, *Association Football*, pp. 30, 40.
12 J. Catton, *The Real Football*, Sands, 1900, pp. 123–6.
13 See I. Nannestad, 'The Early Days of Aston Villa', *Soccer History*, Winter 2004, 10, pp. 21–4.
14 Arsenal FC Archives, Catton Folders (hereafter referred to as 'Catton Folders'), A–B, p. 33.
15 *Birmingham Post*, 1 October 1941, p. 4.
16 Birmingham Central Library, LF25.1, George H. Osbourne Newscuttings, Notes on Aston Villa Football Club, 1874–1907 (a collection of cuttings from contemporary Birmingham newspapers, hereafter referred to as 'Osbourne Newscuttings'), pp. 56, 65.
17 *Aston Villa News and Record* (AVNR), 25–26 December 1907, vol. 2, 66, pp. 11–12; *All Sports Weekly*, 11 October 1924, p. 5.
18 *Birmingham Daily Post*, 8 October 1935, p. 16.
19 Osbourne Newscuttings, p. 170.
20 S. Inglis, *Villa Park: 100 Years*, Warley: Sports Projects, 1997, p. 15.
21 Catton, *Real Football*, p. 71.
22 *Birmingham Daily Post*, 21 December 1911, p. 10; S. Inglis, *League Football and the Men Who Made It*, Collins Willow, 1988, p. 4.
23 *Sports Argus*, 23 December 1911, p. 3.
24 *Birmingham Daily Mail*, 23 December 1911; 'William McGregor', *Dictionary of National Biography*.
25 E. Grayson, *Corinthians and Cricketers*, Sportsman's Book Club, 1957, p. 25.
26 *Preston Herald*, 24 March 1888, p. 5, 13 April 1895, p. 6. It should be stressed that differences between association football and rugby were less marked than they are today, with both games coming under the generic term 'football'. For a fuller discussion on how the two codes emerged see T. Collins, *Rugby's Great Split: Class, Culture and the Origins of Rugby League Football*, Frank Cass, 1998.
27 'Sir Richard Burbidge', *Dictionary of Business Biography: A Biographical Dictionary of Business Leaders Active in Britain in the Period 1860–1980*, ed. D. Jeremy, Butterworths, 1984–6, vol. 1, pp. 510–13.
28 T. Mason, 'Sport and Recreation', in P. Johnson (ed.) *Twentieth-Century Britain: Economic, Social and Cultural Change*, Longman, 1994, p. 115.
29 S. Rae, *W.G. Grace*, Faber and Faber, 1998, pp. 24, 46.
30 D.H. Martinez, *The Book of Baseball Literacy*, Penguin, 1996, pp. 139–40.
31 Young, *Bolton Wanderers*, p. 169.
32 In 1881, the rugby player Teddy Bartram of Wakefield Trinity was appointed assistant secretary of the club to cover the fact that he was paid for playing. Collins, *Rugby's Great Split*, pp. 49–50.
33 For all monetary conversions see Appendix.
34 Young, *Bolton Wanderers*, pp. 19–20.
35 Inglis, *Villa Park*, p. 15.
36 Osbourne Newscuttings, p. 178.
37 *Birmingham Gazette*, 16 June 1887; *Birmingham Daily Gazette*, 2 March 1891; *Birmingham Sporting Mail*, 23 December 1911, p. 1.
38 *Birmingham Daily Gazette*, 30 November 1894, p. 3.

39 A. Gibson and W. Pickford, *Association Football and the Men Who Made It*, vol. 2, Caxton, 1906, p. 54.
40 P. Morris, *Aston Villa: The History of a Great Football Club, 1874–1961*, Sportsman's Book Club, 1962, pp. 4, 7; A. Rippon, *The Aston Villa Story*, Derby: Breedon, 1993, pp. 8–9; S.W. Clives, *The Centenary Book of the Birmingham County Football Association, 1875–1974*, Birmingham County FA, 1974, p. 84; Birmingham City Archives, MS519/1, p. 288.
41 Osbourne Newscuttings, pp. 36, 48, 56; *Albion News*, 2 December 1922, p. 112.
42 Osbourne Newscuttings, pp. 68, 76, 85; *Birmingham Mail*, 6 December 1889.
43 Mason, *Association Football*, p. 69.
44 Williams, *Code War*, p. 93.
45 T. Mason, 'Football', in T. Mason (ed.) *Sport in Britain: A Social History*, Cambridge: Cambridge University Press, 1989, pp. 147–8.
46 *Glasgow Evening News and Star*, 22 January 1887, p. 4.
47 Ibid.
48 B. Butler, *The Football League 1888–1988*, Queen Anne Press, 1987, p. 11.
49 M. Taylor, '"Proud Preston": A History of the Football League 1900–1939', unpublished PhD thesis, De Montfort University, Leicester, 1997, p. 18.
50 Ibid., p. 62.
51 Ibid., p. 26. Professionalism in Scotland was not legalized until 1893, two years after the Scottish League had been established.
52 Bentley, 'Is Football a Business?', *World's Work*, September 1912, vol. 20, 118, p. 383.
53 Catton, *Real Football*, p. 128.
54 D. Tywdell, 'Ghosts of the League . . . No. 5 Bootle', *The Footballer*, January/February 1989, vol. 1, 5 pp. 12–13.
55 Appleton, *Hotbed of Soccer*, pp. 81–4.
56 Vamplew, *Pay Up*, table 8.1, p. 83; table 8.5, p. 94.
57 *Sports Argus*, 16 October 1909, p. 1.
58 Bentley, 'Is Football a Business?', p. 393.
59 *AVNR*, 1 September 1906, vol. 1, 1, p. 5.
60 *Sports Argus*, 16 October 1909, p. 1.
61 S. Tischler, *Footballers and Businessmen: The Origins of Professional Soccer in England*, Holmes and Meier, 1981, p. 61 n52.
62 Mason, *Association Football*, p. 97.
63 *Liverpool Review*, 27 August 1898, p. 9.
64 Mason, *Association Football*, p. 105. The Southern League did not recognize the contracts of players from the Football League until 1909. Players were then able to switch leagues without the fear of being penalized. Vamplew, *Pay Up*, p. 136.
65 The Football League set the £10 signing-on fee in 1891 and the amount was not changed until 1958. S. Inglis, *Soccer in the Dock*, Collins Willow, 1985, p. 11.
66 Taylor, 'Proud Preston', ch. 5.
67 Appleton, *Hotbed of Soccer*, p. 90.
68 Inglis, *Soccer*, pp. 10–18. The other clubs were Queen's Park Rangers, Sunderland, Glossop, Coventry City and Manchester United.
69 Mason, *Association Football*, p. 37.
70 A. Fabian and G. Green (eds) *Association Football*, vol. 3, Caxton, 1960, p. 242.
71 Bentley, 'Is Football a Business?', p. 384.
72 Young, *Football on Merseyside*, pp. 173–6.
73 *Sunderland Daily Echo*, 10 September 1898, p. 3.
74 Vamplew, *Pay Up*, table 6.4, p. 65.
75 *AVNR*, 8 August 1914, pp. 668–9.

76 T. Mason, 'The Blues and the Reds: A History of the Liverpool and Everton Football Clubs', *History Society of Lancashire and Cheshire*, 1985, p. 7.
77 G. Keeton, *The Football Revolution*, Newton Abbot: David and Charles, 1972, p. 52.
78 Mason, *Association Football*, pp. 46, 56 n108, 162; Vamplew, *Pay Up*, pp. 13, 86.
79 Vamplew, *Pay Up*, p. 159, table 10.2, p. 160.
80 D. Kennedy, 'The Split of Everton Football Club, 1892: The Creation of Distinct Patterns of Boardroom Formation at Everton and Liverpool Football Club Companies', *Sport in History*, Summer 2003, vol. 23, 1, p. 24 n103.
81 Mason, *Association Football*, pp. 38, 41.
82 The Co-operative movement also had working-class shareholders.
83 Vamplew, *Pay Up*, pp. 166, 168, table 10.6, p. 160, table 10.2.
84 Tischler, *Footballers and Businessmen*, pp. 75–6.
85 T. Collins and W. Vamplew, 'The Pub, the Drinks Trade and the Early Years of Modern Football', *The Sports Historian*, May 2000, vol. 20, 1 pp. 1–17.
86 J. Harding, *Football Wizard: The Story of Billy Meredith*, Derby: Breedon, 1985, pp. 29, 34.
87 R. Lewis, 'The Development of Football in Lancashire, c.1860–1914', unpublished PhD thesis, University of Lancaster, 1994, p. 14.
88 Tischler, *Footballers and Businessmen* pp. 86, 70.
89 Mason, *Association Football*, pp. 38, 45.
90 R. Day, 'The Motivation of Some Football Club Directors: An Aspect of the Social History of Association Football 1890–1914', unpublished MA thesis, University of Warwick, 1976, pp. 69–80.
91 Arnold, *A Game That Would Pay*, pp. 23–49.
92 Middlesbrough FC Minutes, 23 April 1900.
93 Bentley, 'Is Football a Business?', p. 389.
94 Russell, *Football*, pp. 42–4.
95 Mason, *Association Football*, p. 49.
96 J. Wilson, *British Business History 1720–1994*, Manchester: Manchester University Press, 1995, p. 22.
97 Holt, *Sport and the British*, p. 166.
98 Korr, *West Ham*, pp. 27, 43.
99 See Bentley, 'Is Football a Business?', p. 390.
100 *Birmingham Daily Gazette*, 9 June 1887, p. 7.
101 Middlesbrough FC Minutes, 27 June 1899, 19 April 1900.
102 AVNR, 3 August 1907, p. 8. Fred Rinder attended all forty-one meetings. Other directors and the number of meetings they attended were Howard Toney, 40; John Devey, 39; P.W.M. Bate, 36; and Councillor Jack Jones, 40.
103 Middlesbrough FC Minutes, 1899, *passim*.
104 *Preston Herald*, 24 March 1888, p. 5.
105 *Football Field*, 23 January 1886, p. 4; H. Berry and G. Allman, *One Hundred Years at Deepdale: 1881–1981*, Preston: Preston North End FC, 1982, p. 72.
106 *Football Field*, 22 July 1893, p. 8.
107 *Birmingham Mail*, 27 December 1938, p. 7.
108 Taylor, 'Proud Preston', p. 49.
109 AVNR, 23 April 1913, pp. 545–7; 31 December 1938, pp. 221–2; 3 September 1910, p. 6; *Birmingham Mail*, 27 December 1938, p. 7.
110 Inglis, *Villa Park*, p. 24.
111 Mason, *Association Football*, p. 120.
112 *Birmingham Gazette*, 15 January 1940, p. 3.
113 P. Joyce, *Work, Society and Politics*, Brighton: Harvester, 1980, p. 1.

114 M. Savage, *The Dynamics of Working-Class Politics: The Labour Movement in Preston, 1880–1940*, Cambridge: Cambridge University Press, 1987, p. 103.
115 J.K. Walton, *Lancashire: A Social History, 1558–1939*, Manchester: Manchester University Press, 1987, pp. 221–30.
116 *Preston Herald*, 24 March 1888, p. 5; H. Cunningham, *The Volunteer Force*, Croom Helm, 1975, pp. 104, 119. In 1881 he was a lieutenant of the 522 strong 11th Lancashire Rifle Volunteers. By 1888 he was a captain of the 1st Vol. Battalion Loyal North Lancashire Regiment. *Preston Herald*, 9 November 1881, p. 5.
117 *Liverpool Daily Post*, 23 March 1936, p. 5.
118 Catton Folders, V–W, p. 1897.
119 *Preston Herald*, 24 March 1888, p. 5.
120 *Birmingham Daily Post*, 16 December 1905, p. 10.
121 Harding, *Football Wizard*, pp. 94, 29.
122 Appleton, *Hotbed of Soccer*, pp. 95–7.

2 The pioneers, 1880–1914

1 Bentley, 'Is Football a Business?', p. 383.
2 *AVNR*, 1 September 1906, p. 5.
3 Bentley, 'Is Football a Business?', p. 393.
4 *Birmingham Daily Gazette*, 21 June 1886, p. 2.
5 *Liverpool Football Echo*, 15 May 1915, p. 3.
6 *Ward's Directory of Newcastle, 1887–88*, p. 613. I am also grateful to Neal Garnham for information on Watson's background.
7 *Athletic News*, 10 May 1915; Tyne and Wear Archives Service, S/NFA/13.
8 *Newcastle Daily Journal*, 10 May 1886, p. 3.
9 Catton Folders, W. Correspondence between Watson and Catton.
10 *Newcastle Daily Journal*, 21 December 1887; *Newcastle Daily Chronicle*, 24 December 1887.
11 *Newcastle Daily Journal*, 7 May 1915, p. 11.
12 D. Turner and A. White, *The Book of Football Managers*, Derby: Breedon, 1993, pp. 74, 153, 198–9; J. Holland, *Spurs: A History of Tottenham Hotspur Football Club*, Phoenix, 1956, p. 70.
13 T. Campbell and P. Woods, *The Glory and the Dream: The History of Celtic FC 1887–1987*, Grafton, 1987, p. 54.
14 Turner and White, *Football Managers*, p. 73; *Liverpool Review*, 1 August 1896, p. 12.
15 Young, *Bolton Wanderers*, pp. 68–9.
16 J. Alexander, *McCrae's Battalion: The Story of the 16th Royal Scots*, Mainstream, 2003, pp. 62–3.
17 Catton Folders, B–C, p. 218; *C.B. Fry's Magazine*, November 1904, vol. 2, 8, p. 180.
18 J. Walvin, *Victorian Values*, Andre Deutsch, 1988, pp. 86–7.
19 *Preston Herald*, 24 March 1888, p. 5.
20 Turner and White, *Football Managers*, p. 186.
21 *Tottenham Herald*, 24 October 1899, p. 3.
22 Middlesbrough FC Minutes, 3 May 1900.
23 *Sunderland Daily Echo*, 4 April 1888, p. 4, 4 June 1889, p. 3.
24 *Sunderland Weekly News*, 2 October 1931, p. 7.
25 R. Finn, *Tottenham Hotspur FC: The Official History*, Robert Hale, 1972, pp. 28–32.
26 J. Cameron, 'How to Run a Football Team', in Gibson and Pickford, *Association Football*, vol. 4, pp. 128–33.
27 Holland, *Spurs*, p. 70.
28 *Tottenham Weekly Herald*, 20 March 1907, p. 4.

29 *Sunday Sun*, 7 June 1931, p. 32.
30 Williams, *Code War*, p. 162.
31 *Liverpool Echo*, 29 August 1896, p. 3.
32 Kelly, *Bill Shankly*, p. 73.
33 Alexander, *McCrae's Battalion*, pp. 62–3, 258–9.
34 P. Morris, *Aston Villa: The First 100 Years*, Birmingham, 1974, p. 8.
35 *Sunderland Daily Echo*, 4 June 1889, p. 3, 10 July 1894, p. 3.
36 Mason, 'The Blues and the Reds', p. 7.
37 Middlesbrough FC Minutes, *c*.1899–1900, *passim*.
38 *Birmingham Post* 16 December 1905, p. 10; *Birmingham Mail*, 23 December 1905, p. 3.
39 *Sunderland Daily Echo*, 19 May 1892, 27 May 1893, p. 3.
40 Young, *Bolton Wanderers*, pp. 30–1.
41 Middlesbrough FC Minutes, 4 July 1899.
42 *Birmingham Daily Mail*, 25 February 1893, p. 3.
43 Catton, *Leaguers*, p. 79.
44 Alexander, *McCrae's Battalion*, p. 63.
45 Holland, *Spurs*, ch. 6.
46 J. Catton, *Wickets and Goals*, Chapman and Hall, 1926, p. 138; Lewis, 'Football in Lancashire', p. 139; *Athletic News*, 4 September 1911, p. 4.
47 *Scottish Umpire*, 10 December 1884, p. 11.
48 Catton, *Leaguers*, p. 96; *Preston Herald*, 11 August 1894, p. 5.
49 Lewis, 'Football in Lancashire', p. 139.
50 The origin of this sobriquet is attributed to William McGregor, although its actual meaning may be more ironic than literal as talent can also mean money. *Athletic News*, 26 February 1917, p. 1 Sunderland won three Football League championships in four years between 1892 and 1895.
51 *Football Field*, 10 June 1893.
52 *Athletic News*, 26 February 1917, p. 1.
53 *AVNR*, 3 September 1910, p. 7.
54 J. Harding, *For the Good of the Game: The Official History of the Professional Footballers' Association*, Robson, 1991, p. 54; *AVNR*, 13 November 1909, p. 189.
55 Osbourne Newscuttings, p. 55.
56 *Birmingham Gazette and Express*, 12 August 1910, p. 8.
57 Middlesbrough FC Minutes, *passim*.
58 Taylor, 'Proud Preston', pp. 208–9.
59 Wolverhampton Wanderers FC, Rules for Players, 1914–15.
60 For example, Middlesbrough FC Minutes, 27 November 1899.
61 Middlesbrough FC Minutes, 31 July 1899.
62 Osbourne Newscuttings, p. 80.
63 *Birmingham Mail*, 25 February 1893, p. 3.
64 Middlesbrough FC Minutes, *passim*.
65 T. Mason, '"Our Stephen and Our Harold": Edwardian Footballers as Local Heroes', *International Journal of the History of Sport (IJHS)*, March 1996, vol. 13, 1, p. 80.
66 *Birmingham Mail*, 7 November 1892, p. 3.
67 *AVNR*, 1 September 1906, p. 3.
68 *AVNR*, 8 August 1914, p. 668.
69 *Dictionary of Business Biography*, vol. 5, p. 505.
70 *Sunderland Daily Echo*, 19 May 1892, p. 4.
71 C.E. Hughes, 'The "Spurs" in Mufti', *C.B. Fry's Magazine*, November 1904, vol. 2, 8, pp. 177–83.
72 *Preston Herald*, 7 January 1885, p. 6; *Football Field*, 30 January 1886, p. 5.

73 *Scottish Umpire*, 7 January 1885, p. 9.
74 Williams, *Code War*, p. 159.
75 Harding, *Football Wizard*, p. 40; *Good of the Game*, pp. 5–32.
76 Wagg, *Football World*, p. 8.
77 *Preston Herald*, 4 January 1888, p. 3; Gibson and Pickford, *Association Football*, vol. 2, p. 160.
78 *Football Field*, 22 January 1887, p. 2.
79 J. Cameron, *Association Football and How to Play it*, Health and Strength, 1909, p. 33.
80 *Football Field*, 16 February 1889, p. 2, 23 February 1889, pp. 2, 23, 30 March 1889, pp. 5, 3.
81 D. Terry, 'An Athletic Coach Ahead of his Time', *British Society of Sports History Newsletter*, 11, Spring 2000, pp. 34–8.
82 Harding, *Football Wizard*, pp. 52–3.
83 Hughes, 'The "Spurs" in Mufti', p. 178.
84 Cameron, *Association Football*, pp. 34, 40.
85 Catton, *Leaguers*, pp. 21, 83.
86 *Liverpool Review*, 16 March 1889, p. 18.
87 *Birmingham Sporting* Mail, 5 December 1908, p. 1. The columnist was Charles Johnstone of Aston Villa.
88 *Athletic News*, 4 September 1911, p. 4.
89 Catton, *Wickets*, p. 144; Catton, *Real Football*, p. 152.
90 *Football Field*, 25 January 1890, p. 3.
91 *Football Field*, 3 December 1887.
92 B. Joy, *Soccer Tactics*, Phoenix, 1956, pp. 44–5.
93 Mason, *Association Football*, p. 209.
94 *Preston Herald*, 7 January 1888, p. 2, 11 January 1888, p. 3.
95 *Athletic News*, 1 April 1889, p. 5.
96 Joy, *Soccer Tactics*, p. 48.
97 Mason, *Association Football*, p. 187.
98 Taylor, 'Proud Preston', p. 370.
99 Catton Folders, W.
100 Alexander, *McCrae's Battalion*, pp. 62–3.
101 *Newcastle Daily Journal*, 2 October 1885, p. 4.
102 Catton Folders, W.
103 *Newcastle Daily Chronicle*, 6 June 1887, p. 7.
104 *All Sports Weekly*, 11 October 1924, p. 5.
105 *Liverpool Football Echo*, 24 January 1891, p. 3.
106 *Newcastle Evening Chronicle*, 19 August 1896, p. 3.
107 *Athletic News*, 1 April 1889, p. 5.
108 Ibid., 1 September 1889, p. 5.
109 *Birmingham Sporting Mail*, 24 March 1906, p. 1; *Liverpool Daily Post*, 30 April 1901, p. 6.
110 *Birmingham Daily Mail*, 30 January 1893, p. 4.
111 *Athletic News*, 13 August 1894, p. 1; *Lancashire Daily Post*, 28 May 1894, p. 4; 11 August 1894, p. 3.
112 S. Wagg, 'Organising Victory? A Social History of the Football Manager', in J. King and J. Kelly (eds) *The Cult of the Manager: Do They Really Make a Difference?* Virgin, 1997, p. 22.
113 *Preston Herald*, 13 April 1895, p. 6; *Preston Guardian*, 13 April 1895, p. 2; Public Record Office HO140/161, A58929.
114 *Athletic News*, 18 March 1889, p. 4.

115 Catton, *Wickets*, p. 146. They recovered to win 3–2.
116 *Sunderland Echo*, 7 May 1915, p. 2.
117 *Athletic News*, 10 May 1915.
118 Catton Folders, W; *Liverpool Evening Express*, 6 May 1915, p. 5.
119 *Kicking and Screaming*, BBC Television, 1995.
120 *Sunderland Daily Echo*, 4 June 1889, p. 3.
121 *Sunderland Echo*, 7 May 1915, p. 2.
122 *Liverpool Review*, 1 August 1896, p. 6; *Newcastle Evening Chronicle*, 5 September 1896, Football Edition, p. 3.
123 M. Savage and A. Miles, *The Remaking of the British Working Class, 1840–1940*, Routledge, 1994, table 2.3, p. 26.
124 G. Routh, *Occupation and Pay in Great Britain 1906–60*, Cambridge: Cambridge University Press, 1965, pp. 70–4.
125 Tischler, *Footballers and Businessmen*, p. 74.
126 AVNR, 8 August 1914, pp. 662–3. On the balance sheet it states: Secretary's and Assistant Secretary's salaries – £615 15s. 8d.
127 Middlesbrough FC Minutes, 3 May 1900.
128 P. Joannou, *The Black 'N' White Alphabet*, Leicester, Polar Print, 1996, p. 482; Appleton, *Hotbed of Soccer*, pp. 124–5; R. Hutchinson, *The Toon: A Complete History of Newcastle United Football Club*, Mainstream, 1997, pp. 24–5.
129 E.P. Thompson, *The Making of the English Working Class*, Pelican, 1963, pp. 10–11.
130 J. Melling, '"Non-Commissioned Officer": British Employers and their Supervisory Workers, 1880–1920', *Social History*, May 1980, vol. 5, 2, p. 191.
131 *All Sports Weekly*, 11 October 1924, p. 5.
132 AVNR, 31 December 1938, p. 222.
133 Kennedy, 'The Split of Everton Football Club', p. 20 n87; *Liverpool Courier*, 11 May 1915; *Liverpool Daily Post*, 23 March 1936, p. 5.
134 Day, 'Football Club Directors', p. 55.
135 *Sunderland Daily Echo*, 18 October 1911, p. 8. Football's link with freemasonry continued into the 1990s as a former President of the Football Association, the Duke of Kent, was also the Grand Master of all freemasons. J. Webb, *Freemasonry and Sport*, Addlestone: Lewis Masonic, 1995, p. 28.
136 *Liverpool Echo*, 7 May 1915, p. 4.
137 *Liverpool Evening Express*, 6 May 1915, p. 5.
138 I am grateful to Eric Doig for this information.
139 Turner and White, *Football Managers*, p. 186.

3 'Organizing victory'

1 He managed Northampton Town, initially as player-manager, from 1907 to 1912; Leeds City, 1912–18; Huddersfield Town, 1921–5; and Arsenal, 1925–34.
2 Chapman won the Football League with Huddersfield Town in 1924 and 1925, and then with Arsenal in 1931 and 1933, as well as the FA Cup in 1922 with Huddersfield and with Arsenal in 1930.
3 T. Adams, *Addicted*, Collins Willow, 1998, p. 185.
4 M. Busby, *Soccer at the Top*, Sphere, 1974, p. 135.
5 B. Joy, *Forward Arsenal*, Phoenix, 1952, p. 85.
6 H. Chapman, *Herbert Chapman on Football*, ed. John Graves, Garrick, 1934, p. 125.
7 *Dictionary of Business Biography*, vol. 1, pp. 715–19, vol. 5, pp. 109–13.
8 Turner and White, *Football Managers*, p. 105.

9 His clubs included: Stalybridge Celtic, Grimsby Town whom he joined in May 1898, Swindon Town, Sheppey United in Kent, Worksop, Northampton Town, Sheffield United, and finally, Tottenham Hotspur, leaving in 1907.

10 L. Knighton, *Behind the Scenes in Big Football*, Stanley Paul, 1948, p. 62.

11 I am grateful to Lawrence Aspden, the Curator of Special Collections and Library Archives, University of Sheffield, and Mark Shipway at the Leeds University Archive, for the research they undertook in helping me try to trace Chapman's mining qualifications.

12 PRO MUN 4/4297, Report of J. Gibson, 7 November 1917; R.H. Gummer, *The Story of Barnbow*, Leeds, 1919, 'Staff Lists of Nos. 1 and 1A Filling Factories'.

13 L. Urwick and E. Brech, *The Making of Scientific Management*, Management Publications, 1945, vol. 1, p. 60.

14 *Huddersfield Examiner*, 13 June 1925, p. 11.

15 *Dictionary of Business Biography*, vol. 5, pp. 690–2; *Athletic News*, 29 September 1919, p. 1, 6 October 1919, p. 1; A.J. Arnold, '"Not Playing the Game?" Leeds City in the Great War', *IJHS*, May 1990, vol. 7, 1, pp. 113–18. On 6 October 1919 the FA suspended Leeds City and later that month it was expelled from the Football League. A joint FA and Football League commission had been set up to inspect the club's books following allegations of improper payments to players during the war. Chapman was implicated and then suspended *sine die* together with five others. Chapman's ban was overturned in October 1920 by the same commission.

16 Catton Folders, B–C, p. 263.

17 *Northampton Independent*, 4 May 1907, p. 10.

18 Chapman, *Herbert Chapman*, p. 2.

19 Leeds finished in fifteenth position in 1914–15 before winning two regional wartime competitions: in 1916 the northern group of the Midland League and the following year the Midland League itself. In 1918 Leeds again won the Midland League and also a play-off against the winners of the Lancashire League.

20 *Northampton Independent*, 4 May 1907, p. 10.

21 Arnold, *A Game That Would Pay*, pp. 61, 82–3.

22 *Huddersfield Daily Examiner*, 28 June 1922, p. 3.

23 *Huddersfield Examiner*, 30 June 1923, p. 11.

24 Northampton Town had been competing with Northampton Rugby (Union) Club, the Saints, Leeds City with Leeds (Rugby League or Northern Union as it was known until 1922), and Huddersfield Town, formed in 1908, with Huddersfield (Rugby League), which dated from 1868.

25 Fishwick, *English Football*, pp. 37–8.

26 *Northampton Daily Reporter and Echo*, 2 May 1906, p. 4, 21 August 1906, p. 3, 28 August 1906, p. 3, 24 August 1907, p. 3.

27 Chapman, *Herbert Chapman*, p. 7.

28 He was a member of the Kingsley Lodge of Freemasons. *Northampton Mercury and Herald*, 12 January 1934, p. 15.

29 *Huddersfield Daily Examiner*, 6 January 1934, p. 3.

30 *Huddersfield Examiner*, 15 April 1922, p. 2; Harding, *Good of the Game*, p. 148.

31 Chapman, *Herbert Chapman*, pp. 10–13.

32 *Yorkshire Evening Post*, 6 January 1934, p. 10.

33 Catton Folders, V–W, p. 1870.

34 R. Taylor and A. Ward, *Kicking and Screaming: An Oral History of Football in England*, 1995, p. 27.

35 *Sunday Dispatch*, 7 January 1934, p. 13.

36 Chapman, *Herbert Chapman*, p. 13.

37 T. Say, 'Herbert Chapman: Football Revolutionary', *The Sports Historian*, May 1996, 16, p. 81.

38 Chapman speaks briefly on *Kicking and Screaming*, Part 2, BBC Television, 1995.

39 *Athletic News*, 22 August 1921, p. 5.

40 *Northampton Independent*, 11 May 1912, p. 22.

41 *Northampton Daily Echo*, 4 May 1912, p. 4.

42 *Huddersfield Examiner*, 13 June 1925, p. 3.

43 D. Baines, 'The Onset of Depression', in Johnson (ed.) *Twentieth Century Britain*, pp. 175–6.

44 He was also Mayor of Fulham between 1909 and 1919.

45 Joy, *Forward Arsenal*, pp. 21–7; 'Henry Norris', *Dictionary of National Biography*.

46 *Athletic News*, 11 May 1925, p. 1.

47 Ibid., p. 4.

48 C. Buchan, *A Lifetime in Football*, Phoenix, 1955, pp. 84–6. Norris later came to a peculiar arrangement with the Sunderland manager, Bob Kyle. There was to be an initial down payment of £2,000 and then £100 for every goal Buchan scored. The total cost was £3,900.

49 Knighton, *Big Football*, p. 62.

50 Football Association Minutes, The Arsenal Football Club, Limited, Report of Commission, August 1927; Decisions of the Council, 29 August 1927.

51 Arsenal FC Minutes, 30 October 1928.

52 Arsenal FC Minutes, 23 April 1929. This seems to be the case on the evidence of the minutes from 11 October 1927 to 26 September 1929.

53 Islington Central Library, Arsenal Collection, YH779ARS, *Islington Gazette*, 29 July 1960.

54 Arsenal FC Minutes, 16 June 1930.

55 G. Allison, *Allison Calling*, Staples, 1948, *passim*.

56 Arsenal FC Minutes, 30 August 1928, 20 November 1928.

57 It was eventually decided that Chapman would arrange for them to take tea in the gymnasium. Arsenal FC Minutes, 4 October 1928.

58 Allison, *Allison Calling*, pp. 101, 217.

59 Joy, *Forward Arsenal*, p. 45.

60 Joy, *Soccer Tactics*, pp. 60–1, 25.

61 E. Hapgood, *Football Ambassador*, Sporting Handbooks, 1945, p. 12.

62 Say, 'Herbert Chapman', p. 84; Joy, *Soccer Tactics*, p. 50.

63 A player was now offside if at the moment the ball was played towards him, he did not have at least two opponents in front of him. Under the previous law the number was three.

64 Say, 'Herbert Chapman', pp. 81–98; Joy, *Soccer Tactics*, pp. 50–64.

65 Studd, *Herbert Chapman*, pp. 38–9.

66 Chapman, *Herbert Chapman*, pp. 65–7.

67 Joy, *Soccer Tactics*, p. 59.

68 T. Whittaker, *Tom Whittaker's Arsenal Story*, Sporting Handbooks, 1957, pp. 182–3.

69 Turner and White, *Football Managers*, p. 165.

70 Knighton, *Big Football*, p. 37.

71 Arsenal FC Minutes, 8 January 1929, 15 January 1929, 12 March 1929.

72 *Guardian*, 21 February 1998, p. 17.

73 Taylor and Ward, *Kicking and Screaming*, p. 29.

74 J. Harding, *Alex James: Life of a Football Legend*, Robson, 1988, p. 154.

75 Ibid., pp. 135–9.

76 Joy, *Forward Arsenal*, p. 48. Chapman later found Hardy a job as trainer at Tottenham Hotspur. Islington Central Library, Arsenal Collection, YH779ARS, *Islington Gazette*, 29 July 1960.
77 Arsenal FC Minutes, 1928 to 1929.
78 Studd, *Herbert Chapman*, p. 129.
79 Whittaker, *Tom Whittaker's*, p. 44.
80 Studd, *Herbert Chapman*, p. 108.
81 Arsenal FC Minutes, 27 October 1927, 14 February 1928.
82 Arsenal FC Minutes, 21 February 1928.
83 Arsenal FC Minutes, 31 July 1929.
84 Whittaker, *Tom Whittaker's*, p. 56.
85 *Yorkshire Evening Post*, 6 January 1934, p. 10; *Northampton Independent*, 13 January 1934, p. 9.
86 Arsenal FC Minutes, 20 October 1927, 23 October 1928.
87 BBC WAC, R30/1262/1, Gerald Cock, Internal Memo, 22 February 1928; OB Department letter, 23 February 1928.
88 BBC WAC, George Allison File 1, 1927–32, Letter from George Allison to S.J. de Lotbiniere, 22 June 1932; George Allison File 2, 1933–4, Letter from George Allison to S.J. de Lotbiniere, 13 October 1933. Allison had instead suggested Peter Hodges of Leicester City and Percy Smith of Tottenham Hotspur.
89 BBC WAC, George Allison File 1, 1927–32, Letter from S.J. de Lotbiniere to George Allison, 12 December 1932.
90 *Islington Gazette*, 28 October 1932, p. 6.
91 I. Sharpe, *40 Years in Football*, Hutchinson, 1952, p. 52; *Daily Herald*, 8 January 1934, p. 15.
92 Whittaker, *Tom Whittaker's*, pp. 95, 100.
93 Chapman, *Herbert Chapman*, pp. 156–74; Whittaker, *Tom Whittaker's*, p. 283.
94 Buchan, *Lifetime in Football*, p. 123.
95 Sharpe, *40 Years*, p. 156.
96 Joy, *Forward Arsenal*, p. 86; Chapman, along with the rest of the England party, is later pictured with Mussolini at his residence. Hapgood, *Football Ambassador*, opposite p. 33.
97 I. Sharpe, *Soccer Top Ten*, Stanley Paul, 1962, p. 14.
98 Arsenal FC Minutes, 3 November 1927, 31 January 1928.
99 Catton Folders, B–C, p. 263; *Birmingham Mail*, 6 January 1934, p. 3; *Northampton Chronicle and Echo*, 8 January 1934, p. 4.
100 *Northampton Mercury and Herald*, 12 January 1934, p. 15.
101 Allison, *Allison Calling*, pp. 101, 217.

4 The emergence of the football manager, 1918–39

1 Information based on Turner and White, *Football Managers*.
2 D. Jeremy, *A Business History of Britain, 1900–1990s*, Oxford: Oxford University Press, 1998, p. 206.
3 H. Perkin, *The Rise of Professional Society: England since 1880*, Routledge, 1989, pp. 294–6.
4 R. McKibbin, *Classes and Cultures: England 1918–1951*, Oxford: Oxford University Press, 1998, pp. 44–9.
5 Keeble, *The Ability to Manage*, p. 59; Wilson, *Business History*, p. 177.
6 Baines, 'Onset of Depression', pp. 169–76; D. Baines, 'Recovery from Depression', pp. 188–91; B. Harris, 'Unemployment and the Dole in Interwar Britain', in Johnson, *Twentieth Century Britain*, pp. 203–6.

7 S. Jones, 'The Economic Aspects of Association Football in England, 1918–39', *British Journal of Sports History*, 1984, vol. 1, 3, pp. 281–9; S. Dobson and J. Goddard, 'Performance, Revenue and Cross Subsidization in the Football League, 1927–1994', *Economic History Review*, 1998, vol. 51, 4, pp. 767–8.

8 Szymanski and Kuypers, *Winners and Losers*, pp. 363, 375; Russell, *Football*, p. 82.

9 J. Bale, *Sport and Place: A Geography of Sport in England, Scotland and Wales*, Hurst, 1982, ch. 4.

10 Information based on Turner and White, *Football Managers*.

11 *Huddersfield Examiner*, 22 December 1923, p. 16.

12 *Sunday Sun*, 16 August 1931, p. 21.

13 Turner and White, *Football Managers*, pp. 86, 208; Young, *Bolton Wanderers*, p. 69.

14 *Sunday Mercury*, 20 March 1949, p. 13, 24 April 1949, p. 13, 29 May 1949, p. 17; *Midland Chronicle*, 1 October 1915, p. 4.

15 Catton Folders, B–C, p. 195.

16 *Athletic News*, 17 March 1919, p. 6.

17 'Footballer's Battalion' by Frank Buckley. Information supplied by Wolverhampton Wanderers Football Club.

18 J. Seed, *The Jimmy Seed Story*, Phoenix, 1958, p. 67.

19 B. Murray, *The Old Firm: Sectarianism, Sport and Society in Scotland*, Edinburgh: John Donald, 1984, pp. 204–7.

20 P. Lanfranchi, 'Exporting Football: Notes on the Development of Football in Europe', in R. Giulianotti and J. Williams (eds) *Game Without Frontiers: Football, Identity and Modernity*, Aldershot: Arena, 1994, pp. 23–46.

21 J. Walvin, *The People's Game*, Newton Abbot: Readers Union, 1975, ch. 5.

22 T. Mason, 'Death of the Soccer Exiles', *BBC History Magazine*, June 2000, p. 34; P. Lanfranchi, '"Mister Garbutt": The First European Manager', *The Sports Historian*, May 2002, 22, 1, pp. 44–59.

23 *When Saturday Comes*, March 2001, 169, p. 20.

24 D. Turner, 'A Coach's Trip to Europe', *The Footballer*, March/April 1989, vol. 1, 6, pp. 28–9.

25 Walvin, *People's Game*, pp. 94–5; S. Kelly, 'Charlie Roberts: The Complete Centre-Half', *The Footballer*, March/April 1989, vol. 1, 6, pp. 26–7.

26 Sharpe, *40 Years*, ch. 12.

27 Chapman, *Herbert Chapman*, pp. 166–7.

28 *Topical Times*, 12 January 1935, p. 43.

29 *World Sports*, December 1953, p. 22.

30 *Albion News*, 11 December 1937, p. 139.

31 Turner and White, *Football Managers*, p. 114.

32 Appleton, *Hotbed of Soccer*, pp. 151–61.

33 Murray, *Old Firm*, p. 206.

34 *Sunday Mercury*, 1 January 1939, p. 19.

35 Wolverhampton Wanderers FC Minutes, 23 August 1933, 29 August 1933, 3 October 1933.

36 Middlesbrough FC Minutes, *passim*.

37 Walker, *Soccer in the Blood*, Soccer Book Club, 1960, pp. 36–7.

38 *Dictionary of Business Biography*, vol. 2, 1985, pp. 574–8.

39 West Ham FC Minutes, 7–22 November 1932: Korr, *West Ham*, pp. 88–90.

40 Taylor, 'Proud Preston', chs 5 and 6.

41 *Athletic News*, 2 May 1927, p. 19.

42 *Guide and Ideas*, 1 May 1937, p. 3.

43 P.M. Young, *Centenary Wolves*, Wolverhampton: Wolverhampton Wanderers FC, 1976, p. 109; S. Cullis, *All for the Wolves*, Rupert Hart-Davies, 1960, p. 94.

44 Charlton Athletic FC Minutes, 21 April 1937.
45 Seed, *Jimmy Seed*, pp. 25–31.
46 R. Redden, *The History of Charlton Athletic: Valley of Tears, Valley of Joy*, Print Co-ordination, 1993, p. 32.
47 Fishwick, *English Football*, p. 41.
48 Seed, *Jimmy Seed*, p. 31.
49 Charlton Athletic FC Minutes, January–July 1935; Middlesbrough FC Minutes, 24 April 1927, 18 January 1928, 25 January 1928.
50 Charlton Athletic FC Team Book, 27 August 1934, 10 October 1936.
51 Middlesbrough FC Minutes, 14 December 1927, 12 September 1928, 18 December 1929, 9 April 1930, 16 April 1930.
52 Interview with Jack Curnow.
53 Middlesbrough FC Minutes, 11 April 1930, 8 June 1933, 11 April 1934.
54 Taylor, 'Proud Preston', p. 246.
55 FA Instructional Classes for Boys in Association Football, Committee Report 1936–7, May 1937.
56 *Guide and Ideas*, 8 May 1937, p. 5.
57 *Blackpool Times*, 21 September 1923, p. 4.
58 Murray, *Old Firm*, pp. 205–6.
59 J. Guthrie, *Soccer Rebel: The Evolution of the Professional Footballer*, Newton Abbot: Readers Union, 1976, pp. 141–2.
60 Taylor and Ward, *Kicking and Screaming*, p. 34.
61 R. Calley, *Blackpool: A Complete Record, 1887–1992*, Derby: Breedon, 1992, p. 60.
62 Dunphy, *Strange Kind of Glory*, pp. 56–72.
63 Taylor and Ward, *Kicking and Screaming*, pp. 39–40.
64 Hull City AFC, Season 1939–40, Player's Ticket.
65 Wolverhampton Wanderers Football Club (1923) Ltd, Season 1933–4, Player's Ticket.
66 *Albion News*, 16 January 1937, p. 195.
67 *Express and Star*, 23 December 1964, p. 8.
68 Interview with George Hardwick.
69 I am grateful to Ian Atkins for this information.
70 Guthrie, *Soccer Rebel*, p. 138.
71 J. Seed, *Soccer from the Inside*, Thorson, 1947, pp. 108–10, 67–8. Shortly after the war, Tony Pawson, an amateur, played a few games for Charlton when Seed was manager. Interestingly, he noted that in the changing room before a game against Tottenham, there was no discussion of Charlton's tactics or their opponent's. T. Pawson, *The Football Managers*, Newton Abbot: Readers Union, 1973, p. 7.
72 Murray, *Old Firm*, p. 205.
73 Cullis, *Wolves*, pp. 12–14.
74 Interview with Jack Curnow.
75 *Topical Times*, 12 January 1935, p. 43.
76 Walker, *Soccer*, p. 112.
77 *Kicking and Screaming*, Part 2, BBC Television.
78 *Blackpool Times*, 31 July 1923, p. 12, 7 August 1923, p. 5.
79 *Express and Star*, 3 August 1927; interview with Don Bilton; Cullis, *Wolves*, p. 13; Taylor and Ward, *Kicking and Screaming*, pp. 34–5.
80 See D. Hamilton, *The Monkey Gland Affair*, Chatto and Windus, 1986.
81 Young, *Centenary Wolves*, p. 115; *Express and Star*, 29 March 1939, p. 12; Taylor and Ward, *Kicking and Screaming*, p. 32; Cullis, *Wolves*, pp. 15–16.
82 *Express and Star*, 12 September 1964, p. 37.
83 R. Daniels, *Blackpool Football: The Official Club History*, Robert Hale, 1972, p. 36.

84 Joy, *Forward Arsenal*, pp. 32–3.
85 *Albion News*, 26 August 1922, p. 2.
86 Seed, *Jimmy Seed*, pp. 89–90; *Albion News*, 11 December 1937, p. 139.
87 *Albion News*, 16 January 1937, p. 195.
88 Cullis, *Wolves*, p. 16; Pawson, *Football Managers*, p. 34.
89 Russell, *Football*, p. 85.
90 Seed, *Jimmy Seed*, pp. 35–6.
91 Seed, *Soccer*, pp. 26, 67.
92 *Albion News*, 'Football Programme Supplement', vol. 22, 1930–1.
93 P. Morris, *The Team Makers*, Pelham, 1971, p. 33.
94 Guthrie, *Soccer Rebel*, p. 17.
95 Taylor and Ward, *Kicking and Screaming*, pp. 31–3; Young, *Centenary Wolves*, pp. 112–15.
96 Russell, *Football*, pp. 87–8.
97 FA Council Minutes, 30 April 1937; FA Disciplinary Committee Minutes, 18 January–26 June 1937.
98 The game's broader appeal was also reinforced through the football pools, which in 1936 had an annual turnover of £30 million, twenty times the annual income of all Football League clubs. *The Economist*, 17 April 1937, p. 132.
99 Fishwick, *English Football*, pp. 100–13.
100 R. Taylor, *Football and its Fans*, Leicester: Leicester University Press, 1992, chs 3–4.
101 Middlesbrough FC Minutes, 9 April 1930.
102 Taylor, 'Proud Preston', p. 209. Players did put their names to ghosted articles however.
103 Wagg, *Football World*, pp. 44, 54–7.
104 Russell, *Football*, p. 88.
105 Davies, 'Cinema and Broadcasting', in Johnson (ed.) *Twentieth Century Britain*, pp. 265–9.
106 BBC WAC, George Allison File 1, 1927–32, Letter from George Allison to S.J. de Lotbiniere, 22 June 1932.
107 BBC WAC, R30/915/1, 1 March 1944; *Express and Star*, 3 March 1944, p. 7.
108 West Bromwich Public Libraries, Scrapbook No. 10, p. 29; *Albion News*, 26 October 1946. It was also shown in cinemas on *Pathé News*.
109 Arsenal FC Minutes, 15 June 1934; Catton Folders, A–B, p. 6.
110 Young, *Bolton Wanderers*, p. 69 n1.
111 Walsall FC Minutes, 25 September 1934, 23 April 1935.
112 Darlington FC Minutes, 8 May 1935, 14 May 1936.
113 Ipswich Town FC Minutes, 4 October 1937, 1 November 1937.
114 Charlton Athletic FC Minutes, 8 April 1936.
115 Wolverhampton Wanderers FC Minutes, 24 October 1933.
116 *Express and Star*, 4 December 1943, p. 7, 22 February 1944, p. 7.
117 Routh, *Occupation and Pay*, pp. 72–4.
118 Gourvish, 'British Business and the Transition to a Corporate Economy: Entrepreneurship and Management Structures', *Business History*, 1987, vol. 29, 4, p. 28; *Dictionary of Business Biography*, vol. 5, p. 264, vol. 4, p. 23.
119 McKibbin, *Classes and Cultures*, pp. 44–6.
120 Davies, 'Cinema and Broadcasting', p. 264.
121 I am grateful to Gladys Dutton for this information.
122 McKibbin, *Classes and Cultures*, pp. 87–8.
123 *Sunday Mercury*, 5 June 1949, p. 13; *Albion News*, 5 October 1935, p. 67.
124 Turner and White, *Football Managers*, p. 9.

125 In 1937 only eight managers had been managers of one club for ten years or more. *Albion News*, 25 December 1937, p. 155.
126 Turner and White, *Football Managers*, p. 66; Wagg, *Football World*, p. 47.
127 Dunphy, *Strange Kind of Glory*, p. 103.
128 Korr, *West Ham*, pp. 84–5.
129 *Albion News*, 10 February 1934, p. 245.

5 The modernization of football management, 1945–70

1 Perkin, *Professional Society*, p. 419.
2 Wagg, *Football World*, p. 157.
3 B. Conekin, F. Mort and C. Waters (eds) *Moments of Modernity: Reconstructing Britain 1945–1964*, Rivers Oram Press, 1999, pp. 2–3, 18–20.
4 Perkin, *Professional Society*, pp. 460, 418, 405, 359.
5 N. Tiratsoo, 'Limits of Americanisation: The United States Productivity Gospel in Britain', in Conekin *et al.* (eds) *Moments of Modernity*, pp. 97–110.
6 'English Professional Football', *Planning*, June 1966, vol. 32, 496, pp. 120–4; Butler, *Football League*, p. 223.
7 At the 1952 Olympics Great Britain's amateur team had been defeated by Luxembourg.
8 *Kicking and Screaming*, BBC Television; Bowler, *Winning*, pp. 64–5; *Football Association Year Book 1949–50*, pp. 32–4.
9 *Football Association Year Book 1952–53*, pp. 42–4.
10 U. Hesse-Lichtenberger, *Tor! The Story of German Football*, WSC Books, 2003, p. 114.
11 FA International Senior Selection Committee and Technical Committee Minutes, 22 July 1954.
12 FA Minutes, Regional Meetings of Managers of 1st and 2nd Division Clubs, Plans for England XI-World Cup 1966, October 1962.
13 I am grateful to Pierre Lanfranchi for this information.
14 FA Technical Committee Minutes, 11 August 1961.
15 'English Professional Football', p. 123.
16 Interview with Pat Carter; *Kicking and Screaming*, BBC Television.
17 Anon., *Talking With Wolves*, Derby: Breedon, 1998, p. 15.
18 Hopcraft, *Football Man*, p. 112; J. Rogan, *The Football Managers*, Queen Anne Press, 1989, pp. 24–5.
19 *Express and Star*, Newspaper Library, 'Stan Cullis' file; Hapgood, *Football Ambassador*, p. 130; Interview with Andrew Cullis.
20 Kelly, *Shankly*, p. 15; Rogan, *Football Managers*, p. 1; Turner and White, *Football Managers*, p. 73.
21 Rogan, *Football Managers*, p. 93.
22 Interview with George Hardwick.
23 Bowler, *Winning*, pp. 25–6.
24 Hopcraft, *Football Man*, p. 112; *Independent on Sunday* (Review), 30 June 1996, pp. 11–12.
25 *Observer* (Sport), 23 January 1994, p. 20.
26 Anon., *Talking With Wolves*, p. 75.
27 Bowler, *Winning*, pp. 95–6.
28 Morris, *Team Makers*, p. 70.
29 *Express and Star*, 21 August 1944, p. 7, 26 April 1945, p. 7.
30 'English Professional Football', pp. 110–13.

31 J. Obelkevich, 'Consumption', in J. Obelkevich and P. Caterall (eds) *Understanding Postwar British Society*, Routledge, 1994, pp. 141–54.
32 P. Clarke, *Hope and Glory: Britain 1900–1939*, Penguin, 1996, pp. 250–3.
33 Inglis, *Soccer*, Chapter 8.
34 A. Marwick, *British Society since 1945*, Penguin, 1990, p. 152.
35 'English Professional Football', pp. 108–10.
36 *Football Association Bulletin*, September 1952, p. 31.
37 D. Bowler, *Danny Blanchflower – A Biography of a Visionary*, Victor Gollancz, 1997, p. 54.
38 Durham County Record Office, D/XD 97/4, Darlington FC Minutes, 16 December 1952, 13 October 1953, 25 November 1957, 2 October 1958.
39 Busby, *Soccer*, pp. 17–19.
40 Kelly, *Shankly*, pp. 135–7, 74–5.
41 Young, *Football on Merseyside*, pp. 76, 105 n3, 146–52.
42 Turner and White, *Football Managers*, p. 162.
43 *Daily Herald*, 10 March 1956, p. 10.
44 Young, *Football on Merseyside*, pp. 152–3.
45 Kelly, *Shankly*, pp. 136–41.
46 Prior to his retirement, Shankly had improved the salaries of all the playing staff, with Kevin Keegan's doubled. M. Dononvan, 'Football as a Life and Death Struggle: A Critical Analysis of the Management Style of Bill Shankly', unpublished MA thesis, University of Warwick, 1992, p. 54.
47 A. Johnson, *The Battle for Manchester City*, Edinburgh: Mainstream, 1994, p. 22.
48 Szymanski and Kuypers, *Winners and Losers*, p. 360.
49 Kelly, *Shankly*, p. 159.
50 *Express and Star* Newspaper Library, 'Stan Cullis' File, *Sporting Star*, 7 May 1960.
51 Dunphy, *Strange Kind of Glory*, pp. 147–8; Rogan, *Football Managers*, p. 6.
52 Dunphy, *Strange Kind of Glory*, pp. 124–5, 254.
53 *FA Handbook: Rules of the Association and Laws of the Game*, 1960–1.
54 FA Consultative Committee Minutes, 6 April 1959.
55 *Observer* (Sport), 2 January 2000, p. 4.
56 *Guardian*, 10 December 1993, p. 4.
57 *Express and Star*, 9 May 1949, p. 11.
58 *Guardian*, 21 January 1994, p. 4; Dunphy, *Strange Kind of Glory*, pp. 105, 129, 144–6.
59 Anon., *Talking With Wolves*, p. 13.
60 Interview with Bill Slater.
61 Anon., *Talking With Wolves*, p. 15.
62 T. Farmer, *The Heartbreak Game*, Wolverhampton: Hillburgh, 1987, pp. 53–4.
63 *The Times*, 27 July 1962, p. 12f; Szymanski and Kuypers, *Winners and Losers*, p. 354.
64 G. Best, *The Good, the Bad and the Bubbly*, Pan Books, 1991, pp. 30, 64, 166.
65 R. Flowers, *For Wolves and England*, Stanley Paul, 1962, pp. 90–2; *The Times*, 18 July 1962, p. 4c.
66 Kelly, *Shankly*, p. 92.
67 *Sunday Correspondent*, 11 March 1990, p. 58.
68 *Sunday Times*, 4 October 1981, p. 31.
69 Flowers, *Wolves*, pp. 57–63.
70 Kelly, *Shankly*, pp. 50, 194–9; *Sunday Correspondent*, 11 March 1990, p. 58.
71 Dunphy, *Strange Kind of Glory*, pp. 257, 295.
72 B. Ferrier, *Soccer Partnership: Billy Wright and Walter Winterbottom*, Heinemann, 1960, p. 168.
73 *FA Bulletin*, August 1951, pp. 8–9.
74 Wagg, *Football World*, p. 159.

75 A. Stock, *Football Club Manager*, Sportsmans Book Club, 1969, p. 149.
76 BBC WAC, R30/915/1, Letter from OBD, S.J. de Lotbiniere to Victor Smythe, Manchester, 27 August 1946; Memo from OBD, S.J. de Lotbiniere to Victor Smythe, Manchester, 4 September 1946.
77 Cullis, *Wolves*, p. 205.
78 Wolverhampton Wanderers FC Minutes, 7 February 1957.
79 Bowler, *Shanks*, pp. 93–4; Kelly, *Shankly*, p. 143.
80 Bowler, *Winning*, p. 228.
81 F. Chisari, 'Football and TV – The Case of the 1966 World Cup', paper presented at FIFA: A Century of World Football Conference, Lausanne, December 2004.
82 Stock, *Football Club Manager*, pp. 51–8.
83 Kelly, *Shankly*, p. 115.
84 *Sunday Times*, 4 October 1981, p. 31.
85 *Express and Star*, 15 March 1956, p. 28, 17 March 1956, p. 15.
86 Ibid., 9 September 1964, p. 36, 18 September 1964, p. 1, 19 September 1964, p. 1.
87 Farmer, *Heartbreak Game*, p. 82.
88 Wolverhampton Wanderers FC Minutes, 27 February 1957, 4 April 1957.
89 Cullis, *Wolves*, pp. 98–9; Anon., *Talking With Wolves*, p. 75.
90 Charlton FC Minutes, 2 May 1946.
91 Busby, *Soccer*, p. 16. By contrast, the maximum wage for players in 1945 was £9; in 1961 it was £20.
92 *Observer*, 9 May 1999, p. 11.
93 Ipswich Record Office, GC 426/2/2/2, Ipswich Town FC Minute Book, 8 August 1955, 5 December 1955, 9 April 1956.
94 Bowler, *Winning*, p. 153.
95 FA International (Senior) Committee Minutes, 26 September 1966.
96 *Observer* (Sport), 2 May 1999, p. 5.
97 Durham Record Office, D/XD 97/4, Darlington FC Minutes, 1 April 1952, 31 January 1957, 9 May 1958, 28 December 1959, p. 8.
98 *Observer* (Sport), 2 May 1999, pp. 1, 5.
99 *Guardian*, 11 November 1997, p. 18. It is not known if the figure was an annual salary.
100 Stock, *Football Club Manager*, pp. 144–5.
101 S. Webb, *Footballers' Wives*, Yellow Jersey Press, 1998, p. 92.
102 *Express and Star*, 10 September 1948, p. 7.
103 Webb, *Freemasonry*, pp. 29–30.
104 *Express and Star*, 23 November 1962.
105 *Sunday Times*, 4 October 1981, p. 31; Kelly, *Shankly*, pp. 87–8.

6 Managers in the television age, 1970–92

1 L. Hannah, 'Crisis and Turnaround? 1973–1993', and M. Sanderson, 'Education and Social Mobility', in Johnson (ed.) *Twentieth Century Britain*, pp. 340–3, 374–91.
2 C. Handy, 'Great Britain', in C. Handy, C. Gordon, I. Gow and C. Randlesome, *Making Managers*, Pitman, 1988, pp. 163–91; Tiratsoo, 'Management Education' pp. 123–4; Aldcroft, 'Missing Dimension', pp. 93–125.
3 N. Tiratsoo, '"You've Never Had It So Bad"?', in *From Blitz to Blair: A New History of Britain since 1939*, Phoenix, 1997, pp. 181–2.
4 *FA News*, November 1970, p. 4, December 1970, p. 4, April 1971, p. 8, April 1972, p. 4; *FA Newsletter*, February 1984.
5 Of the 39, 32 were Italian, 4 Belgian, 2 French and 1 British.
6 Russell, *Football*, pp. 182–8.

7 T. Arnold, 'Rich Man, Poor Man: Economic Arrangements in the Football League', in J. Williams and S. Wagg (eds) *British Football and Social Change: Getting into Europe*, Leicester: Leicester University Press, 1991, p. 49.

8 *FA News*, October 1972, p. 4.

9 Arnold, 'Rich Man', p. 56.

10 Russell, *Football*, pp. 195–6.

11 D. Birley, *A Social History of English Cricket*, Aurum, 1999, pp. 317–19.

12 *Express and Star*, 10 September 1964; 'English Professional Football', p. 101.

13 D. Conn, 'The New Commercialism', in S. Hamil, J. Michie and C. Oughton (eds) *A Game of Two Halves? The Business of Football*, Mainstream, 1999, pp. 50–1.

14 M. Crick and D. Smith, *Manchester United: The Betrayal of a Legend*, Pan Books, 1990, pp. 273–6.

15 *Guardian*, 1 November 1990, p. 16, 30 November 1990, p. 16, 7 December 1990, p. 14.

16 S. Jamieson, *Graeme Souness: The Ibrox Revolution and the Legacy of the Iron Lady's Man*, Edinburgh: Mainstream, 1997, pp. 20–8, 76–83.

17 R. Atkinson, *Big Ron: A Different Ball Game*, Andre Deutsch, 1998, p. 160.

18 M. Wilders, 'The Football Club Manager – A Precarious Occupation', *Journal of Management Studies*, May 1976, pp. 158–9; Johnson, *Manchester City*, pp. 73–7.

19 FA Annual Coaching Report, 1972.

20 FA Instructional Committee Minutes, 10 December 1969; FA Annual Coaching Report, 1970; *FA News*, December 1971, p. 4.

21 FA Joint Liaison Committee of Football Association and Football League Minutes, 29 June 1973.

22 FA Instructional Committee Minutes, 3 October 1977, 26 February 1980, 10 September 1980, 20 November 1980.

23 J. Smith and M. Dawson, *Bald Eagle: The Jim Smith Story*, Edinburgh: Mainstream, 1990, pp. 7–10; Rogan, *Football Managers*, pp. 228–9, 174; B. Clough, *Clough: The Autobiography*, Partridge, 1994, pp. 1–19.

24 Rogan, *Football Managers*, pp. 174–5.

25 D. Bassett, *Harry's Game*, Derby: Breedon, 1997, pp. 21, 228.

26 Atkinson, *Big Ron*, pp. 49–51.

27 *Guardian*, 23 October 2001, pp. 22, 30.

28 J. Charlton, *Jack Charlton: The Autobiography*, Partridge, 1996, p. 38; Clough, *Clough*, pp. 15–21.

29 A. Ferguson, *Managing My Life*, Hodder and Stoughton, 1999, p. 127.

30 K. Dalglish, *Dalglish: My Autobiography*, Hodder and Stoughton, 1996, pp. 1–12.

31 Charlton, *Jack Charlton*, p. 51.

32 Bassett, *Harry's Game*, p. 33.

33 Clough, *Clough*, p. 51.

34 Ibid., pp. 61, 92–106, 246–9.

35 Ferguson, *Managing My Life*, pp. 140–1.

36 *The Ferguson Factor*, BBC Television, 2002.

37 Crick and Smith, *Manchester United*, p. 175; Atkinson, *Big Ron*, p. 22.

38 *Observer* (Sport), 12 December 1999, p. 6.

39 Scottish Industrial Tribunals Office, Case No. S/3151/78.

40 Pawson, *Football Managers*, pp. 19, 213–14.

41 R. Hutchinson, *The Toon: A Complete History of Newcastle United Football Club*, Mainstream, 1997, pp. 211–12.

42 *Guardian* (Sport), 25 January 2004, p. 13.

43 L. Brady, *So Far So Good . . . A Decade in Football*, Newton Abbot: Readers Union, 1980, pp. 108–11.

44 T. Adams, *Addicted*, Collins Willow, 1998, pp. 50, 183–6.
45 E. Harrison, *The View from the Dugout*, Manchester: Parrs Wood, 2001, p. 18.
46 Dalglish, *Dalglish*, pp. 134–5.
47 A. Gowling, *Football Inside Out*, Newton Abbot: Readers Union, 1977, pp. 82–92; Hutchinson, *The Toon*, pp. 216–17.
48 T. Brooking, *Trevor Brooking*, Pelham, 1981, p. 140.
49 Charlton, *Jack Charlton*, pp. 227–8.
50 Clough, *Clough*, pp. 186–91.
51 Ibid., ch. 12.
52 Ibid., p. 190.
53 Atkinson, *Big Ron*, ch. 6.
54 S. Kuper, *Football Against the Enemy*, Orion, 1994, pp. 52–4, *Guardian*, 15 May 2002, p. 18.
55 Charlton, *Jack Charlton*, pp. 238–41.
56 Taylor and Ward, *Kicking and Screaming*, p. 302.
57 Wagg, *Football World*, p. 193.
58 Wilders, 'Football Club Manager', p. 159.
59 Crick and Smith, *Manchester United*, p. 233.
60 M. Crick, *The Boss: The Many Sides of Alex Ferguson*, Pocket Books, 2003, pp. 108, 212, 256.
61 Clough, *Clough*, pp. 106, 146–7, 233–4.
62 *Guardian* (Weekend), 12 February 2000, pp. 37–46.
63 Jamieson, *Graeme Souness*, pp. 81–91.
64 *Guardian*, 2 February 1994, p. 14.
65 *Guardian* (Weekend), 12 February 2000, p. 46.
66 Jamieson, *Graeme Souness*, pp. 98–100, 192–3.
67 Dalglish, *Dalglish*, pp. 161–88.

7 The 'postmodern' football manager?

1 *Guardian* (Sport), 23 September 2000, p. 7
2 *Guardian* (Sport), 10 January 1997, p. 2
3 *Independent*, 2 May 2002, p. 19.
4 *Guardian*, 25 May 2001, p. 7.
5 *Guardian*, 15 August 2001, p. 25.
6 *Observer* (Sports Magazine), 7 March 2004.
7 *The Ferguson Factor*, BBC1, 2002.
8 D. Conn, 'The New Commercialism', in S. Hamil, J. Michie and C. Oughton (eds) *The Business of Football: A Game of Two Halves?* Edinburgh: Mainstream, 1999, pp. 43–51.
9 *Guardian*, 7 September 1998, p. 3, 10 September 1998, p. 8, 21 March 2000, p. 35.
10 *Observer* (Business), 29 March 1998, p. 7
11 'On the Line', BBC Radio 5 Live, 11 June 2001.
12 D. Conn, *The Football Business: Fair Game in the 90s?* Edinburgh: Mainstream, 1998, p. 63.
13 *When Saturday Comes*, February 2004, p. 13.
14 Turner and White, *Football Managers*, p. 9.
15 *Guardian*, 15 May 2001, p. 32.
16 Green, *Sack Race*, p. 14.
17 J. Williams, *Is It All Over? Can Football Survive the Premier League?* Reading: South Street Press, 1999, p. 41.

18 *Guardian*, 16 May 2001, p. 30; *Guardian* (Sport), 16 October 2001, p. 5; *Financial Times*, 17–18 May 2003, p. 14.
19 *Guardian*, 22 September 2003. One black coach who has held a prominent post is Hope Powell of the England women's team.
20 *Guardian*, 14 July 2000, p. 31. By 2002, however, seven teams had British coaches. *Guardian* (Sport), 2 March 2002, p. 19.
21 *Guardian*, 1 November 2000, p. 34.
22 Tony Banks MP, quoted on *BBC News*, 12 October 2000.
23 M. Sanderson, *Education and Economic Decline in Britain, 1870 to the 1990s*, Cambridge: Cambridge University Press, 1999, p. 90.
24 Green, *Sack Race*, p. 114.
25 I am grateful to Pierre Lanfranchi for this information.
26 *Observer*, 18 May 2003; *Guardian*, 4 May 2004, 20 May 2004; *Guardian* (Sport), 14 August 2004 p. 14.
27 *Daily Telegraph*, 29 December 2003.
28 *Guardian* (Sport), 12 February 2000, p. 2.
29 *FA Premier League Handbook, Season 2002–2003*, p. 91. In recognition of his achievements and management experience, Alex Ferguson was awarded an honorary qualification.
30 *Observer* (Sports Magazine), 6 October 2002.
31 Green, *Sack Race*, p. 118.
32 *Guardian* (Sport), 15 May 2004, p. 6.
33 See T. Bower, *Broken Dreams: Vanity, Greed and the Souring of British Football*, Simon and Schuster, 2003.
34 *Guardian* (Weekend), 12 February 2000, p. 37.
35 Ibid., 10 June 1999, 31 July 1999.
36 Ibid., 6 March 2003.
37 Ibid., 1 May 2002.
38 *Guardian* (Sport), 30 August 2004, p. 21
39 *Independent on Sunday* (Sport), 16 May 1999, p. 3.
40 *The Times*, 31 August 2004, p. 64.
41 *Guardian*, 27 April 2000, p. 35.
42 Ibid., 17 January 2001.
43 Madeleine Bunting, 'Sweet Smiles, Hard Labour', *Guardian* (Weekend), 12 June 2004, pp. 17–22.
44 *When Saturday Comes*, December 2003, p. 22, January 2002, p. 16.
45 *Observer* (Sports Magazine), 6 October 2002.
46 *Independent on Sunday* (Section 2), 22 November 1998, p. 7.
47 Bunting, 'Sweet Smiles, Hard Labour', pp. 17–22.
48 *Observer* (Sport), 23 May 2004.
49 *Guardian* (Sport), 2 May 1998, p. 1.
50 *The Ferguson Factor*, BBC1, 2002.
51 *Observer*, 9 April 2000.
52 *Guardian* (Weekend), 12 February 2000, p. 43.
53 *Footballers' Diaries*, BBC 2, 2004.
54 Crick, *The Boss*, pp. 356–7. The other two players were Willie Miller and Bryan Robson.
55 *Inside the Mind of Alex Ferguson*, Channel 4, 2002.
56 *Independent on Sunday* (Sport), 2 November 1997, p. 11.
57 *Independent on Sunday* (Section 2), 22 November 1998, p. 7.
58 *Guardian* (Sport), 23 October 2000, p. 1.
59 *Guardian* (Review), 13 June 1998, pp. 6–7; *Guardian* (Sport), 21 May 2000, pp. 14–15.

60 *Guardian*, 22 August 2000, p. 26, 23 August 2000, p. 27.
61 *Guardian*, 12 June 2001, p. 1.
62 Crick, *The Boss*, p. 561.
63 *Guardian*, 8 October 1998, p. 21.
64 *Observer* (Sports Magazine), 6 October 2002.
65 'The Panic Room', *Observer* (Sports Magazine), 6 October 2002.
66 *Guardian*, 22 April 2003.

8 What difference does the manager make?

1 Wagg, *Football World*, p. 174.
2 Russell, *Football*, p. 171.
3 Busby, *Soccer*, p. 20.
4 *Guardian* (Sport), 2 July 1998, p. 1.
5 *Coventry City FC Official Matchday Magazine*, 10 April 2004, pp. 27–8.
6 *Metro*, 2 November 2000, p. 38.
7 *Observer* (Sports Monthly), July 2000, pp. 29–35.
8 King and Kelly, *Cult of the Manager*, pp. 260–2.
9 P. Dawson, S. Dobson and B. Gerrard, 'Estimating Coaching Efficiency in Professional Team Sports: Evidence from English Association Football', *Scottish Journal of Political Economy*, September 2000, vol. 47, 4, pp. 399–421.
10 See, for example, L. Kahn, 'Managerial Quality, Team Success, and Individual Player Performance in Major League Baseball', *Industrial and Labor Relations Review*, April 1993, vol. 46, 3, pp. 531–47; G. Scully, 'Managerial Efficiency and Survivability in Professional Team Sports', *Managerial and Decision Economics*, 1994, vol. 15, 5, pp. 403–11. One dissenting view is provided by I. Horowitz, 'On the Manager as Principal Clerk', *Managerial and Decision Economics*, 1994, vol. 15, 5, pp. 413–19. For a view on baseball in Japan see Y. Ohkusa and F. Ohtake, 'The Relationship Between Supervisor and Workers – The Case of Professional Baseball in Japan, *Japan and the World Economy*, 1996, vol. 8, pp. 475–88.
11 P. Porter and G. Scully, 'Measuring Managerial Efficiency: The Case of Baseball', *Southern Economic Journal*, January 1982, vol. 48, 3, pp. 642–50.
12 S. Szymanski, 'Suits in a League of Their Own', *Observer* (Business, Work), 1 November 1998, p. I.
13 S. Szymanski, 'Why Money Talks Louder Than Managers', *Observer* (Sport), 22 February 1998, p. 7.
14 Szymanski and Kuypers, *Winners and Losers*, pp. 162–70.
15 The top ten in order were: Kenny Dalglish; Joe Kinnear; Lawrie McMenemy; Howard Kendall; Alex Ferguson; Keith Burkinshaw; Dave Bassett; Trevor Francis; Bruce Rioch; Kevin Keegan.
16 P. Sloane, 'The Economics of Professional Football: The Football Club as a Utility Maximiser', *Scottish Journal of Political Economy*, 1971, vol. 17, 2, pp. 121–46.
17 Vamplew, *Pay Up*, pp. 80–7.
18 Szymanski and Kuypers, *Winners and Losers*, p. 16. There were further periodic rises; in 1920, 7.5 per cent; 1974, 10 per cent; 1983, 15 per cent.
19 Dobson and Goddard, 'Performance', p. 769.
20 Vamplew, *Pay Up*, pp. 81, 328 n28, 137.
21 Arnold, *Game*, p. 124.
22 Taylor, 'Proud Preston', p. 277.
23 T. Arnold and I. Benveniste, 'Cross Subsidisation and Competition Policy in English Professional Football', *Journal of Industrial Affairs*, 1988, vol. 15, 1, p. 3.

24 K. Sandiford and W. Vamplew, 'The Peculiar Economics of English Cricket Before 1914', *British Journal of Sports History*, 1986, vol. 3, pp. 311–26.
25 Horowitz, 'Manager', p. 415.
26 See D. Kennedy, 'The Split of Everton Football Club, 1892: The Creation of Distinct Patterns of Boardroom Formation at Everton and Liverpool Football Club Companies', *Sport in History*, Summer 2003, vol. 23, 1, pp. 1–26.
27 An independent tribunal set the transfer fees of out-of-contract players.
28 Obelkevich, 'Consumption', p. 142.
29 In 1958, the third divisions, north and south, were replaced by third and fourth divisions.
30 Turner and White, *Football Managers*, p. 157.
31 Wilson, *Business History*, p. 13.
32 *Guardian* (Sport), 8 November 1999, pp. 6–7.
33 R. Audas, S. Dobson and J. Goddard, 'Team Performance and Managerial Change in the English Football League', *Journal of the Institute of Economic Affairs*, September 1997, vol. 17, 3, pp. 30–6.
34 *Guardian* (Jobs), 3 February 2001, p. 43.
35 *Tottenham Weekly Herald*, 19 April 1935, p. 11; *Sunday Dispatch*, 21 April 1935, p. 9; Szymanski and Kuypers, *Winners and Losers*, p. 375.
36 Korr, *West Ham*, ch. 6.
37 Russell, *Football*, pp. 81–2; Szymanski and Kuypers, *Winners and Losers*, p. 351; I. Sharpe, *Soccer Top Ten*, Stanley Paul, 1962, p. 117; Turner and White, *Football Managers*, p. 165.
38 *Guardian* (Sport), 3 July 2004, p. 12.
39 Only one substitute was allowed at first. It was later increased to two in 1987–8, then three in 1995–6.
40 *Football Association Handbook: Rules of the Association and Laws of the Game for Season 1960–61*, p. 186. Law 5, Referees.
41 *Express and Star*, 10 January 1955, p. 20.
42 *Guardian* (Sport), 3 July 2004, p. 14.
43 Szymanski and Kuypers, *Winners and Losers*, pp. 243–4.
44 Bowler, *Winning*, p. 221.

Conclusion

1 *The Times*, 3 February 1997, p. 33; *Independent on Sunday* (Sport), 21 January 2001.
2 *Guardian* (Jobs and Money), 26 August 2000, p. 17; *Guardian* (Sport), 2 September 2000, p. 2.
3 M. Brearley, *The Art of Captaincy*, Hodder and Stoughton, 1985, pp. 263–4.

Index